740005737994

STRICTLY OFF THE RECORD

Summersdale Publishers Ltd
46 West Street
Chichester
West Sussex
PO19 1RP
UK

www.summersdale.com

Printed and bound in Great Britain

ISBN: 978-1-84953-069-9

Substantial discounts on bulk quantities of Summersdale books are available to corporations, professional associations and other organisations. For details contact Summersdale Publishers by telephone: +44 (0) 1243 771107, fax: +44 (0) 1243 786300 or email: nicky@summersdale.com.

STRICTLY OFF THE RECORD

On the Trail of World Records with Norris McWhirter

Anna Nicholas

In memory of the 'one and only'
Norris McWhirter, CBE, (1925–2004)
co-founder and editor of *The Guinness Book of Records*.

CONTENTS

AUTHOR'S PREFACE

It is said that all great men, even fictional heroes, have need of a trusty companion. Holmes had Watson, Robinson Crusoe his Man Friday, even Alexander the Great relied on his trusty steed Bucephalus; but Norris McWhirter, founder of *The Guinness Book of Records*, picked the short straw and ended up with me.

Back in the eighties as a young rookie, I was lucky enough to have been offered a job as press officer at *The Guinness Book of Records* but at the time hadn't the slightest notion of the kind of roller coaster ride I was about to embark on, the madcap adventures in store, nor the utterly extraordinary record-breakers I would meet.

Years beyond that crazy period I happened to be up in my attic where I discovered a treasure trove of memories, proving to me once again the benefits of being an inveterate hoarder! For nigh on 25 years I have been the custodian of two enormous boxes of *The Guinness Book of Records* memorabilia, press cuttings and news releases, letters, books, diaries, photographs and several bizarre and dubious record-breaking objects that hailed from that eccentric and unpredictable time in my working life. As I dusted down the musty boxes and blew away the cobwebs, I made up my mind to write a book about that magical epoch, and what it was like to work closely with the brilliant and charismatic Norris McWhirter.

I'm writing about a time of great change in Britain. Prime Minister Margaret Thatcher was calling the shots, yuppies bounded around the City with clunky white mobile phones pinned to their ears, Sloane Rangers strutted the Shires in green Barbours squawking 'OK yah!' and Duran Duran, Spandau Ballet and Prince blasted from every radio. That pesky toy My Little Pony was omnipresent, just about everyone was going on strike and we were still in the midst of the cold war.

Back then, *The Guinness Book of Records* was run by a small team from a modest office in Enfield. Although we had some computers, much of the work was painstakingly manual and the book had only just started to experiment with big, eye-catching images. Of course, researching facts was never a problem for us all because we had Norris in our midst, a walking encyclopaedia of knowledge with an unnervingly high intellect and an uncanny, almost photographic, memory. There was never a dull moment in the editorial office and no two days were ever the same. All of us lived and breathed the book, which celebrated a vast range of eccentric human endeavours and achievements as well as containing many records of academic value.

In his capacity as record king, Norris was a much-loved personality and yet he wore many hats. Born in Enfield on 12 August 1925 to Scottish parents William and Margaret 'Bunty' McWhirter, Norris was an identical twin to his brother, Ross, with whom he was inseparable. William McWhirter was an extraordinarily successful newspaperman and record-breaker himself, being the first ever to become the editor of three national newspapers, the *Sunday Pictorial*, the *Daily Mail* and the *Sunday Dispatch*. It was therefore not surprising that Norris, twin brother Ross and older brother Kennedy were all high achievers and obsessed with research and current affairs from their infancy. Norris cheerfully admitted to me once that he and twin Ross were very independently minded as toddlers, with a great sense of mischief. On one occasion they slipped out of their nursery unnoticed and pedalled off in little toy cars, Ross to a level crossing to watch the trains and Norris to the local park, causing their poor mother Bunty, who raised the alarm, near panic. That independence of spirit and maverick humour was to keep me on my toes on many occasions while working with Norris.

In his youth Norris had been an outstanding athlete and an Oxford scholar, managing to complete a three-year economics degree in just one year, followed by a degree in contract law. During his student days he also served as a sub lieutenant in the Royal Navy Voluntary Reserve, undertaking minesweeping missions in the Atlantic and Pacific.

In 1951 Norris and Ross set up a business in Holborn, known as McWhirter Twins Ltd, which supplied facts and figures to newspapers, yearbooks and advertisers. At the same time Norris juggled sports commentating for the BBC. It was while running their fact-finding agency that on 12 September 1954 the McWhirter twins were approached by Sir Hugh Beaver, Managing Director of Guinness, to create a book of records to settle pub arguments. The rest, of course, is history.

In 1975, at the age of fifty, Ross McWhirter was shot in north London by two members of the IRA. The killing was in retaliation for a £50,000 reward he had publicly offered for information leading to a conviction of IRA members carrying out bombings on the mainland. Earlier the same year, he and Norris had co-founded The National Association of Freedom, which continues to exist today as The Freedom Association. Its main aim was, and still is, to protect the liberty of the individual and at the time challenged the trade union movement and Britain's membership of the EEC. Norris continued to edit *The Guinness Book of Records* after the death of Ross and later in 1985 became editorial director until his official retirement in 1996.

Norris had a magical sense of humour and was a brilliant mimic and wit. His impersonations and word-perfect recollections of ludicrous conversations and situations would often reduce me to tears on long journeys while on book promotional tours together. As a fellow prankster and someone who appreciated the eccentricities of English life and revelled in bizarre facts and feats, I couldn't have found myself in a more fitting job or working with a more like-minded companion.

When Norris decided to diminish his role as editorial adviser before retiring, I took the decision to move on, accepting a new post with a luxury goods company in Jermyn Street. However, I agreed to act as a consultant to the book for some years thereafter and Norris and I continued our friendship beyond Guinness. It was in 1999, while running my own public relations company in Mayfair, that I helped Norris in negotiating the publication of a new tome, *The Millennium Book of Records*, with Virgin Publishing. This afforded us the opportunity to work together promoting the new title.

One unforgettable memory I have of Norris was on my wedding day. Norris had agreed to give me away and so together we had set off to the church by car. Despite the heavy traffic in Knightsbridge we were well on course to reach St Colomba's Church ahead of schedule but Norris suggested instead that we took the next turning so that he could stop to listen to the cricket scores. Unfortunately, it was a one-way street so our poor chauffeur lost his way and we arrived at the church late. When I remonstrated with him, Norris merely chuckled and said, 'AN, it doesn't do to arrive on the dot.'

In years to come my husband Alan, son Olly and I would become frequent fixtures at Norris's home in Kington Langley, spending relaxing weekends with his wife, Tessa, and often with his children Alasdair and Jane. I remember commenting once on the chic bathroom taps in his home, an exclusive label, but he just laughed and said he'd never heard of the brand and neither had he ever bothered to examine the taps. On another occasion when we were discussing different car models, he shrugged and said that for him a car was merely 'to get from A to B and B to A'. It was this complete lack of pretension and interest in materialism that in some ways I respected most about Norris.

Even when I set up home with my family in Mallorca, Norris and I remained firm friends, meeting in London on my frequent forays back to England, and habitually discussing politics and current affairs by telephone. Rather lazily I still relied on his immense brain to provide me with little-known facts and figures, rather than researching the information for myself, and he would always dryly chastise me as he did when we worked together.

And then on 19 April 2004, Norris succumbed to a heart attack while playing a vigorous game of tennis with Tessa and friends at his Wiltshire home. At the memorial service that followed at St Martin-in-the-Fields in Trafalgar Square, an immense gathering of people squeezed into the church. Gospel singers belted out some inspiring scores, and Norris's son, Alasdair, gave a moving address followed by tributes from Sir Tim Rice and Sir Roger Bannister. I too was honoured to give an address about my adventures with Norris while at Guinness and our enduring friendship. Aside from his close family, Baroness Margaret Thatcher attended as well as politicians, celebrities, record-breakers and old university friends and colleagues, illustrating abundantly how Norris had touched so many people's lives.

So this little tome is a celebration of *The Guinness Book of Records,* which Norris and his brother, Ross, created. By the time Norris had relinquished his role, the brothers' creation had become the best-selling book in the world after the Bible, having sold 75 million copies and having been translated into 37 languages.

Together the twins established a brand recognised and revered by millions of record-breakers and readers across the globe. I hope, therefore, that through the humorous events and escapades that I recall, to offer a fun and light-hearted tribute to a truly great man: a man who put record-breaking firmly and forever on the map.

ONE

★ ★ ★

THE ODYSSEY BEGINS

There are some things you never forget; unforgettable moments that can change the course of a life. One of mine was walking into the small library of a fairly anonymous building in Enfield, Middlesex, and meeting the man who had made dreams come true for countless millions. His name was Norris McWhirter, a man who, like a magician, had turned the ordinary into the extraordinary with the creation of *The Guinness Book of Records*, which to this day remains the best-selling copyright book in publishing history.

In all honesty I had never before even glimpsed a copy of the famous record-breakers' bible, which is why some friends questioned what on earth I was doing applying for the job as the book's press officer. In my twenties and working in London within the PR department of the national charity Help the Aged, I was looking for a fresh challenge. When a headhunter phoned me out of the blue, suggesting I seemed like a suitable applicant for the new role at Guinness Publishing, I was flattered. Of course I had heard of Norris McWhirter and had seen him co-presenting the BBC *Record Breakers* television show with the ever-cheerful, tap-dancing and trumpet-blowing Roy Castle, but I had never before felt motivated to rush out and buy a copy of the book. That was until now.

As soon as my lunch break came, I rushed to the nearest bookshop, bought a copy of *The Guinness Book of Records*

15

and began scouring the pages. Surely in the interview I would need to demonstrate a genuine passion for the book if I was to stand a chance of being offered such a prized post?

So there I was, sitting in some anxiety at a pale, beechwood table in the library of Guinness Publishing's head office awaiting the arrival of the great man. For the last week, whenever an opportunity arose, I had immersed myself in the pages of the best-selling tome, desperately trying to retain record-breaking facts that I could knowledgably spill out in an interview to impress the book's founder. My patient flatmate Jane, a trainee insurance broker, who shared a modest flat with me on the upper floor of a terraced house in Haringey, north London, had painstakingly spent every evening quizzing me on aspects of the book, and had become increasingly frustrated by my dismal lack of recall.

Drumming my fingers on the shiny polished table, I surveyed my surroundings with some ennui. The floor of the library was covered in dreary brown acrylic carpet tiles, and the view from the grimy, half-blinded rear window was of unremitting greyness, drizzling rain and suburban red rooftops. One side of the room was constructed entirely of glass and shielded by white blinds. Peering between the slits I could make out a tantalising hive of activity going on beyond my cell in the neighbouring room, although all sound was blocked out. I got up and wandered over to the wall directly in front of me, which was lined with books, mostly factual titles – the history of aviation, several atlases, encyclopaedias, economic tomes and sporting and scientific titles – presumably all there for research purposes. There were several of Guinness's pop and rock titles, such as *The Guinness Book of British Hit Singles* and *The Guinness Hits Challenge*. As an English and Classics graduate I scanned the spines in vain for something of a literary nature but was disappointed. Observing my watch, I realised that ten minutes had elapsed since I'd been shown into this semi-glass cage. It was ten past five. When would Norris McWhirter appear? Was this waiting game a calculated move on his part?

As I twiddled my thumbs, the door swung open and a motherly figure with a shock of wavy grey hair swept into the room. I discovered that this was Muriel, who informed me she had been Norris's secretary for many years. She gave me a beatific smile, then chuckled.

'I've brought you a coffee. I'm so sorry that Mr McWhirter isn't here yet. He's only just arrived in the office. He's always rushing about, bless him.'

As she departed, I felt a sudden flutter of butterflies in my stomach. What on earth was I doing here? Within a few minutes, the world's most famous chronicler of records would arrive and in some frustration and dismay deduce that I was a complete fraud. He would expect me to wax lyrical about my favourite records, fondly recall childhood memories of when I received my first ever copy of *The Guinness Book of Records*. I would have to tell the truth; in other words that I had never broken a record nor been remotely interested in anyone else who had.

In some panic I now saw the door handle being turned. It was too late to make a run for it. Norris, for it was he, walked briskly into the room, a pile of files and books balanced underneath one arm. It was odd meeting him in the flesh. Of course he was instantly recognisable from his many appearances on television but his face seemed gentler and more sculpted, his gaze direct and piercingly intelligent. For a man past sixty he had a very youthful gait and slim physique, which hinted at his former days as an amateur athlete. Despite having his hair cut short, it was thick and wiry and sported an unruly kink and a few rogue curls. I jumped to my feet to shake his hand and was greeted with a bemused smile. Placing his files and books on the table, he looked momentarily around the room, sniffing the air.

'Can you smell something odd?'

'Glue,' I suggested.

'Yes. Well done. Let's hope the editorial team hasn't taken to glue-sniffing. We don't want them dropping off with hypoxia or hypercarbia, do we?'

He gave an amused grunt and sat down next to me, the sleeves of his heavy tweed jacket resting on the table. I was struck by his eyes, a clear blue that fixed unwaveringly on my face.

'Terrible problem with solvent abuse in the Republic of Ireland. Can you believe that twenty-two per cent of teenagers over there take to solvent abuse?'

'Gosh, that's dreadful.'

'Pathetic. And what's being done about it?'

'I'm not sure,' I replied awkwardly.

'So when do you start?' he said, a tad impatiently.

This wasn't the sort of question I'd been anticipating. 'Well, Mr McWhirter, I suppose that all depends on how I fare in the interviewing process, doesn't it?'

He eyed me curiously. 'Oh, I see. So what do you want to know?'

This was turning out to be one of the strangest interviews I'd ever experienced. Who was interviewing whom?

I shrugged. 'I suppose it would be useful to know about the day-to-day workings of the editorial department and how you envisage my role.'

He brushed the air with his right hand. 'Oh, it's quite straightforward. Once you start here, Alan, the editor, and

David Hoy, Guinness Publishing's managing director, will explain everything.'

I took a small sip of coffee just as Muriel reappeared bearing a cup of tea for the maestro himself. She placed the cup reverentially down in front of him, and positioned a plate of custard creams on the table.

He rewarded her with a schoolboy smile. 'Custard creams! Just what the doctor ordered.'

He pushed the plate towards me. 'Do eat some, or I'll scoff the lot.'

I took one in my hand, uncertain whether to crunch on it at the risk of spraying biscuit crumbs everywhere. I had been told by a former boss never to accept any drink or food at an interview in case of spillage or incurring some other mishap, so now I had broken two important interview rules. She'd also warned about the dangers of bringing along a child or animal, though for the life of me I couldn't imagine why anyone would ever consider such an idea. Norris was looking at me expectantly.

I cleared my throat. 'I've been told that the role of press officer is completely new. Who handled the PR for the book before now?'

He munched on a biscuit. 'In the early days my twin brother, Ross, and I acted as joint compilers and PR spokesmen for the book, and when he died in 1975 it fell to me to carry on alone. Recently I decided to step down from day-to-day editing and so we've appointed Alan as editor. He's a former producer of *Record Breakers*. You'll no doubt meet him today. My role is editorial advisor, which means I can spend more time out of the office, meeting record-breakers and carrying out editorial research.'

'A sort of roving PR ambassador?'

He laughed. 'That too, I suppose.'

'And so what might you expect of me in the office?' I persisted.

He regarded me uncertainly. 'I'm honestly not sure what your role would be here and probably no one else does either. If I were you I'd just make it up as you go along.'

I nodded, wondering what kind of eccentric company I might be joining. Norris gave a little cough and began studying one of the books at his side. I watched as his silvery grey head hovered over the pages of a rather dilapidated old hardback. He selected a passage and pushed it towards me.

'I believe you read Classics at university. What's your view of this passage?'

I pulled the book towards me and examined the cover. It was a copy of *The Odyssey* by Homer in the original Greek.

'My Ancient Greek isn't as good as it once was,' I mumbled and began surveying the text. 'Oh, this is book eleven when Odysseus meets the dead Achilles in the underworld.'

He nodded encouragingly.

'It's not terribly cheerful, is it?' I ventured. 'When you consider what a celebrated hero Achilles had been in the battle of Troy, only to have wound up dead and suffering from eternal boredom in Hades.'

He glanced at the ceiling. 'Yes, it's rather poignant. All that worldly glory for what?'

I read on. 'All Odysseus can think about is Achilles' track record in battle, while poor Achilles can only focus on the unremitting gloom of the underworld now he's no longer alive.'

We sat in sombre silence.

'Are you a fan of Socrates?' he suddenly asked.

'Socrates was pathetic,' I blurted out; years of translating Plato's *Republic* from the original Greek had resulted in my intense and childish dislike for the key protagonist.

'Pathetic?' he giggled, banging his cup on to his saucer. 'I've never heard him described as pathetic before.'

'Well, take the notion of the City State...'

The door opened. David Hoy poked his head through the crack, a huge grin playing on his face.

'Sorry to butt in, but how long are you guys likely to be? I'd like to see Anna before I leave for the day.'

Norris drained his cup and gave a cursory nod in David's direction.

'I don't think we need any more time, do we? Better you draw up the contract so she can get cracking.'

'So you want the job, then?' smiled David.

Rather bewildered I rose to my feet. 'Well, yes, of course. Is there anything else you'd like to ask me, Mr McWhirter?'

'Yes,' he said. 'When might you start calling me Norris?'

And so I became press officer, spokeswoman, and soon-to-be adjudicator – although as yet I didn't know it – and whatever else anybody wanted me to be at Guinness Publishing. From the very first day I walked through the door, the telephone trilled unceasingly. In the open-plan office it was hard not to bob up from behind the desk partition to eavesdrop on every new call. These weren't the sort of calls that you heard in normal office life. For instance, just that morning Ashrita Furman, the man who had somersaulted the longest distance at 12 miles and 390 yards, had rung for a chat; the world's greatest memory man, Creighton Carvello, wanted to alert the editorial team to his forthcoming new record attempt; and Mr Mangetout, a Frenchman and the world's greatest omnivore, had notified the editor about his latest guzzling record of a supermarket trolley.

The department consisted of Alan, the editor, Muriel, who discreetly handled both his and Norris's secretarial work, and two editorial assistants who answered all incoming calls before passing them on to one of four section deputy editors. Each one was responsible for several of the 11 chapters of *The Guinness Book of Records* and jealously guarded their own subject matter and its prominence in the overall book. The only exception was chapter 12, the sports section, which was so dense that it needed an editor and a deputy all to itself. Then there was David, the art editor, and Alex, the witty and wily picture editor, whom everyone feted. He was the one who made the final decision with Alan and Norris about which visual would make its debut on the front cover of the annual edition and also the images that would be used within each section of the book. In my confusing first days at the publishing company it was Alex who constantly kept me enthralled with hilarious behind-the-scenes anecdotes about the book.

My induction period was not without its trials and tribulations. Alan, a theatrical and extrovert character at times, was constantly on the phone or dashing to meetings; the scholarly deputy editors kept their heads glued to their computers behind screens and Norris was always on the road attending record-breaking events or appearing on television and radio shows worldwide. Although friendly and welcoming, none of the editorial team quite understood the role of a press officer, and so seeing a window of opportunity to rid themselves of calls from the weird and, quite frankly, barking mad, began having them diverted to my phone. They gained a sort of sadistic pleasure from this little ruse as I tried valiantly to fob off the persistent and pesky callers who wouldn't take no for an answer. My line flickered.

'Hello, it's Jack Tidsworth. I'm still waiting to hear back from the section editor about my rubber band ball record?'

'Your WHAT?' I asked, incredulous.

'Me rubber band ball is now blocking the road and the neighbours are complaining. And me mum and dad are fed up. When are you going to put me in the book?'

I told him to hold and hissed across the desk divides at Shelley, one of the younger and more lively of the deputy editors. She giggled, sweeping her wild, red curly hair from her face.

'Oh, he's in the nutter file. Just keep fobbing him off. He's sixteen years old and has built a rubber band ball bigger than his parents' garage and refuses to accept that it isn't a record.'

'But rubber bands aren't that big?'

'Don't you believe it! He gets them specially manufactured by a rubber band supplier.'

I shook my head in disbelief and released the hold button, trying to choose my words carefully. 'I'm sorry Jack, but it doesn't look like the editor feels it appropriate for the book. You see creating a big rubber band ball does not in itself constitute a competitive record. It's the first of its kind.'

'You don't think it's amazing?' he yelled in broad northern tones.

'It sounds fantastic but I'm just the press officer, so I can't really interfere with the editor's final decision. I'm so sorry.'

I replaced the receiver only to find the entire editorial department in spasms of hysterical laughter.

'Oh very funny,' I sniffed.

One of the perks of the job was to scan every national newspaper, including all the tabloids and my favourite publication, *The National Enquirer*, for cheap laughs. It was critical that we kept abreast of the weird and wacky, and news of forthcoming record attempts that hadn't already reached our ears. In those early days I soon got to know those journalists with a heightened interest in record-breaking and so was born my idea to create a Record News monthly bulletin which would keep the media up to speed on new records being broken. One of my early fervent supporters was Geoff Smith, head of news features at the Press Association, who immediately saw the mileage in being able to distribute a monthly update on record-breaking attempts through his news agency to all the regional press. In time he was to become one of my greatest media allies.

Despite the frenetic atmosphere of the office, and the lack of interest in my role, I wasn't entirely left to my own devices. My activities and workload were overseen by the company's marketing director, Chris, and also David, the managing director. This was probably a wise decision given my penchant in a previous post at Help the Aged for dreaming up crazy publicity stunts with celebrities using bizarre props to promote the cause of the elderly. Much as I had been hired for my creative input, Guinness was a traditional company that grew twitchy at anything too innovative or off the wall.

It was late one afternoon when Chris invited me to his office for an update. He was a petit man with pale skin, soft blue eyes and a constant look of irony sketched on his face.

'What news?'

'Well, we've had a fantastic response to the first Record News bulletin. The press seems to love it.'

He nodded cheerlessly. 'Good. A cost-effective promotion. What else?'

'I was wondering about the launch of the next book. What normally happens?'

He pushed out his lower lip. 'Not a lot. We organise book signings for Norris at some major book stores and there's obviously a fair amount of media coverage by dint of it being the best-selling book every year. Why?'

He noted the glint in my eye and frowned.

'I wondered whether we might do something different this year. Something fun and a bit more exciting.'

'Go on...'

'How about we create the biggest *Guinness Book of Records* in the world, hold a party for record-breakers and press and do a major regional book tour.'

He tittered to himself. 'And where do you suppose we get the budget for this extravaganza?'

I smiled confidently. 'Oh, I'm sure you can find it, Chris. I'll go and discuss it with David and Norris if you like.'

He grimaced. 'Oh God, I've a feeling you're going to make this a crusade.'

'It's going to be spectacular. Thank you for supporting the plan.'

'But I haven't agreed to anything,' he protested.

'No, but I know you will.'

With a spring in my step, I left his office, suddenly realising that if I stuck to my guns and forged ahead with new ideas, my new role could prove a gateway for greater things.

★ ★ ★

Norris was sitting on my desk peering at *The National Enquirer*.

'Pathetic! Where do they dream up such nonsense?'

'What? You mean you don't think it's all true? Not even the green alien story in Oklahoma?' I gave him a wink.

He laughed. 'I can't believe you're being paid to read this rubbish.'

'No, neither can I. It's great.'

He took a seat opposite me, chomping on a chocolate bourbon dished out to him by our indulgent office tea lady, Eileen, on her afternoon round.

'So how are you finding things?' he suddenly asked.

'Oh, OK. I'm just developing my own role and building up media contacts. The deputy editors have finally quit passing all the nutter calls on to me. I simply put my foot down.'

He shook his head impatiently. 'What were you supposed to do about them anyway?'

I smiled. 'Nothing. It was a sort of boarding school ritual for the new girl to see whether I cracked up or not.'

'We haven't got time for such silliness. Now then, how are you getting on with launch plans for the new book?'

'I'm getting the guest list together and a plan for the regional tour. My idea is that we visit some new and existent record-breakers in different parts of the country and invite the media along. It's far less boring than conventional book signings.'

He nodded. 'Yes, book signings aren't so effective these days. I hope you'll run the programme by me first though. There may be one or two troublesome record-breakers who should be avoided at all costs.'

'Oh?'

'You know, imbibers and obsessives. We don't want to encourage the pathological either.'

'No, quite.'

He got up and flattened the collar of his tweed jacket. Norris had a fondness for tweed jackets, dark blue and striped ties, light blue shirts and blazers teamed with beige twill trousers.

I was becoming familiar with his wardrobe, a walking advert for Gieves & Hawkes.

'I thought you might like to come on to the *Record Breakers* set next week. We're filming the new series at BBC Television Centre and Roy Castle would like to meet you. A young girl will be attempting a ball juggling record on the first show.'

'How exciting.'

He gave me an old-fashioned look then, realising that I wasn't being ironic, continued.

'She can't possibly beat the current record, of course. It would be impossible.'

'True. It would be difficult to beat Albert Lucas. Didn't he juggle ten balls simultaneously in 1984?'

Norris stared at me, wordlessly, a smile of satisfaction on his lips. He knew the symptoms. In just over a month, I'd been well and truly bitten by the record-breaking bug.

★ ★ ★

It was six thirty on a chilly morning in May. Jane sleepily wandered into the hallway as I made my way to the front door.

'My God, are you leaving for work already?'

'You won't believe it! Craig Caldwell, the man who climbed every Munro and Corbett, is coming into the office this morning. Alex and I want to set up some good shots for local press.'

'What's a Munro when it's at home?'

'You know, the two hundred and seventy-seven mountains over 3,000 feet in Scotland. He also climbed all two hundred and twenty-two Corbetts.'

'The only Corbett I know has Ronnie in front of it. Why on earth do you have to get in so early?' she yawned.

I shrugged. 'Because I'm so busy.'

She gave me a concerned look. 'You're not becoming obsessed with this job are you?'

'Obsessed? What ever gave you that impression?'

★ ★ ★

Yawning heavily at my desk, I stared out at a grey day. Tears of rain glided down the windowpanes as I sat contemplating the selection of record-breakers I might involve for the book's promotional tour later in the year. A press cutting winked at me from the desk which showed Dean Gould, the champion beer mat flicker and coin snatcher, in action with a pile of loose change. He was able to catch 132 ten pence pieces, flipping them from his forearm to his hand. Sneaking a glance over my desk partition to check the coast was clear, I took some coins from my pocket, placed them on the back of my forearm and attempted to flip them into the same downward palm. They flew in all directions, jangling as they hit the carpet. A polite cough. I looked up to find Muriel smiling down at me as I gathered up the coins. Her bouncy hair was carefully flicked back and she wore a shoulder-padded silk blouse with a floppy bow at the neck which gave her an air of importance.

'Having fun?'

'Ah, yes, just a little experiment.'

Her eyelashes flickered. As I scrambled to my feet she took on a confidential air.

'Alan would like you to pop into his office. I think he'd like a quick update on your activities.' She seemed a little guarded.

'Is everything all right?'

'Just remember, his bark's worse than his bite,' she said with a slightly prim smile.

In some trepidation I hurried through the warren of desks to the editor's office. Rather theatrically, the door was thrown wide open as usual as if to invite in the whole world but the reality was different. Ruddy faced and highly charged, Alan was pacing about his office, dramatically throwing his arms about in the air. I noticed his 'ready for action' rolled-up shirt sleeves as he pushed a fretful hand through his wiry grey hair. To my relief I also observed Alex sitting back in one of the chairs in front of Alan's desk, his legs crossed in front of him as he twiddled a biro between his fingers.

Alan ignored my entrance. 'Look, Alex, if Branson's doing this hot air balloon record in July and providing he and Lindstrand make it, surely there'd still be time to get an image of the balloon on the front cover?'

Alex nodded slowly. 'Yes, but we'll have to keep another first-class image up our sleeve in case for any reason Branson fails.'

Rather unwisely I interrupted. 'You're talking about the first Atlantic crossing by hot air balloon? It sounds fantastic and the PR potential would be great.'

Alan fixed me with fiery eyes. 'There's no PR potential if the damned thing crashes, is there?'

'Well, maybe not the sort of PR we might have had in mind.'

He gave a cynical snort. 'That's true enough. OK, Alex. I'll leave it with you but I want this cover to be superb. Nothing lame or boring.'

'I don't do lame or boring,' said Alex, surreptitiously giving me a wicked grin as he sauntered out of the office.

Alan surveyed me intently. 'So what are you up to right now?'

'Getting out the Record News monthly bulletins, building up a media database and planning the book launch. Have you had a chance to look at the updated press pack I wrote?'

'No,' he said, biting ferociously at the air. 'Now listen, keep me in the loop on everything, do you understand? What are you discussing with Norris?'

'Just the launch.'

He grunted and stomped back to his desk, flinging himself in the leather swivel chair.

'And don't get up the noses of the deputy editors, OK? They've got an important job to do.'

'Fine by me,' I replied curtly.

His telephone began bleating. He snatched at it and growled into the receiver. I took the opportunity to smile and wave and shot out of his wired den. I often pondered in those first months whose decision it had been to employ a press officer for the book. It didn't take much imagination to work out that it could never have been the editor himself. Without doubt, he regarded me as a new irritation in his hectic working life, a fly that needed swatting, but for all that, was I perhaps taking his brusque manner and impatience a little too personally? He had a big job and was under considerable pressure. And maybe Muriel was right too, that his bark really was worse than his bite. I stood by my desk lost in my thoughts until I noticed my internal line flickering. It was one of the editorial assistants.

'I've got that grumpy Rixi Markus on the phone again and she insists that she only speaks to you. That'll please Stewart in sport,' she tittered.

For once I didn't mind this particular difficult caller. Rixi Markus was the first woman World Grand Master of the game bridge and a regular contributor to the magazine *Harpers & Queen*. A skilled player, she often won bridge tournaments and would call Stewart, the deputy sports editor, imperiously demanding that he include the new feat in a future edition.

Much as achieving the premier slot in a competition was a great achievement, it didn't necessarily qualify Rixi for a place in the existing category of bridge. Several weeks earlier Stewart had told her in no uncertain terms that he could not guarantee that all of her regular competition wins would gain entry in the next edition and she had furiously asked to speak to the press officer. Stewart had put the call through to me, barely concealing the irritation in his voice. She was frosty and uncompromising at first but after I had reassured her that one of her records would definitely appear in the new edition, she calmed down. I realised that having her name in *The Guinness Book of Records* meant everything to her. After all, it was firm proof of her status in the world of bridge. We had chatted for a while and suddenly and unexpectedly we had touched common ground.

'My dear girl, you're a classicist? Why ever didn't you say so? From now onwards I shall only speak with you.'

Now as I waited for her imperious voice to flood the receiver, I wondered what new battle she'd had with Stewart. Instead she was full of sweetness and good cheer. 'My dear girl, I just wanted to thank you for your advice and kind words the other day and to invite you to a private lunch at the Carlton Tower Hotel. It will be with my good friend and fellow bridge player, Bernard Levin. I've told him all about you.'

I stopped in my tracks. Bernard Levin, the brilliant journalist and broadcaster? Why on earth would he want to meet me?

'I'm afraid I'm no bridge player, Rixi, and so I doubt Mr Levin would want to meet me.'

'Nonsense. Our lunch has nothing to do with bridge. Just a fun get-together between friends.'

She gave me the date some months hence, insisting that I mark it immediately in my diary. When she rang off, I sauntered down the corridor to the editors' desks. Two of them looked up expectantly.

'I've been invited to a private luncheon with Bernard Levin.'

They regarded me with some puzzlement.

Shelley popped her head over her divide. 'Really? Lucky you!'

'How did you pull that off?' asked Stewart, peering at me from his desk.

'Well,' I said mischievously. 'I suppose it all comes down to who you know. Rixi Markus, whose calls no one ever wants to take, happens to be one of his best friends.'

Muriel stifled a snigger and gave me a triumphant wink while the others regarded me in wonderment. I breezed off down the corridor and when I glanced back found them staring after me, their faces etched with amusement and maybe even a hint of respect.

★ ★ ★

It was seven in the evening when David, the managing director, strolled downstairs and leaned over my desk. As usual he was immaculately groomed and wore one of his chic dark blue suits. 'Still working? Haven't you got a home to go to?'

'I won't be long. I'm just trying to finish some press releases.'

He sat down, thumping a metal toolbox on the floor beside him. I'd already become familiar with this hefty object. David was an early bird like Alex and me, and it became a standing joke between us that we would always find him in the office fixing a loose wire or replacing a plug or fuse, his trusty toolbox in tow. I appreciated that some managing directors liked to be hands-on but this was taking the concept to a new level.

'What are you fixing this evening?' I asked.

He looked down fondly at the toolbox and pushed a hand through his sleek brown hair. 'There's always something the maintenance men forget. Actually, I've just fixed the photocopier but the telex machine's still on the blink.'

He stood up and looked wistfully out at the darkening sky, his eyes widening at the sound of a police siren. He rose to his full height and tried to glimpse the speeding car down below on street level but it had evidently disappeared in a flash.

'Gosh, that police officer was in a hurry. Mind you, I'm glad he wasn't heading our way.' He gave me a wry smile. 'We've come a long way, you know, Norris and I. Who would have thought that creating a book for settling pub arguments in 1955 would take the world by storm and become a publishing phenomenon?'

'How long have you been with the book?'

He pondered the question. 'Too long. Actually, it was in 1966 that I first met Norris and Ross when I was employed by Dunlop and they were producing the *Dunlop Book of Facts*. I ended up working with them a year later.'

'As managing director?'

He laughed. 'I was brought in to create some kind of order to their administrative systems.'

'Why? Weren't they very organised?'

He shook his head. 'At that time they were running their own rather eccentric show, producing *The Guinness Book of Records* and some other factual titles from a small office in Enfield. Quite frankly the last thing on their minds was admin or making budget!'

I grinned. 'Now I know why I like Norris. So when did Guinness take over the company?'

He eyed me with humour. 'You do ask a lot of questions. Thankfully a year after I joined them, Guinness took hold of the company and we had a little more structure.'

'It must have been extraordinary working for identical twins,' I said.

'You bet. It was great fun and they were such a source of inspiration.' He gave a heavy sigh. 'I was around when Norris's brother Ross was assassinated by the IRA in 1975. In fact, it happened just round the corner from here.'

I shuddered.

'Anyway,' he said poignantly, 'life must go on. Norris is an example to us all.'

'But why did the IRA kill Ross?'

He took out a perfectly creased white handkerchief and blew his somewhat prominent nose.

'That's a long story and probably best kept for another day. I'm going to pack up now and go home and I suggest you do the same. See you tomorrow.'

I watched as his tall, slightly bowed frame disappeared from view at the end of the corridor. A moment later I heard him plodding up the stairs to his office on the floor above.

The sound of a distant vacuum cleaner assailed my ears and then a door thumped open. Phyllis, the office cleaner, approached my desk and, with arms on hips, gave a loud tut.

'What's wrong with you? Ain't got no home?'

I rose wearily. 'Don't worry. I'm on my way.'

She strode off, returning with a ruffled and dog-eared newspaper.

'Seen this?' she quizzed.

'The *News of the World*? No, I can't say I have.'

She pushed the front page under my nose. I took a closer look and was amused to see a photo of a woman with two heads smoking what appeared to be two cigarettes simultaneously.

I laughed. 'Very droll.'

She thumped me on the arm, aghast. 'What you laughing about? Poor cow! Imagine having two heads and having to buy two lots of fags every week?'

I attempted a look of contrition. 'You're absolutely right, Phyllis. It must be a pain.'

'I tell you what, working here makes you realise that everything you read like this is absolutely true.'

With a feeble smile, I made my way to the front door. I wanted to add that if that was the case, working at *The Guinness Book of Records* must gradually but assuredly send you quite mad, but I felt it would have been churlish to say so.

TWO

★ ★ ★

FULL OF HOT AIR

Staring out of the office window at a faded blue sky I dreamily began tracing the path of a distant plane as it ploughed white furrows overhead before melting away in the haze, a tiny sun-spangled dot. Enfield in late June was certainly more palatable than Enfield in January, when I would wait for the bus at the end of Haringey Street with numb toes and ice-caked breath, wondering why I wasn't flush enough to own a car. Now at least a wedge of sun was winking at me from the top of a dingy block of flats and shedding honeyed light on the trees and cars in the street below. I was snapped out of my reverie by the sound of a creaking shoe. Norris's to be exact.

'Did you know,' he said quietly, peering through the window at the billowing clouds, 'that in 1986 Dick Rutan and Jeana Yeager flew non-stop around the world without refuelling?'

'I do now,' I replied, daring to give him a pert smile. 'What was the distance?'

He chortled. 'Well I'm hardly going to tell you that. Look it up. That's what reference books are for.'

He pulled a copy of the previous year's *The Guinness Book of Records* from a shelf and dropped it on the desk in front of me.

'I haven't got time,' I grumbled. 'The phone never stops ringing and I'm up to my eyes in getting out press releases.'

On cue the telephone rang. 'Press office,' I trilled.

Norris pottered over to my filing cabinet and began inspecting a folder. I listened as a reporter named Tony from the *Birmingham Mail* enthusiastically quizzed me about a new kiss of life record that he'd seen in my latest monthly Record News handout.

'Yes that's correct, a seventy-three-hour CPR demonstration was carried out at Birmingham's NEC last month by two ambulance crew members.'

He rumbled on. Had the crew carried out the CPR attempt on a living person he wanted to know?

'On a living person? For seventy-three hours?' I exclaimed, rolling my eyes. 'No of course not, they used a dummy.'

Norris observed me wryly, the file lying open in his hands. 'Hah! Tell him that if they did that, the victim would be in need of CPR!'

I gave him a warning grimace. 'Sorry, can you repeat that, Tony? The last record for the longest CPR demonstration? Let me see...'

I clamped my hand over the receiver and turned to Norris.

'I don't suppose you'd happen to know the previous record, would you?'

'If by CPR you mean cardiopulmonary resuscitation, the last record was 53 hours, carried out by two chaps in Illinois in September 1985.'

I relayed the information to Tony in Birmingham, who appeared mightily impressed by my lightning response. With brass-necked modesty I accepted his compliment and replaced the receiver.

Norris shook his head. 'I like that! Taking credit for something you haven't done.'

I shrugged. 'It's called using one's initiative and the tools at one's disposal.'

He gave a little snort and then, replacing the file in the cabinet, held up a hand. 'Listen, the sound of a heaven-sent chariot. Do you hear jingling and the dulcet tones of the tea goddess of Enfield?'

The noise of clattering cups and jangling teaspoons was drawing ever nearer.

'Wanna cuppa?' called Eileen over the partition.

'You bet. And biscuits, please.'

Glimpsing Norris, she broke into an ecstatic smile. 'Oh, I didn't see you there. Treble rations in that case.'

With a thud she placed a plate of assorted biscuits on my desk and lovingly passed a cup of tea to him. Distractedly she offered one to me too.

'You're keeping an eye on her I hope?' she winked.

'Oh, constantly,' Norris winked back.

With a fluttery wave she hurtled off, her trolley clinking along as she headed for the editorial department.

'I'm appearing on *Blue Peter* again this afternoon,' I yawned.

'Again?'

'Well, I was on twice last month when everyone was busy here. I judged a baton-twirling attempt which was pretty hopeless and then watched a lad trying his hand at record onion peeling.'

'What happened with that one?'

'It all ended in tears of course.'

He shook his head. 'Don't be inane.'

'It's a tough record to beat. Fifty pounds of onions in 3 minutes and 18 seconds. He gave up after his tenth onion.'

'So why have you got to go back today?'

'The deputy editors are frantic and anyway, they're not mad about adjudicating records on TV. In fact they're all fairly shy and prefer to be at their desks rather than out in the public domain.'

He looked thoughtful as he munched on a biscuit. 'There's no reason why you shouldn't start invigilating records. You've been out and about with me enough times in the last few months witnessing record attempts so you should know the ropes by now.'

I nodded. 'Well, it kills two birds with one stone. I can judge the record and then handle the media immediately afterwards at any live event.'

'And it would free Alan and me up. There's a limit to how many records we, as a team, can adjudicate when we've got the book to edit. We simply don't have the staff.'

'Well, I think that's another reason Alan's been getting me to judge some simple records on *Blue Peter* – to get the feel of it. I'm actually really enjoying it.'

'Good, but if it gets too much with all the press work, let us know.'

I grabbed a file on my desk. 'Today some teenage girl is attempting to blow the largest bubblegum bubble.'

He took a sip of tea. 'She won't make it. The largest diameter recorded is 22 inches. Impossibly difficult.'

'Yes, but the English record is only 16 and a half inches.'

'Only?' he scoffed. 'I'd like to see you attempting to beat that.'

'Surely it's just a case of sticking to your gums?'

He erupted into laughter. 'That has to be one of the worst puns I've heard in a long time.'

The telephone was going again. He rose and gave me a nod. 'I'll leave you to your busy day. Let's catch up about the Branson record tomorrow. It's but weeks away.'

He disappeared behind the partition as I picked up the phone. An aggressive female journalist from one of the tabloids began droning on about the dangers of gluttony record attempts.

I dealt with her firmly. 'But we don't encourage people to eat or drink themselves silly, and besides these eating competitions shouldn't be about volume, but about improving the rate of consumption.'

She told me sternly that it wouldn't be long before some obsessives died from gorging or imbibing themselves into oblivion in order to enter the book's hallowed portals and it would be the fault of *The Guinness Book of Records* if that happened. She had touched a raw nerve. Now in my sixth month at Guinness Publishing, I had begun fretting about the prospect of some fool eating too many clams or kippers and keeling over on the spot. It would be muggins here who'd have to handle the fallout when the snarling press calls came rattling down the line. I would have to discuss the matter with Sheila, the deputy editor for the gluttony section, and maybe even Alan. But then hearing the familiar roar from the open door of his office, I decided to postpone that idea for another day.

★ ★ ★

Cindy was popping pink bubblegum behind a stage set in the BBC television studio. She was fourteen and told me that she blew at least a hundred bubbles every day.

'Can't be good for your teeth,' I muttered.

'Yeah, but that's what dentists are for,' she said with her soft Perthshire lilt. 'I mean, I'd do anything to get into *The Guinness Book of Records*.'

'Walk through fire?' I suggested.

She nodded.

'Eat two thousand slugs?'

She shrugged. 'Simply anything.'

Another completely hopeless case, and at such a young age too. I paced around, regarding my watch with some irritation. *Blue Peter*'s revered and at times quite frankly terrifying producer Biddy Baxter insisted that all participants on the show should turn up punctually, but often I'd find myself hanging around the dim studio waiting for my miniscule slot in the limelight to arrive. As a Guinness adjudicator, my role was simply to stand inanely with a stopwatch or measuring tape on the sidelines every time someone attempted to better an existing record, and express excitement and delight. It was practically impossible to beat anything in the limited time allotted on the show, but it didn't really matter; a nail-biting attempt at a record was enough to thrill young audiences.

'Anna, you're on,' presenter Caron Keating called softly from her studio chair. She whisked her fair hair over one shoulder and gave me a winning smile. 'You'll be away in twenty minutes, honestly.'

I watched as she put an encouraging arm around young Cindy's shoulders while her male co-presenters continued to consult with Biddy some way off. A few minutes later and the cameras rolled. Pint-sized Cindy stood in the sharp camera light, bubblegum firmly in mouth while I stood close by, a look of studious excitement on my face. Caron and I chatted on air about bubblegum records and then stepped back in time for the drum roll and countdown as Cindy, with enormous concentration, began to inflate her fuchsia pink bubble. As it grew and grew, I took a sharp intake of breath. Will she, won't she, will she, won't she? Minutes and seconds seemed to tick by as Caron gave a detailed commentary on the bubblegum girl's slow but sure progress. Perhaps, just perhaps, for the first time in my six months of work at the book, I could declare a world record. In some anticipation I sidled up to her with a ruler and carefully began to estimate the overall diameter of the bubble. The law of gravity would affect the height of the bubble so this was the only option. It was nearly at eight inches. This could be it. One for the book. Or not. POP! At barely nine inches, it was all over. Pink gum hung in long strands from Cindy's face as she looked at us both in bewilderment, blinking away tears. Whoever said breaking records was easy? Having delivered a few comforting cheerleader words to her, I whizzed out of the studio at four o'clock and caught a train back to Enfield. Chris Greener, the UK's tallest man, was coming by the office later. A date I simply could not miss.

★ ★ ★

It was five thirty. I hadn't had time for lunch, and now it was simply far too late. For the umpteenth time there came the shrill sound of a telephone. Richard Branson's PR manager at Virgin Atlantic was on the blower.

'It's about Richard's forthcoming record attempt. Is there any chance of featuring the Virgin hot air balloon on the cover of the new edition?'

Although I knew Alan already had this in mind, I decided to keep it to myself.

'Very few records make it to the front or back cover,' I replied. 'It really is the editor's decision.'

'But when will that be?' she persisted.

'Not yet. Besides, I'd advise your boss to break the record first.'

She laughed. 'Good point. I guess we'll know in a week's time.'

In attempting to be the first to cross the Atlantic by hot air balloon, Richard Branson and his Swedish pilot, Per Lindstrand, would be embarking on a perilous, 3,000-mile journey in the Virgin Atlantic Flyer. Rather them than me.

Alex breezed up to my desk, a devious smile on his lips. 'Was that Virgin's PR? Was she fishing?'

'Branson's after a front cover slot. As our esteemed picture editor what would you say are his chances?'

He shook his head. 'Out of the question. Already allotted to Madonna and Michael Gross, the fastest swimmer, but we're thinking of sticking the balloon on the back. Worth a mint to Virgin in PR terms.'

I nodded. 'Very true.'

'Ha! That's got the cogs turning. What's it worth to them? Just think, nearly three million copies worldwide would be carrying the Virgin logo for a year.'

Alex perched on my desk and began fiddling with my paper clips. 'Fancy a cuppa?'

We pottered into the cramped departmental kitchen and made some instant coffee. Like a frenzied bear in search of honey, Alex began pulling open the door of every cupboard.

'Where does that woman hide the biscuits?'

'Eileen knows what you're like. She locks them away upstairs. If you're good I'll let you have one from my own supply.'

We returned to my desk where I revealed a packet of chocolate digestives stowed under a filing cabinet.

'Crafty,' he grinned. 'Your secret's safe with me. Anyway, what time's Chris Greener popping by?'

'About now, actually. He said around 6 p.m. Shame the editorial team has gone home.'

Alex slumped in my chair and took a slurp of coffee. 'As usual it's like a morgue. Just the slaves left in the bowels of the ship. And of course, David, our chief engineer.'

A door banged at the end of the corridor and David strode towards us, a screwdriver firmly in his grasp.

'Do you know that Chris Greener is upstairs? Just arrived.'

We both rose to our feet.

'I couldn't borrow that screwdriver, could I?' said Alex.

'Why, is something broken?' David asked expectantly.

'Just a loose wall plug.'

'Aha! Leave it to me,' he smiled.

I watched as they loped off towards Alex's desk. 'Don't you want to meet Chris?'

Alex turned and sighed. 'Love to, but I've got a stack of images to file before I go home.'

I plodded up the stairs to the first floor where I found a giant of a man pacing around the empty reception area. He stopped momentarily by the main entrance and it was then that I appreciated his true height as he towered above the wooden frame of the front door. If Chris Greener's head was close to touching the ceiling at seven feet and six and a quarter inches, I could barely imagine what it would be like to meet Gabriel Estavao Monjane, the tallest man in the world at just over 8 feet. I noted that, like me, Chris had untamed curly hair, albeit a darker shade.

'It's like the *Marie Celeste* up here,' he boomed, fixing his gentle brown eyes on me.

'Chris Greener, I presume?'

He held out a massive hand, his deep voice reverberating around the silent office.

'The one and only.'

'So can I get you a coffee or something stronger? We've got a few cans of Guinness knocking around somewhere.'

He emitted a deep roar of laughter. 'Good grief. Trying to get me drunk already? No, I'm fine, thanks. I just wanted to pop by to say hello. I've just been opening a local store.'

I directed him to one of the sofas. 'So do you do a lot of promotional work?'

He nodded. 'Thanks to *The Guinness Book of Records* I get a lot of invitations to open events and stores across the country. I do a fair amount of TV work too. It's good fun, although quite hard work.'

'So you've become pretty famous?'

He rapped his large knuckles on the coffee table in front of him. 'I'll tell you a funny story about that. I was doing a gig in north London and two old ladies stood and watched me getting into my car. They were obviously fascinated that I had an adapted car with only two seats to accommodate the length of my legs. I heard one say to the other, "He's that famous jolly green giant from the TV ad, isn't he?" and her mate raised her eyes and said, "Nah, he's a nobody." So I shouted over to her, "I'll tell you what, love, I'm a bigger nobody than you are!" That's the God's honest truth.'

'How rude people are!' I exclaimed.

He gave me a wolfish smile. 'Yes, but I give as good as I get. You have to learn to deal with the stares and comments. People are generally lovely and kids come up and ask me if I'm a giant and I say that of course I am. Right out of a fairy tale but a nice one.'

I smile. 'Well I do hope you'll join us at the forthcoming book launch. Norris will be there of course. We're holding it at the Savoy.'

'He's an amazing man, Norris. We once went on a hilarious record-breaking tour to Austria with a whole bunch of other record-breakers. It was a riot, I can tell you, people getting drunk and misbehaving but Norris, he was always a gentleman and never lost his cool. He's one in a million.'

He rose like an enormous oak and beamed down at me. 'Time to be off.'

At the door, he turned to me. 'And don't forget to send me that invitation.'

★ ★ ★

The wind was pulling violently at my hair as I stood clutching a jacket about me on Bristol Bridge. Far below in the choppy waves, yellow water buses and ferries struggled laboriously up the River Avon, buffeted by the gales and swaying from side to side. Buildings old and new flanked both sides of the river, as well as a floating harbour and a rather prominent landing stage. Maybe I was imagining it, but I thought I could make out the docks and Bristol Cathedral. I turned round and studied the landscape on the other side of the river. The church spires of St Nicholas, St Mary-le-Port and All Saints popped up on the murky horizon. A moment later I felt a shove against my arm. Roy Castle, presenter of the BBC *Record Breakers* TV programme was grinning at me, pointing up at the grey sky.

'Not the best day for ballooning, eh?'

I shook my head. 'No! What are we going to do?'

He shrugged. 'Wait and see, I guess. The balloonists think it will clear up in an hour or so. The wind's good but a bit fierce.'

He looked at his watch. 'Our crew should get here in half an hour and then we can get cracking with some interviews and background stuff before filming the balloons.'

He beckoned me to follow him along the bridge towards Norris. Absentmindedly looking up into the sky, Norris gave a cursory nod of acknowledgment as we approached.

'I think the mass ascent of hot air balloons might have to wait until a little later,' he said crisply. 'Unless of course we're looking for a bit of drama in the River Avon.'

Roy cackled. 'I don't think we want any dramas today, do you? Come on, let's grab a coffee before the crew gets here.'

We found a simple cafe a few minutes' walk from the bridge. Heads bobbed up as we entered, a look of incredulity sketched on various faces. Seemingly oblivious to their celebrity, Norris and Roy seated themselves next to me and smiled disarmingly at the motherly waitress.

She flushed pink. 'Ooh, you're Roy Castle, aren't you? And you're, you know, that Norris McWhirter from Guinness Records?'

'That's right, love,' said Roy with a cheery smile. 'Could you rustle us up some drinks?'

'Right away!'

She bustled back to the kitchen overcome with excitement, returning with menus. We ordered coffee and toast.

'I reckon we'll get good footage even if we just get twenty balloons up in the sky altogether,' mused Roy.

Norris nodded. 'Yes, we just need something visually strong.'

'So will this mass ascent of hot air balloons constitute a record?'

'No,' Norris replied. 'You should know that. There isn't a category for it.'

'So what's the point?' I asked in some exasperation.

'None, really,' Roy smiled. 'It's just a show filler to accompany the piece we're doing about Branson's Atlantic record attempt.'

Norris turned to Roy. 'Are we interviewing Don Cameron?'

'Sure. Great guy,' he replied, cheerfully taking a cup of coffee from the waitress.

'Who's he?' I asked.

Norris fixed his blue eyes on me. 'If you stopped answering all those wretched telephone calls in the office, you'd have time to read about people like Don Cameron. He's a hot air balloon designer. He and members of Bristol Gliding Club built the first modern day hot air balloon in 1967.'

'Interesting. Now look, if you genuinely want me to get to grips with record-breaking and work as an adjudicator I really could do with an assistant for all the press work in the office.'

He nodded. 'Good idea. Ask David.'

Roy smiled. 'If you don't ask, love, you don't get in this life.'

I nodded, putting it on my mental list of requests for our beleaguered managing director. David would rue the day that he ever employed me.

'How long have you been on *Record Breakers*?' I asked Roy.

'Believe it or not, I started presenting the show fifteen years ago, back in 1972.'

'Gosh, that must be a record in itself.'

'Yeah, I'm a bit of a dinosaur. The thing about this show is that it's a one-off,' he enthused. 'Did you know that Alan came up with the original concept?'

I frowned. 'What, Alan, my editor?'

'That's right, love. That man came up with a winning idea. I thought you'd know that.'

I sighed. 'We don't talk that much. He's always busy.'

'I know that feeling. Don't you, Norris?'

They both laughed.

'Well, get him to sit down with you one day and talk about it. He's a brilliant man.'

I raised my eyebrows. The thought of Alan discussing the good old days of the BBC with me over a cuppa seemed an alien concept.

'So,' I asked Roy, 'you've got a few records of your own?'

Roy regarded me somewhat sheepishly and gave a modest shrug.

'He's pretty remarkable,' said Norris. 'Fastest tap dancer of a million taps last year, and he even managed to play the same tune on forty-three different instruments in four minutes.'

'Can I ask why?' I laughed.

'Because I could, I guess. Nothing like a fun challenge.'

We finished our breakfast and returned to the bridge to find the BBC film crew setting up shots.

'Nice windy day,' beamed the cameraman. 'Just heard from the studio that the balloons will set off in an hour all being well.'

'Great,' beamed Roy. 'Let's get going.'

Feeling slightly redundant in the hive of activity taking place around me, I leaned on the bridge and flicked through my copy of *The Guinness Book of Records*. Norris strolled over.

'It's good for you to see this sort of event. I always think you learn more being out and about than stuck in the office.'

'True, but I feel a bit useless.'

He chuckled. 'You won't be idle. We've got you down for welcoming the balloonists when they've landed and also assisting the BBC continuity team.'

For the next hour I watched as Norris and Roy performed a double act to camera, interviewing the ballooning fraternity and previewing the record attempt, two maestros at work, unfazed by the variety of guests and working effortlessly without scripts. Suddenly a cheer rose from the crew. Floating high over the river a mass of colourful balloons came into view. I counted at least 20. Then to everyone's relief, a gentle sun emerged from the clouds and the sky blushed blue. I watched mesmerised as the film crew captured the big moment. A few minutes later, the balloons sailed overhead and beyond the river.

'Great stuff!' yelled Roy, tapping Norris on the arm. 'They did it!'

Members of the film crew were already packing up equipment and heading for their BBC van parked beyond the bridge.

'Come on,' said Norris with schoolboy glee. 'We'll drive to Ashton Court Estate to greet them as they come into land. It's only a short journey.'

We strode off to Norris's car, and were soon joined by Roy, who jumped into the back seat. After a 20-minute drive we arrived at the wide-open space of Ashton Park just in time to see a glorious multicoloured cloud of globes gliding towards land. We parked and walked briskly to the landing area, where the BBC crew was already stationed, their eyes trained to the blue sky.

'I'd love to go up in a hot air balloon one day,' I said wistfully to Norris as I watched the enormous coloured orbs descending slowly towards us.

'Yes, I think you'd enjoy the experience,' he remarked.

Some moments later the balloons landed, one by one. We rushed to greet them and when all were assembled, Norris and Roy carried out interviews with the pilots and crew. Two hours later, the BBC film team began packing up. Roy yawned and tapped me on the shoulder.

'Wasn't it a great day? I've got to push off now and head back to London. I've got filming in the studio first thing tomorrow.'

'You never stop! I'm meeting up with some of the Bristol media in the morning so I'm staying overnight here.'

'I know,' he said with a wink.

I frowned. 'Do you?'

Norris came over and clapped his hands together, a roguish smile playing on his lips.

'This is a perfect wind for ballooning.'

'Absolutely,' giggled Roy, looking into the sky.

I observed them both in some puzzlement. 'What's so funny?'

'I hope you've got a head for heights,' said Norris. 'We've arranged a balloon flight for you.'

'Seriously?' I squeaked.

Norris grinned. 'Well you said you wanted to try ballooning, so now's your chance.'

'Have fun!' yelled Roy as he clambered into the BBC van. Norris and I watched as the vehicle slowly pulled out of the car park, Roy waving from the window.

Norris turned to me. 'I've got to head back to London now so I've arranged for John, one of the balloonists you met earlier today, to sort out your trip.'

I stood by his car as he wearily lowered himself into the driver's seat.

'Thank you for organising this for me. It's such a wonderful surprise.'

He gave a cursory nod and started the ignition. 'A word of advice, don't lean over the side of the basket and don't attempt a trapeze act at 16,420 feet like Ian Ashpole did in Suffolk a few years back.'

I laughed. 'I wasn't planning on it but now that you come to mention it...'

He gave me a wry grin. 'See you back in the office, that's if you don't end up over the Atlantic.'

As his car disappeared along the rough track and out of the front gates of the park I began thinking about Colonel

Joe Kittinger, the first man to complete a solo transatlantic crossing by helium balloon in 86 hours. How incredible was that? Some credit Father Bartolomeu de Gusmao with the first ever ascent by a model hot air balloon, flown indoors at the Casa de India in Portugal in 1709, but others firmly believe that ballooning began in Ancient Egypt and that the mace-head of the Scorpion King, made in 3100 BC, was in reality a depiction of a panelled hot air balloon. I was rudely awoken from my reverie by someone calling my name. It was John the balloonist, plodding towards me across the muddy grasslands.

'Ready for the big event?' he grinned.

I nodded. 'Just try and stop me.'

★ ★ ★

A week later I sat at home late afternoon glued to the television. Just as I'd been leaving the office for the weekend, Alex had given an ominous prediction: with the blustery weather hitting the Scottish coast, the landing of Richard Branson and Per Lindstrand's hot air balloon might not go according to plan. In fact, he believed it might be somewhat precarious. I was firmly hoping it wouldn't be. Apparently Richard Branson and Per Lindstrand would be setting off from Sugarloaf Mountain in Maine at dawn on 2 July with the aim of arriving in daylight in the UK the next day. Both Norris and Alan had busy travelling schedules the day of their take off and over the weekend, so when and if the balloon did come down, wherever that might be, it was likely I'd have to deal with the fallout on behalf of Guinness. Still, at least I had the telephone number of Michael, our aviation expert, if needed, and Alan's telephone number overseas. I didn't welcome the prospect of having to make a final decision alone about whether or not Richard Branson had broken the record. Surely, as a novice adjudicator I didn't have the necessary experience for that just yet? In truth I just wanted it to land successfully and for a new record to be established. I calculated that the balloon had been in the air for 30 hours or more. While keeping an eye on the television for any news bulletin, I decided to call the Virgin operational team. Rupert, one of the staff, answered in one ring.

'No updates at the moment, but the winds are quite strong and there's low cloud, so we're not sure when or where it's going to be able to land. Hopefully the Mull of Kintyre as planned but if not...'

'There isn't a problem?' I probed.

'Not yet. I'll keep you in the loop.'

I paced around the room. I'd got a bad feeling about this. Pulling a dog-eared atlas from one of the bookshelves, I homed in on the North Channel. If the balloon was on course it would end up on the Scottish coast, but if not, it could just as easily find itself in Irish waters. I heard the sound of a key turning in a lock and the thud of the front door. My flatmate Jane breezed in, wearing a gypsy-style summery dress and pearls, and smiling cheerfully.

'Thank God it's the weekend! Bad day at work?'

'It looks like there might be a hitch with the balloon attempt.'

She dropped her handbag on the sofa and pottered into the kitchen, helped herself to a bottle from the fridge and returned clutching a glass of orange juice. She sat down heavily on the sofa and took a few long swigs.

'Well, whatever the outcome, remember it's not really your problem.'

'That's where you're wrong. It's Friday night and the world press will be salivating to know whether Branson's got into the book or not. If there should be any ambiguity, it'll be for me to make a decision with advice from our aviation expert.'

She tutted. 'That doesn't seem awfully fair when you've only been in the job for a short time. On the other hand it might be quite fun to act like the Red Queen having the press and the Branson crew at your mercy.'

'Ha! I don't think so.'

'I can't see what all the fuss is about. After all, it's just another record attempt. You handle them every day.' She drained her glass and stood up. 'Look cheer up. I'm just going to change out of my work things and then I'll pour you a calming glass of wine. Won't be a moment.'

A few minutes later I could hear 'Notorious' by Duran Duran blaring from her bedroom. She was a sucker for the New Romantics. I was tapping my foot to the beat when the shrill cry of the telephone jolted me from my temporary daydream. It was Brendan, an old and cynical university contact, now working as a rookie on one of the tabloids.

'Heard the news about the Virgin Flyer?'

I felt my heart miss a beat. 'What news?'

He gave a snort. 'Not very on the ball, are you? Looks like the weather's getting worse and Branson's going to cop it.'

Precisely what I did not want to hear.

'But Brendan, I've just spoken to the Branson camp and...'

'They're just giving you the usual spin. Things are falling apart. I reckon it could end up being a life or death situation out there in the ocean.'

Knowing how Brendan revelled in his new junior role as the harbinger of grisly news, I decided to feign nonchalance.

'That's absurd. There'll be search craft everywhere even if the balloon does get into difficulties. Sounds like pure speculation, Brendan.'

'Gotta run. I'll call when I hear anything new. Prepare yourself for tragedy,' he said with a mock sob.

Jane re-emerged from her bedroom in pale blue pedal pushers and a pink T-shirt, her hair pushed back with a blue velvet headband. She observed me impatiently. 'Was that Brendan? What did he say?'

I rolled my eyes. 'What do you think? He's already writing up Branson's obituary.'

She got up and scrutinised the atlas. 'At least we're both in tonight. So, apart from Brendan, which other media might have your telephone number here?'

'All of them of course. I'm on call.'

She absentmindedly flicked open a copy of *Cosmopolitan*. 'Well, not to worry. We'll cope. I'll get us both a glass of wine.'

'Are you sure that's such a good idea?'

She gave a grunt from the kitchen. 'It'll be good for your nerves.'

I decided to put a call through to Alan and Norris to give them an update and also Michael, the aeronautical expert for the book. Forewarned was forearmed.

I called all three numbers and received no response. I left messages. Humph. Jane and I sat sipping our wine and discussing the balloon's flight path. An hour later the *Mirror* called, followed by the *Daily Mail*, *Evening Standard*, *London Daily News*, *Express*, *The Times* and *The New York Times*, oh, and some obscure title in Delhi and an infuriatingly persistent freelancer from Canada. The Press Association was next.

'We're getting reports that the Virgin Flyer is in difficulties and may not be able to land on the Mull of Kintyre. What's your take?'

Buggeration.

'Well, until the craft has landed I don't think I can really add much...'

Could he feel the rising panic in my voice?

'But if the balloon doesn't hit dry land, it won't constitute being a record, will it?'

Most certainly not.

'As I say, until it touches down, I can't make any comment.'

'Yes, but if it lands in the sea, it won't be a record, will it?'

I wanted to thump the man on the nose.

'Call me when it lands,' I replied firmly, 'and I'll give you an answer.'

Jane sat opposite me at the living room table absorbed in *Cosmo* and munching on a slice of cheese on toast.

'What do they want me to do, look in my crystal ball and tell them the future?'

She gave me a sympathetic glance. 'Oh can't you just fob them off'? Say it'll all be fine.'

The phone was bleating again. It was Rupert.

'The balloon is veering off course and heading towards the Irish coast. Have you had any press calls?'

'Are you kidding, the phone hasn't stopped. Look, the balloon has to hit land or I can't officially declare it a Guinness record.'

'Sure, I appreciate that.'

There was a pause.

'And another thing, Rupert. I'll have to take counsel from the FAI, you know, the Fédération Aéronautique Internationale. It has very strict criteria about ballooning records.'

'So I understand. OK. We'll keep in touch.'

I had a certain amount of sympathy for the Branson team. They'd worked round the clock and were desperate to see their tycoon boss given a hero's triumphant welcome on the Mull of Kintyre. The sky was darkening. I pottered into the kitchen, made myself some tea and toast and resumed my position at the table. If the balloon was heading north, it would pass Limavady in Northern Ireland, Rathlin island and head up to the Kintyre Peninsula. Ring, ring. Jane reluctantly got to her feet. She tutted and handed the receiver to me. 'Brendan.'

'Anything new?'

He laughed manically. 'Told you. The pillocks are going way off course. Could end up in the Antarctic at this rate.'

'I'm glad you find this entertaining, Brendan. There are lives at stake here.'

He yawned. 'Lighten up. We could be looking at a great front page, "Balloon record bid ends in tragedy… tycoon lost at sea,"' he giggled inanely, exhausted by his own wit.

'If you've nothing sensible to say…'

'OK, heads up. The balloon is heading for Limavady and may touch down any time soon, so cheer up.'

I felt my mood lighten. Thank heavens. It would soon be over and we could all get on with our lives. Jane looked up.

'Good news?'

'Yes, I think they'll land soon. Just imagine, they'll have been in the air for more than thirty hours.'

'Fancy another glass of wine? There's half a bottle of Blue Nun in the fridge.'

I nodded wearily. We sat staring at the television for another hour. There were no news bulletins and I saw no point in driving the Branson team mad with calls when they were no doubt frantic. Ring, ring.

'The balloon's hit land near Limavady,' Brendan was yelling, 'but it's taken off again. Looks like it lost some fuel tanks and Branson and Lindstrand are still aboard.'

'Oh God! Where's it heading?'

'Christ knows, out to sea, and the conditions are rough. You couldn't dream of a scoop like this! I'd prepare one of those tear-jerker statements if I were you. "It was with deep sadness that we at *The Guinness Book of Records* heard the tragic news…"' his voice trailed off. 'Hang on. Apparently they're nearing Rathlin Island and have tried to land on shore…'

'Phew…' I breathed deeply as I rammed the receiver against my ear.

'Nah! They've missed! I guess it's curtains for both of them. I'll call you in a minute. Get scribbling. 'Poor things!' I exclaimed as I replaced the receiver.

Jane suddenly looked interested. 'Are they both dead?'

'Don't you start! You're getting as bad as Brendan, the grim reaper.'

'Sorry, just didn't sound too good.'

I grabbed the telephone again and called the Branson team. A girl answered, sounding harassed. 'There's been a bit of a glitch. It looks like they tried to disembark as the balloon touched land but the release bolts for the capsule wouldn't work and they rose up on a gust of wind to about sixty feet. Then Per leaped off over the sea.'

'What did he do that for?'

A nervous cough. 'I don't think he had much choice.'

'And Branson?'

A sigh. 'Still in the crippled capsule. For some reason he stayed. The RAF and the Royal Navy are mounting a rescue. We'll keep you informed.'

I tapped the receiver against my head and sighed.

'What a night. Poor Lindstrand's lost at sea and Branson's apparently clinging on to the capsule.'

Jane sipped at her wine. 'You wonder why people are silly enough to do these stunts.'

She curled up on the sofa and began watching *Dynasty*, her favourite soap.

I paced around the room, looking out at the charcoal sky. The evening seemed to have passed by in a flash and yet the saga wasn't over yet. Thirty minutes elapsed and then... ring ring. It was a contact at Reuters.

'In case you didn't know, in the end Branson jumped out of the capsule but was picked up by the Royal Navy off Rathlin Island. No sign of Lindstrand. We fear the worst,' he said.

I thanked him and replaced the receiver. Now what? No word from Norris, Alan or Michael, the aeronautical consultant. What to do? Only one thing for it. I'd have to consult with the FAI, the governing body of aeronautical records.

'*Bonsoir?*' I stammered in my best schoolgirl French and proceeded to speak with one of their operators. The man listened to my appalling French for some minutes and replied somewhat coldly and officiously.

'*Ah oui,*' he said, 'The Virgin Flyer attempt? It has failed, you will agree?'

I frowned. 'Well, no, I'm still awaiting final details. Apparently it touched down in Limavady...'

'*Regarde, mon amie,* it did not touch land. It kissed land, that is different. *Une bise.*'

'But have you details of exactly how long it landed for?'

He gave a long, bored sigh. '*Écoute*, in order to achieve this record, the balloon should have landed intact and either on land or fresh water. It broke up and it ended up in the sea. *Voilà. C'est fini.* I am sorry for Britain, but *Messieurs* Branson and Lindstrand cannot claim any record. You must feel disappointment.'

Feeling tired and grumpy, I was not enjoying the man's patronising tone.

'*Merci*, but I shall wait before making a decision.'

There was a pause. 'Forgive me, but Guinness and the Federation should comply on this. It is better that we give a consistent message, *non*?'

'I shall consult with the book's own aviation expert and let you know.'

He took on a haughty tone. 'Be careful. This is very serious. You have a responsibility to make an unemotional decision on behalf of the book.'

I thumped the receiver down and made myself a coffee. Minutes later the press calls streamed in. Was it a record or not? Why couldn't I announce a decision? Where was Norris McWhirter? Did I agree with the FAI? Exhausted, I slumped down on the sofa with the map.

Jane glanced at me. 'Cheer up. Seems to me that if it hit land, he should get the record, don't you think?'

'Yes but if it doesn't meet the right criteria, there's nothing I can do. We need a small miracle.'

The telephone rang yet again. In some exhaustion I looked at my watch. It was getting very late. No doubt it would be Branson's team on the line. They had been urgently requesting a decision and were still hopeful that Per Lindstrand would be found at sea, despite a few hours having passed since his jump into cold and briny waters. But it wasn't them. It was Michael, the book's expert aviation man.

'Sorry, been out and about but I've been following the news. Interesting dilemma, isn't it?'

'What's your view?'

He inhaled deeply. 'Tricky. If we go with the record, we'll fall foul of the FAI and yet...'

'The balloon did touch dry land.'

He sniffed. 'Yes, not for long, admittedly, but nevertheless a direct hit.'

Silence.

'What does Norris or Alan think?'

'I can't get hold of them. They're both away.'

'Ah. Well then, it's up to you to make the right decision.'

'Thanks, I feel better by the second.'

'On balance, and given the facts, I'd say they do deserve the record. Be good for Britain too.'

'True. So should I declare it a record?'

He laughed. 'I can only tell you what I think, given the facts at this stage. They made the first crossing of the Atlantic in a hot air balloon and hit dry land. I know the FAI will have a problem with the nature of the landing, but we at Guinness abide by our own rules.'

I replaced the receiver and sat and stared out at the gloomy sky.

'Oh, why not just give them the record?' sighed Jane, 'and we can get to our beds.'

I called the FAI yet again and told them of my decision. They were not amused and told me that I was making a grave mistake. They believed Mr McWhirter would not approve. Great, that's just what I didn't want to hear. The Branson team called and seemed immensely relieved to report that Per Lindstrand had been recovered from the sea, in shock, concussed but alive. I called the Press Association, Reuters, Associated Press and the nationals with my decision. It. Is. A. World. Record. There was a general sighing of relief down the line.

Brendan was somewhat petulant.

'God, how I hate happy endings. Lucky sods. Not only do the buggers get to live but they get the record too. Where's the excitement in that?'

Jane smiled and pushed a glass into my hand. '"*Santé*,"' as your friends at FAI would say. A victory for Britain and common sense.'

★ ★ ★

After a fretful weekend in which many newspapers quoted me as having declared the Virgin balloon crossing a record, I sloped into the office. The deputy editors peered at me from inside their warren of desks.

'Brave decision,' said Sheila, provocatively. 'Norris is in later. Let's hope he agrees with you or you've had your chips.'

'So did you think it was the right decision?' I asked.

There was a general titter and then Shelley popped her head up from her desk. 'It's not in my section but it seemed a bit complex. I wouldn't be able to give an informed decision.'

Miserably I sat at my desk, piles of weekend newspapers glaring at me accusingly. Images of a smiling Lindstrand and Branson festooned the front pages. Yeah, it was all right for those two. All they had to do was fly a mere 37 hours across the Atlantic, fall 60 feet from the sky into freezing dark water off the Irish coast, get rescued by the RAF and smile at the camera. Little did they know what was going on behind the scenes, or the weekend they'd ruined for a poor lowlife like me. Alex stalked up to the desk, grinning from ear to ear.

'Great stuff! Now we can stick the balloon on the back cover.'

'I hope it was the right decision.'

'Who cares, it makes a great shot! Mind you, Norris might not agree.'

Eileen arrived like Boadicea with her chariot, and gave me an extra helping of biscuits. 'Why the long face? The worst he can do is sack you!'

Mid-afternoon, Norris ambled over to my desk, a pile of newspapers under his arm. 'Can you spare a minute in the library?'

Back to square one, the scene of my start – and now sudden end – with the company.

'Had a good trip?' I asked weakly, when we were sitting down at the table.

He rubbed his eyes. 'Oh, long flight but it was good to catch up with the American editor, David Boehm. Good chap.'

'When did you fly in?'

'This morning. Is Alan back yet?'

'Not that I know of.'

He pulled a pair of reading glasses from his pocket, examined them carefully, frowned, then tugged out his powder blue shirt tails and began using them to rigorously clean the lenses. Without tucking his shirt back in, he stuck the glasses on his nose and began studying a copy of *The Times*.

'So you had a busy Friday?'

'You could say that.'

'A difficult decision, I imagine.'

'Very.'

'What constitutes a landing, I wonder.'

'That was the problem,' I sighed. 'Michael even pondered that one.'

'Indeed.'

'Is your French as good as your Ancient Greek?' he asked with a hint of humour.

'Probably worse.'

'So you didn't hit it off with our friends at the FAI?'

'Not hugely. We didn't find much common ground and it was late. I was crotchety and tired.'

He rose and walked slowly over to the small window. 'They really should clean these panes. Covered in dust. Can't even see your own reflection.'

'I'll talk to Phyllis.'

He waved the thought away.

'It's a funny old thing,' he said. 'We consult with regulatory bodies and experts, create rules for each and every record, and yet, there are occasions when there is an element of doubt. It's at times like that when sensible and logical decisions need to be made. And decisively.'

A pause.

'So, on balance and having carefully studied the facts, I agree that Branson and Lindstrand deserved the record.'

Visibly relieved, I got to my feet. 'That's a huge relief to me.'

He broke into a wicked smile. 'I know, but I enjoyed watching you sweat. Shall we organise some tea? What do you say?'

THREE

★ ★ ★

THE BIGGEST BOOK IN THE WORLD

There was something very therapeutic about taking a bus to work early in the morning. For one thing it gave me time to contemplate and prepare myself for the madness I might expect that day in the office, and also allowed me to catch up on my record knowledge. I got to know Eric, my regular bus conductor on the 121 route, who would catch at the rails with the dexterity of a gibbon as he swung down the rickety bus in between collecting fares. Then he would thrust his crumpled and stubbly face towards the book cradled in my hands and command me to read some records out loud. Predictably, he was always most interested in sport but occasionally took interest in the gluttony and human endurance feats. Other early risers catching the bus would interrupt and often we'd hold small, lively debates about new record attempts and those who broke them.

This morning I was feeling on edge. The launch of the new *Guinness Book of Records* was less than a week away and although I had worked like a woman possessed to get everything in place for the big event, I felt uneasy. The biggest catch had been getting Richard Branson to agree to take part in the photocall in Covent Garden's piazza. Remembering wily Alex's words about the brand value of having the Virgin Flyer balloon on the cover of the book, I had bartered with Virgin's PR manager to loan us Richard Branson for an hour on the big day.

'Who you got coming to your launch then?' asked Eric, jamming a new roll of paper into his ticket machine.

'Well, apart from Richard Branson, I've got Sooty and Matthew Corbett...'

'You're kidding? I used to love that puppet when I was a kid. What's he got the record for?'

'Most durable show. Matthew's father launched Sooty on the BBC back in 1952 and the show's still going strong.'

'Amazing. Anyone else coming?' He pulled the cord above his head and the bus drew to a halt at its shrill ring. An elderly lady with a shopping bag on wheels clambered aboard, aided by another passenger. I peered out of the window into the gloomy street, noting that we were already on the Great Cambridge Road. Eric pulled the cord twice – ding ding – and we were off again. He turned to me. 'Carry on.'

'Well, there's Jean Leggett, the champion fire-eater, and Chris Greener, the UK's tallest man, and Dean Gould, the beer mat flipper, and Norman Johnson, the cucumber slicer – oh, and Mike Solomons with the longest moustache. We're also inviting some celebrity record-breakers such as Nicholas Parsons and Gyles Brandreth too.'

'What did them two do?'

'Funnily enough they both hold records for longest and most entertaining after dinner speeches. Eleven hours, I think.'

He whistled. 'Easy for Parsons being a comedian and all that.'

'Well, it's still a long time to keep talking.'

He gave a loud sniff and wobbled off down the bus, grabbing at a metal rail as we turned sharply round a corner. I thought back to the night before. Jane had held a dinner party for some work colleagues and old university friends and for some inexplicable reason I seemed to have driven them all to distraction with my recounting of recent record feats. Brendan, he of the tabloids, had roared with laughter when I'd thoughtfully shared the new 'mantle of bees' record with them, especially when it wasn't yet in the public domain.

'Who gives a flying toss that some sicko covers himself with a hundred and fifty thousand swarming bees? These geezers should be locked up, not posing in your bloody book, woman!' he had roared. After the guests had left Jane had rolled her eyes and sternly told me that in future I'd be banned from uttering a word about record-breakers at social dinners. Was I really becoming obsessive?

'Oi! It's your stop, dreamer!'

I got up and wavered, suddenly remembering that the longest dream of 2 hours and 23 minutes, or as it was known medically, longest recorded rapid eye movement while asleep, was held by a man named Bill Carskadon in 1967 when he was under observation at an Illinois hospital. Thinking about it, there seemed to be one heck of a lot of records happening in Illinois. Why, there was...

'Are you getting off or not?!' Eric was standing by the exit with his hands on his scrawny hips, observing me impatiently. I raced down the aisle and jumped onto the pavement, a stone's throw from the office. Puffing furtively on his lean hand-rolled cigarette, Eric waggled a nicotine-yellowed finger jokily in my direction as the bus drove away. It got me thinking about the world's most famous cigarette which as any fool knew was Marlboro, but what about UK brands? Possibly Benson and Hedges but then again... I set off at a stride, my record bible firmly under my arm. No, I wasn't obsessive about records at all.

★ ★ ★

As I walked into the office, Lisa was sitting coquettishly on her desk, her big brown eyes fringed with dark curling lashes and her long, wavy hair swept up into a wispy bun. For a woman still clinging to her teen years, she was extraordinarily knowing and grown-up in a way I could never hope to be. A few young males from the administration department upstairs floated by, sneaking glances at her pert little figure and perfectly groomed nails.

'What are they staring at?' she said to me with a giggle, as the third drifted by.

'That's a tough one. I'll have to think about that, Lisa.'

She thumped me on the arm. 'Watch it. Anyway, fancy a tea?'

I nodded and watched as she rose gracefully and with a little wiggle smoothed down her ultra short, fitted skirt and sashayed off to the kitchen. Lisa was my new assistant and the daughter of Eileen, the tea lady. They had a few things in common. Both were incredibly slim and both jingled when they walked. While Eileen had her rattling tea trolley, Lisa had her deadweight of a charm bracelet which tinkled away on her wrist as she wrote, typed, walked or wiggled. Lisa's arrival in my life was a godsend. Overnight she had transformed the heaps of files, letters, newspaper cuttings and books that sat like unwelcome molehills on my voluminous desk into neat and orderly piles. She had begun creating colour-coded files, hurled out the old dog-eared dossiers, sorted the pens and stationery and controlled the phone calls.

With her no-nonsense, yet girly and at times giggly manner, she had most callers eating out of her hand, whether male or female. She would tuck the phone under one ear and carry on typing a letter while chatting away about Guinness rules and regulations or advising the press on a newly broken record. When I was at my most frazzled she would appear on cue with a cup of coffee and a pile of Bourbon biscuits, or during an interminable phone call would dial her own telephone from another desk so that I had an excuse to cut short my tormentor with the familiar line of, 'So sorry, my other line's ringing. Got to go!'

Yes, we were a good team and together were able to turn the press office into a hive of activity, a small but valuable little fiefdom of two. I threw my woolly coat and scarf over a redundant chair and sat down at my desk. Lisa shook her head and tutted, picking them both up in some disdain and hooking them over a coat stand.

'So, d'you want to know attendance numbers for the Savoy launch party?' she asked.

I yawned. 'Go on.'

She tapped a biro against her jaw. 'I reckon we're up to two hundred punters.'

I sat up with a start. 'How many people are yet to reply?'

She shrugged. 'At least another eighty but I don't think they'll pitch up. They'd have replied by now.'

I snorted. 'Don't you believe it. There are always the stragglers who say yes at the very last moment.'

She shrugged. 'Well, if it is a full house, I'm sure the Savoy will cope.'

'That's the least of my worries. I'm supposed to be keeping within budget. Chris and David will have a fit. And don't forget we've ordered those Guinness T-shirts and promotional pens as giveaways for the launch. That little lot is already over budget.'

She giggled. 'Actually, Glen Bascock called. He was supposed to be dropping by with the promotional pens this morning but he rang to say he's got a chesty cough.'

I groaned. 'Not again. The man's always got a bad chest. He's a complete hypochondriac. I wonder how he does his job as a sales rep when he's always ill.'

'Not to worry, he's getting a colleague to deliver them tomorrow instead.'

My internal line bleeped. It was Chris.

'Ah, Miss Nicholas, any chance of a brief update today on the launch's progress?'

I countered the mildly sardonic tone. 'Absolutely. Shall I pop up now?'

'Why not, I can hardly contain myself.'

Lisa bit her lip. 'Be foggy about the numbers… we don't want to wind him up.'

I scooped up my launch file and headed for the stairs. Chris's secretary, Jacquie, a sun worshipper who even now in October was sporting a mild tan, gave me a radiant smile. She tossed her mane of Farrah Fawcett-style curls back from her face and pointed with her pen towards Chris's door.

'Don't give him a heart attack today, please. Softly-softly.'

I nodded reassuringly, knocked on the door and entered. Chris was sitting at his squeaky-clean desk. Where did he put all his stuff? He took one look at the enormous file in my hands, called to Jacquie and asked her to bring us strong coffees.

'I hope you're not going to wade through that entire file,' he said quietly, placing both hands defensively on top of his sandy hair – perhaps to indicate the true meaning of the term 'keeping one's hair on'.

'I thought you might be at a loose end today.'

He gave a small, reedy laugh. 'Very droll. Actually, all I really care about is the budget.'

'That's very dull. I mean think of the publicity we're going to get...'

'We always get publicity. We produce the best-selling book in the world, which means that technically we don't need you at all. And insanely we've just got you a secretary.'

'Assistant.'

'Oh, pardon me,' he said in mock horror, tapping himself on the hand and stifling a snort.

'You know you're rather like Eeyore. Can't you get excited about anything?'

He eyed me wearily. 'Yes, when I make budget. That's what marketing directors do. We look at the bottom line all the time. Anyway, wasn't Chesty Cough supposed to have delivered those promotional pens today?'

'Yes, but unfortunately he's just rung to say that he's got a...'

He interrupted, one hand held in the air. 'Chesty cough? Don't tell me.'

I broke into a grin. 'You're psychic.'

He shook his head. 'No, he's just predictable. Do you think we should fire him and look for a new brand merchandise outfit?'

'No, I like Glen Bascock. Besides, what'll we do for laughs if he goes?'

'True,' he replied, gratefully accepting a coffee from Jacquie. She set one down on his desk in front of me and gave a surreptitious wink.

'Dean Gould's agreed to do a record attempt at the Savoy.'

'The beer mat flipper?'

'The same.'

'Very Savoy,' he sniggered.

'Well, he may be coin snatching too. I'll have to check.'

He sat back in his chair, his pale blue eyes fixed on me. 'Spare me the fun stuff. Are you over budget?'

'Only slightly but don't forget that making the prop of the largest book in the world cost more than planned – the wood bumped the price up – and then of course we decided not to hold the launch at McDonald's...'

He raised his eyes. 'Very witty, missus. So, run through the photocall again.'

'OK. We're going to have Norris, Richard Branson, Sooty, Matthew Corbett and Jean Leggett appearing from different windows in the giant book, bang in the middle of Covent Garden. We'll do some general shots in the piazza too.'

'What's Jean Leggett's claim to fame?'

'She's eaten 6,607 flaming torches in less than one hour.'

'God help us. Now look, is this wooden prop secure? I mean if it fell down and flattened Branson, it wouldn't look too good for us. Picture the headlines. Branson risks his life in a hot air balloon only to be flattened by the very book he tried to enter.'

'Look, the guys making this prop are experts. It's stabilised with ropes.'

He sighed deeply. 'Why do you have to make everything so complicated?'

'Because it's more fun.'

'You're absolutely sure Branson's going to turn up?'

'Trust me, he owes us. The Virgin PR manager has promised.'

The thin reedy laugh again. 'You believe PR people? That's sweet. And what does Norris think about it all?'

'He's happy with it all of course because he's a trooper. He thinks the giant book will look great. Actually Alan does too – and David.'

'Oh God. Am I the only sane soul left in the building?'

'Possibly. Do you want me to run through the whole event?'

'Sadly time is not on my side. Besides I think I'd rather be surprised on the day. Then I can call a shrink directly afterwards.'

I finished my coffee and rose from the chair. 'It's going to be a huge success, I promise. You won't regret having signed this off.'

Chris chuckled to himself as I left the room. 'Keep taking the happy pills.'

★ ★ ★

Alan swanned up to my desk with a grin on his chops.

'Is Norris up to speed with the launch plans?'

'He gets back from the US tomorrow night so I can run through last-minute details with him then but so far he's happy with arrangements.'

He punched my arm. 'Well done. It's looking good. Quite a coup getting Branson.'

He gave me a wink and a cheeky smile and sauntered back to his den. Lisa grinned.

'Wow, that's high praise coming from our esteemed editor. He's quite a softy really, you know. Just don't blow it.'

'Thanks for the confidence boost. Uh-oh, here comes trouble.'

Alex, secret squirrel extraordinaire, was hissing at me from the corridor. 'Got a minute? In the kitchen, now!'

I followed him into our favourite hush-hush meeting place.

'What's up?'

He gave me a furtive look, keeping his voice down. 'I don't know but a stockbroker friend's just called to say something's going on in the market.'

'What's that got to do with anything?'

'Well, he's worried that something's brewing. Apparently the Dow Jones Index has dropped more than ninety-five points today.'

I stared at him in amusement. 'Alex, that's all gibberish to me. I haven't the faintest clue how the stock market works and nor do I want to. Now if you asked me about the role of the chorus in *Aeschylus* I might be able to join in the discussion.'

He tapped the work surface impatiently. 'What I mean is that if something's going down, it might affect Virgin's shares and then Branson would find himself in a bit of a crisis.'

The penny dropped along with my stomach. 'You don't mean he'd pull out of the launch?'

'I've no idea. Look, I'm sure things might stabilise but there's something fishy going on in the money markets.'

I left the kitchen in some concern. If the damned stock market had to crash, why now, right on the eve of my launch?

I looked out on a cold but bright day and shook my head. No, everything was going to be fine. Alex was probably reading too much into things. The stock market couldn't possibly affect a book launch. Could it?

★ ★ ★

I awoke in the night, my heart beating hard. Something or someone had just thumped my window. Shaking, I got out of bed in the chill and dared to raise the curtain. A maelstrom was raging outside. In the dark garden belonging to our downstairs neighbour it seemed as though the trees were dancing wildly to some disco beat, their branches waving in crazy abandon while plant pots hurtled about the lawn, lifted high on the wind then dropping heavily to the ground. Some shrubs appeared to have been uprooted and lay wasted on their sides and, in the corner of the patio, the dog kennel had rolled over onto a sack of cement. The sound of loose tiles slithering from the roof and smashing on to the ground below made me jump. This was one hell of a storm. I heard the click of the bathroom light, then Jane knocked on my door. 'Are you OK?'

I could see the whites of her eyes in the dim light. 'Yes, but it's a bit frightening.'

'The lights aren't working. I've just tried the bathroom. Shall we light some candles?'

I followed her into the kitchen and, in the icy chill, located candles and finally a box of matches. I watched the concentration on her face as she struck the match and finally got the candle to light.

'Do you think the roof's secure?' she asked.

'God knows!' I replied and as if on cue a loud thud came from above, quickly followed by the sound of something crashing to the ground below. 'That could have been a disorientated flying pig.'

'I don't think so,' Jane replied crisply.

'A witch whose broomstick went out of control?'

'Stop being silly.'

'It makes you think about the Eider and Canvasback, doesn't it?'

She narrowed her eyes. 'What are you on about?'

'Well, those species of birds can reach speeds of about 80 miles per hour. Imagine one swooping down on to our roof at that kind of speed.'

'You really are beyond help,' she muttered. 'Can we find out what did cause that crash?'

A groan of thunder sounded overhead and the wind was deafening.

'The weather report didn't say anything about this,' Jane sighed crossly. 'I listened to the late-night news and they just said it would be a blustery evening.'

We stood shivering in the half light listening to plant pots dancing along the gravel paths below. A moment later there came another almighty crash except this time from the street. We ran into the living room and pulled back the curtains. A massive plane tree had been uprooted and lay drunkenly across the bonnet of a car.

'Someone's not going to be happy in the morning,' I said. 'Can't see anything that's come off our roof.'

Jane peered below in disbelief as bushes, litter, tiles and rubbish bins flew threw the air, landing in front gardens and in the middle of the road.

'There's a large bush lying in the front garden. Do you think that could have come off our roof?'

'Curious. I didn't know we had any growing up there,' I remarked.

'No, you fool. It could have been swept up on to the roof with the wind and crashed down again.'

'Interesting theory,' I replied.

'The wind must be incredibly strong to have uprooted that plane tree. Maybe we should just try to sleep through it. Wake me if anything worries you.'

I nodded. 'Likewise.'

We tripped off to our rooms. I tossed and turned for what seemed like hours until I began thinking about wind speed records. The highest surface wind speed of 231 miles per hour was recorded at Mount Washington in New Hampshire, but what about tornados? Ten minutes later I fumbled for the matches and candle by my bed, and finally my copy of *The Guinness Book of Records*. Turning to the meteorological record page, I discovered that the fastest ever recorded tornado was in Texas and travelled at 280 miles per hour. Silly me, I'd been thinking it was the Tri-State tornado that hit America in 1925. Of course, one of the states affected just happened to be Illinois. What was it about that place that seemed to attract records? In weariness I closed the book and finally dropped off, hoping that a disorientated flying pig wouldn't come crashing down on me before daylight.

★ ★ ★

I walked into the office. It was nine o'clock. I had been forced to walk part of the way to work because few buses seemed to be running. Main roads were covered in debris and fallen trees and it was only after walking for nearly forty minutes that a bus came into view. It was crowded with worried-looking passengers, their eyes pinioned to the destruction on the streets around them. I wondered how Eric the conductor was.

Lisa was sitting at her desk in a big-shouldered short-skirted suit, a smudge of black kohl under her eyes and her hair lacquered to perfection. In marked contrast, Shelley was perched on my desk wearing a denim jacket, open-necked pastel shirt and long skirt. They both had mugs of tea in their grip.

'You made it! What a night, eh?' greeted Lisa.

'Tell me about it. How did you both get in this morning?'

Shelley flipped her fiery tresses back behind her ears. 'I got a lift, thank heavens, but it's still pretty horrible out there. The traffic was unbelievable and we had at least three diversions because of trees having fallen down.'

'It was a bit easier for mum and me because we only live nearby,' said Lisa.

I sat down heavily in my chair. Muriel popped her head round the partition. 'Have you got a minute? Alex is summoning you for one of your secret pow-wows in the kitchen.'

She gave me a grin. 'Go on, he says it's important.'

The others laughed as I plodded off. Alex was pacing around the kitchen.

'The markets have been closed due to the storms,' he blurted as I entered.

'Jolly sensible too. I doubt I'd want to do any veg and fruit shopping in this weather.'

'I'm talking about the financial markets, you oaf.'

'What about them?'

'You don't get it, do you? Something's happened. I checked the Dow Jones Index, and it's fallen another hundred points. It's serious.'

Feeling exasperated I grabbed the kettle and filled it with water. 'I'm sorry, Alex, but what is your fixation with Dow Jones anyway?'

'I don't know but I feel it's going to directly affect Virgin.'

Muriel padded into the kitchen. 'I hope you don't mind me interrupting, but even if Branson was affected, he wouldn't pull out of the launch, would he?'

Alex regarded us both solemnly. 'That would depend on how serious it was.'

'But surely a promise is a promise?' I replied.

'Bless,' said Alex, patting my arm with a look of pity.

I watched as he darted out of the kitchen to answer a telephone. Muriel gave me an encouraging smile.

'Don't worry. I'm sure a man in his position wouldn't let you down.'

I returned to my desk in time to grab the telephone on its first ring. 'Norris, how are you?'

'Perfectly fine. Interesting weather conditions last night.'

'That's one way of putting it.'

'You know it's the worst storm since the Great Storm of 1703 – in fact, they're calling it the Great Storm of 1987. They recorded winds of up to 134 miles per hour last night.'

'Fascinating. Where are you?'

'At home, of course. I got in late last night.'

'Have you got time to catch up about the launch?'

He laughed. 'Have you forgotten that I'm coming in later?'

'What? That would be madness. The roads are in chaos.'

'Nonsense. If there's a will and all that.' He paused. 'Did you know that Daniel Defoe based his first book, *The Storm*, on the Great Storm of 1703?'

'What a coincidence, I was just discussing that at three in the morning with my flatmate, Jane.'

He gave a scratchy cough. 'You may mock but as a supposed literature scholar, you jolly well ought to have known that.'

'Yes, but what's the point when I have you around to constantly keep me on track?'

'Pathetic,' he muttered to my amusement. It was Norris's response to most of the things ailing society from apathy to political ineptitude to full-scale wars.

I got down to work, irritated that few people I needed to call had made it into the office. Lisa and I shared some sandwiches at lunchtime and went through our checklist for Monday's event.

'If we forget anything, we can sort it out over the weekend,' she said breezily.

'Let's just hope everyone turns up. Apparently some people are stranded in certain parts of the country.'

She tutted. 'It'll be fine, just you see. Besides, we've got Branson coming, what more do we need?'

★ ★ ★

It was early afternoon when Norris wandered over to my desk.

'You see, I got here. Shall we meet in an hour or so? I must have a quick catch up with David.'

I nodded and watched as he walked decisively along the corridor, greeting editors and accepting a cup of tea from a beaming Muriel along the way. Somehow when Norris entered the office, everyone bucked up. He was adored by one and all. The telephone rang. Lisa grabbed at it and then with a puzzled look put the call through to me.

'It's Virgin's PR manager. She sounds odd.'

I picked up the receiver.

'Hi, I'm so sorry, but I'm afraid, um, Richard, um, isn't going to be able to make your launch after all. He's obviously really, really sorry about it but something pretty urgent has cropped up.'

I sat in silence. Alex was prophetic. I was cross.

'Look, what can be so dramatic that he can't make the launch?'

'We're having a few problems, and Richard really can't make it. I know this must be disappointing...'

'We agreed that he'd do this,' I said icily.

'Yes, I know, but the circumstances are exceptional. Again, my sincere apologies.'

The line went dead. I took a deep breath. Lisa stared across the desk at me with a sick expression on her face. 'Oh no, don't tell me he's pulling out?'

'Something's cropped up apparently,' I said.

'Yeah, right. That's very nice, leaving us in the lurch just before a major launch.'

I called Alex. He was at my desk in a matter of seconds.

'I knew something was up. Virgin must be worried.'

I got up and stomped around my desk. 'You know what, Alex, I'm not remotely worried about Virgin's problems. A deal's a deal and I will get Richard Branson to my launch, whatever it takes.'

He smiled weakly at me. 'Sure. Well, let's have a cup of tea and think about this rationally.'

I was not feeling rational. Grabbing my business card folder I found the telephone number of Mike, a business associate of Richard Branson with whom I'd had dealings during Virgin's Atlantic air balloon crossing. He listened patiently as I ranted furiously into the receiver. He understood how angry I was feeling.

'You know, Richard wouldn't pull out unless things were pretty serious. I know you're upset and this launch is a big deal for you but just imagine what might be happening at his end.'

Stubbornly I refused even to try to contemplate what was happening in the Virgin office. I worked for Guinness, not Virgin, and my loyalties lay with the book.

'I tell you what, Mike, I am going to have a complete tantrum, and go to the press with this unless you do something.'

He groaned. 'OK, leave this with me. There's maybe been a bit of a misunderstanding. Probably Richard's PR people are trying to protect him. He may not even be aware of all this.'

I threw down the phone. Norris appeared.

'Something wrong?'

'I'm fuming.'

'Ah, never mind. Always good to breathe deeply and read a few pages of a book and then reassess the situation.'

I burst out laughing. 'What would we do without you, Norris?'

He shrugged. 'Carry on as usual, I suppose.'

We adjourned to the library where I told him blow by blow what had transpired. He frowned. 'I understand your disappointment but if he can't get there it's not the end of the world. Life goes on.'

'It's the principle of the matter.'

He laughed. 'Ha! Don't expect principles to play a part in this. Look, we have a good event planned with excellent record-breakers coming regardless of Richard Branson.'

Muriel brought in a tray of tea and biscuits. She touched my arm encouragingly. 'I know it's disappointing but it will all go brilliantly, mark my words.'

Norris regarded me with kind eyes. 'You know, life's full of disappointment, AN.' This had become his nickname for me. 'You just have to take it on the chin and plough on.'

I munched on a biscuit, not willing to give in to reason just yet.

'I had sporting disappointments in my youth, as did my brother Ross. On one occasion when we were both recruits in the Royal Navy, Ross and I had to compete in two races against some chaps from the RAF. I managed to get the medallion in the 100 yards sprint but Ross was in the 220 yards race, negotiated a bend badly and ended up with a nasty leg and arm injury. He took defeat with good grace.'

I gave him a smile. Silence. 'Do you mind me asking why the IRA killed Ross?'

Without hesitation he shook his head. 'No, of course not. Ross had a very good chum named Professor Hamilton-Fairley; he was a leading cancer researcher. Anyway, he was killed by an IRA bomb. My brother was enraged and wrote to the lily-livered Home Secretary suggesting that a substantial reward be offered to anyone who blew the whistle on terrorists. The IRA apparently didn't like that. They lay in wait in his garden one late afternoon and when his wife, Rosemary, arrived home, they forced her at gunpoint to ring the doorbell. When Ross answered they shot him dead.'

I sat in horrified silence. 'I'm so sorry.'

He gave a long sigh. 'It was many years ago, but the memory never goes away. You know it's much harder to forget something than to remember it. That night often flashes before my eyes. I can still picture my brother in the mortuary and thinking it was like half of me lying there. We were identical as you know and shared everything. It was hard.'

I felt utterly ashamed. Here I was boring Norris with my pathetic gripes about a press photocall when he had been forced to bear such untold grief in his life.

'Life has to go on though,' Norris resumed.

The door opened. Muriel apologised for interrupting. 'I've got Mike on the line.'

I excused myself and bolted from the room.

'You owe me big time,' Mike was saying. 'I've spoken with Richard and he's agreed to come to your launch after all. I think something got lost in the translation.'

I thanked him profusely and returned to the library. Norris smiled when I told him about the call.

'Saved by the bell, AN, but remember that there are always alternatives and that problems only exist if you allow them to become problems.'

I bit my lip uncertainly. 'But you're pleased he's showing up?'

He rose from the table. 'I'm glad to hear he's attending, but equally the event would have been perfectly fine without him. We all make too much out of small matters that are utterly unimportant in the greater scheme of things.'

Duly chastised, I made my way back to my desk, relieved that one potential disaster had been averted. I thought about Ross and the unimaginable loss to Norris and his family. Norris was right, there were far more important things to focus on in life.

★ ★ ★

Richard Branson, in chinos and a big sweater, was sitting cross-legged on Covent Garden's cobbled piazza. If he'd wanted to strangle me he showed remarkable forbearance as he flicked back his golden locks, smiled cheerfully for the barrage of cameras and chatted animatedly with Matthew Corbett, Jean Leggett the fire-eater, and Norris. I felt a twinge of guilt for having dragged him over here when quite obviously Virgin needed him. It was Monday – forever after known as Black Monday, 19 October 1987, the day share prices tumbled and markets around the world crashed. Did I care? Of course not. I only had eyes for the number of media converging on the piazza and the number of press headlines we'd hopefully make the next morning. Just doing my job. After the ferocious wind that had rocked the country for several days, things were gradually getting back to normal, but not quite. Several guests were unable to make their way to London for the reception and others were delayed due to cancelled trains. The giant wooden prop, an exact replica of the latest edition of *The Guinness Book of Records*, stood at the southern end of the piazza between two pillars. At the press's insistence, Norris, Richard, Matthew Corbett with puppet Sooty, and Jean Leggett climbed up ladders at the book's rear and popped their heads through the small windows that had been created in the huge replica's facade. All went smoothly until the assembled photographers asked them for a few last shots sitting together on the cobbled piazza.

A voice shouted from the line-up of cameramen. 'Jean, lean in, love!'

And another. 'Closer, Jean. Snuggle up to Richard. That's it, lovely!'

Obligingly, Jean, balancing two flaming torches, crouched lower and then just as the shutters blinked, a gust of wind triggered a tongue of flame to lick Richard's locks and a wisp of smoke rose from the top of his head. I looked on in horror just as Matthew Corbett, quick as a flash, leaned forward and aimed Sooty's water gun at the offending patch of smoke. Richard blinked as water showered him but cottoned on quickly to the situation. The photographers whooped and clicked their lenses. Oh God. This would probably be the very last time he would cooperate with the book ever again. A reporter from *The Sun* approached him.

'Close shave, Richard. Thought you were going up in smoke there. Good old Sooty!'

Richard merely scrunched his nose and laughed. 'It wasn't a problem.'

As the protagonists of the photocall and press made their way to the Savoy for the launch reception, Richard Branson casually strode over to me and shook my hand.

'I need to get back to the office I'm afraid.'

'Well thanks for your support this morning and I'm really sorry about your hair getting singed.'

'No harm done,' he replied with a shrug and a bashful smile.

To my relief he didn't allude to the earlier discussions that had taken place between his PR department, Mike and me. Perhaps he never knew. With a wave, he strolled across the piazza alone, a man clearly on a mission and yet without fanfare or seemingly any sense of urgency. Norris pottered over to me having just polished off another impromptu TV interview.

'Seemed to go off OK,' he said quietly.

'Pity about Branson's hair,' I replied.

'He's got plenty of it,' he smiled roguishly. 'Everything went perfectly well, don't fret.'

I nodded. 'I suppose so but I hope the stock market crash isn't going to steal every headline tomorrow. Just our luck!'

He patted my arm. 'AN, you can bring a horse to water but you can't make it drink. What will be will be. You couldn't possibly have done any more.'

Matthew Corbett and Jean Leggett gave us a wave in the distance. Norris waved back and turned to me with a grin. 'Come on, we'd better get going or Sooty will scoff all the sandwiches.'

★ ★ ★

The River Room of the Savoy was throbbing with guests of an unusual kind because they were either record-breakers or had association with superlatives. A gaggle of photographers hovered about the entrance excitedly clicking their cameras when the likes of Dame Barbara Cartland, David Frost, Pat Coombs and Roy Castle entered. Applause broke out as the final speech was given. Norris and Alan stepped down from the stage and took their seats at the top table while Lisa and I chatted with the press and directed guests to their seats. Actresses Thora Hird and Carmen Silvera appeared breathlessly at the door and were besieged by photographers. The flower arrangements adorning each table had been carefully colour coordinated representing *The Guinness Book of Records'* livery of red, yellow and black. In the absence of black tulips, black vases had been provided for red roses and yellow freesias and red rose petals ran along the tables. While standing talking to a journalist from the *Telegraph* I noticed the singer and actor Adam Faith sidling in. With a cheeky wink he came up and gave me a hug. Ever since I'd involved him in one of my crazy photocalls at Help the Aged he had become an ally, loyally pitching up for any event I orchestrated. He was probably the only guest with no record association, although he had once survived a near fatal car crash that had practically left him for dead. Perhaps he should have had a record for that alone.

'Wotcha!' he grinned. 'Anyone interesting here apart from me and you?'

'Barbara Cartland's over there. You could discuss romantic novels with her?'

He pulled a face. 'Give me a break!'

'Well, go and talk with Roy Castle and Norris. I've put you on their table.'

'Thank God for that.'

He wandered off, smiling and stopping to chat to guests. No matter where he went, the public eulogised him. Perhaps it was the irresistible combination of cheeky schoolboy charm and total unaffectedness. Norris and Roy looked delighted to see him and soon they were deep in conversation.

Meanwhile across the room, Dean Gould, lean and pale and concentrating hard, was demonstrating to Creighton Carvello, the world's greatest memory man, and Norman Johnson, the fastest cucumber slicer, how to balance and catch a pile of beer mats in one hand. He was preparing himself for a new record attempt that day. Barbara Cartland, her perfectly starched white halo of hair bobbing in one single move above her heavily powdered face, looked on from her chair until curiosity got the better of her and she came over to watch. She flagged me down.

'Has he got abnormally large hands to do that?' she asked in loud, cut glass tones.

'Well, they certainly are larger than average but it's also got a lot to do with dexterity and dedication.'

She gave a curt nod and gave a flutter of her long spidery false eyelashes. I observed her hands which were weighed down with enormous rocks, the nails deep pink. 'Yes, take my writing, for example. How could I possibly be the top-selling authoress in the world unless I took my work very seriously?'

'Absolutely,' I conceded. 'What is it now, four hundred and fifty million sales globally?'

'Correct – and in twenty-one languages.'

'Staggering.'

She turned to me in some alarm. 'Who is?'

'I was just saying how staggering your sales are.'

She took on a confidential air. 'You know, I have an awful time of it with those people at *Who's Who*. They make a terrific fuss about the size of my entry – apparently the longest in the book – and I have explained quite clearly to them that all my titles must be listed.'

'And why is that?' I asked before I could stop myself.

She gave an impatient sigh. 'Well, obviously it's because my dear friend Norris McWhirter insists on it!'

Without more ado, she swept back to her table where her ever-patient son awaited her return. Norris gave me a discreet nod from afar and beckoned me over. I squeezed through the tables until I reached him and squatted down by his chair.

'Our esteemed authoress loves that necklace,' he said. 'It has seven strings of pearls and she matches it with those large pearl earrings. I think it's a favourite of hers.'

'She also likes pink,' I replied.

He laughed. 'What else do you expect a romantic novelist to wear? Every Christmas she sends me an enormous card with the mark of a real pink kiss planted on the inside.'

'Careful, people will start talking.'

'Did you know that she has the longest entry in *Who's Who*?'

'So she tells me, and it's you who bossily insists that her publishers list all her works.'

'Not at all!' Norris protested. 'She uses me as her buffer. I am innocent of all charges.'

'Have you ever read one of her books?' asked Adam Faith with a grin, leaning from his chair to face us.

'I can't say I have,' I said sniffily.

Norris pulled a face of mock disappointment. 'And she calls herself a literary scholar. Pathetic!'

There was a hush as Alan took to the stage and addressed the guests. I turned to Norris and whispered. 'You'd better go up there. You're on next.'

He took a sip of water and turned to me. 'There's plenty of time before I need to make a move.'

Alan's speech was greeted with enthusiastic applause. It was then that I saw his eyes roam the audience and rest on Norris, at which point the book's founder rose to his feet and with a shy smile made his way through the tables. With a few jaunty steps, Norris was up on to the small stage and sharing a few quiet words with Alan before taking the microphone and addressing the assembled guests. The River Room fell silent as he delivered a word-perfect, unfaltering speech. As always I wondered at his ability to combine gravitas with humour while demonstrating his astonishing memory and enthusiasm for facts and figures, and of course records old and new. As he delivered his thanks rapturous applause broke out. He returned to his seat and very modestly accepted compliments from fellow guests, a slight blush on his cheeks, whether of pride or shyness I couldn't say, though possibly both. The event rolled on. Waiters darted about the room, refilling glasses and replenishing plates until a few guests gradually began rising from their seats and making a move towards the exit.

I checked my watch and decided it was time to start packing up the leftover press packs. Lisa had already started handing out goodie bags to the early departing guests.

'I must get on,' I whispered to Norris.

He nodded. 'Yes, I'll have to be away shortly. It's already three o'clock. Anyway, it seems to have gone well, don't you think? Now all we've got to worry about is the promotional tour.'

Before I had a chance to reply, a massive cheer rose from the centre of the room. Alan was giving Dean, the beer mat flipper, a pat on the back and announcing a new world record. Dean had surpassed his previous record of catching 90 beer mats all at once, by an extra three. We watched as several guests bent down to gather up the fallen beer mats. A reporter from New York's WNYC radio station rushed over to interview him along with various national newspapers.

'Another record in the bag for that young man,' said Norris. 'What's your claim to fame?'

I shrugged and rose to my feet. 'Can't compete, I'm afraid.'

'That's not good enough, AN, can't you think of anything?'

I hesitated. 'Perhaps. How about being the first person to persuade Richard Branson to stick his head through the largest book in the world without paying him a penny?'

He paused to digest the thought. 'That's pretty impressive. Yes, well done, I think that might do.'

FOUR

★ ★ ★

THE LONG AND THE SHORT AND THE TALL

Lisa was sitting at her desk sipping a mug of hot chocolate. The perfectly sculpted, rose-hued nails of one hand were visible against the white china as she raised the mug to her red lips in small mouse-like movements. I wondered how long it took Lisa to get ready in the mornings. Always immaculately dressed in her hugging miniskirts and starched shirts, she would arrive with carefully applied, full make-up, and enough bright gold jewellery to rival a Ratner's store. Her hair was always blow dried with the utmost care and lacquered so that it stubbornly resisted the harshest gale. By contrast I donned whatever was clean and crease-free from my wardrobe each day, shunned make-up and had hair that would rival the wildest angora goat – talking of which, an angora goat had been recently sold in Gloucestershire for the record-breaking price of £14,700, but I digress. Lisa would look at me pityingly, at times subtly suggesting that I might consider ditching my university duffel coat for a smart mac or camel hair coat but on my meagre salary I couldn't see the sense in such a flagrant waste of valuable funds. Fortunately, after about six months in the job, David suggested I buy an Austin Reed blazer on the pocket of which was sewn an expensive gold-beaded *Guinness Book of Records* official logo, all at the company's expense. This meant that I might at least be taken seriously when officiating at record attempts.

I looked out of the window at the descending rain, a typical English November, and contemplated the short train ride I would soon be making to the Trocadero Centre in Piccadilly. Norris had suggested we meet at the *Guinness World of Records* exhibition on the top floor of the building so that he could give me a grand tour of the new exhibits. We would later join Biddy Baxter and the *Blue Peter* team at the BBC White City studios to meet Zeus, an old English mastiff, the heaviest dog ever recorded at 22 stone and 6 pounds. He would fortunately be accompanied by his owner so it wouldn't be down to any of us to control him.

'By the way,' Lisa said. 'Geoff Smith called earlier. Can you ring him back?'

I picked up the telephone and rang the Press Association. Geoff sounded perky.

'Didn't we do well with all the coverage of the book launch? I had regional newspapers fighting for the story. A real scoop.'

It was true, the book launch had thankfully resulted in so much fantastic press coverage that Chris had chosen to ignore discrepancies in the budget.

'Did you see what *The Sun* wrote?'

'I missed that,' said Geoff.

I grabbed the cutting from my in tray. 'Listen to this, "Branson really did look hot stuff in London when a fire-eater accidentally set part of his hair alight".'

He roared with laughter. 'It's all great publicity, honey!'

'So far book sales have been phenomenal. We've notched up about two million sales so far.'

'Unbelievable! How many sales since the book began back in the fifties?'

'We'll soon be hitting sixty million copies at this rate.'

Geoff gave a low whistle.

'Now listen, I just called about one of the stops on your book promotional tour with Norris. It's a pub in Stalybridge called The Old Thirteenth Cheshire Astley Volunteer Rifleman Corps Inn. Is that for real?'

'Absolutely. It's got the longest name of any pub in England.'

'That's quite a laugh. I wonder if they pull the longest beer?' he tittered.

'I'll check it out when I visit it later this month.'

Something suddenly clunked onto my desk. Puzzled, I looked down to find one of my cheap dangly Indian earrings staring back at me. That's odd. How could it have fallen from my ear when it was firmly secured at the back with a butterfly clasp? To my horror I discovered that the earring had somehow ripped right through the lobe. The skin was sliced in two. I gave a shriek. Lisa looked up.

'You all right?' yelled Geoff.

'NO! My earring's just fallen off. It's torn right through my lobe.'

'Urgh!' he cried while Lisa, in some disgust, rushed over to witness the spectacle.

She picked up the earring. 'These weigh a bomb. No wonder! Where on earth did you get them?'

'Camden Market.'

'Classy,' she said with heavy sarcasm. With the phone cradled against it, somehow it must have gone right through.' Pause for effect. 'Just like a hot knife through butter.'

'Oh stop it, Lisa!' I groaned, clutching at my now throbbing ear which stung like mad but curiously wasn't bleeding much.

Geoff sounded faint. 'I'll have to go. You've completely put me off my lunch. I'm not good with blood.'

Lisa hurriedly called her local doctor who suggested that I make all haste to his surgery. She bit her lip and frowned.

'He says he's not good at sewing but he could probably do a temporary job.'

'That sounds comforting. Look, maybe it can wait.'

'Don't be ridiculous! Go now. It's a five-minute walk.'

She wrote down the address on a Post-it and rammed it into my hand. As I headed for the door, Alan popped his head out of his office. 'Thought we might have a brief catch up later when you're free?'

'Not a great time, Alan. I've just torn my ear and am off to have it stitched up. Then I've got Norris and *Blue Peter*.'

He nodded, slowly digesting the news. 'Sure you're feeling OK?'

'Yes, never better. I'll see you later today.'

He smiled weakly and returned to his desk, puzzlement etched on his craggy visage.

★ ★ ★

In the street I surveyed Lisa's neatly drawn mini map and found the surgery easily enough. Mr Singh was courteous, if a little serious.

'You say it just fell through your ear?'

'That's right.'

He joggled the earring up and down in his hand and took a sharp intake of breath. 'You young women sometimes ask for trouble. Look at your lobe. It is too small to sustain this heavy stone.'

I felt my tram ticket earlobe. 'The earrings were a gift from a friend in India. They didn't feel that heavy.'

'But you have to have long and deep lobes for this sort of weight.'

He sighed and, after wiping an icy fluid on my ear, got out a needle and thread. 'My eyes aren't what they used to be,' he mumbled, reaching for some reading glasses. 'Now hold still while I sew you up. I'm very bad at this but at least I can try.'

After a few painful minutes, he cut the thread. 'There. Job done. It's not totally straight but it'll do, after all, you don't strike me as a vain girl. '

With an awkward grimace, he directed me towards a mirror on his surgery wall and, sure enough, his sewing was wonky. I might not be vain but I was a bit disappointed by his handiwork, self-consciously pulling a curl in front of the offending ear.

I set off back to the office and called Norris. He listened calmly to my tale of woe.

'It could of course be elephantiasis.'

'WHAT?'

'That can cause severe swelling. Mind you it's usually in the legs and feet. It's the fault of a parasitic worm passed on by infected mosquitoes.'

I protested. 'But my ear isn't swollen.'

He grunted. 'Maybe you have a deformed ear lobe.'

'I certainly do not!'

'You know, the largest shoes are usually bought by people suffering from elephantiasis although the largest pair ever sold was used for a Harley Davidson promotion.'

In some frustration, I cut short the call.

'Norris thinks I've got elephantiasis,' I remarked to Lisa.

'Sounds nasty,' she said sympathetically. 'Never mind, I'm sure it'll clear up soon.'

I grabbed my bag and headed for the door, suddenly aware of the muffled laughter emanating from behind the wooden partitions of the editorial team.

★ ★ ★

Norris was staring up at Robert Pershing Wadlow. It was impossible to do anything else when faced with the 8 feet and 11.1 inches exact replica wax model. It depicted a rather shy, bespectacled young man in a formal tweed suit and tie, his short, dark gelled hair neatly parted at the side.

'Poor chap. You know he suffered from a terrible back. Only lived until he was twenty-four.'

I peered at the caption beneath the exhibit. 'It says he was born in 1918.'

'Yes, in Illinois.'

'Not Illinois again! What is it with that place?'

He gave a little giggle. 'You're right. There seem to be an inordinate number of records broken in Illinois. Maybe we should investigate that.'

'The tallest living man is Gabriel Estavao Monjane in Mozambique at just over eight feet, isn't he?'

He sniffed. 'Yes, there are photos of him here, and Sandy Allen, the world's tallest woman. Sandy might have grown taller than 7 feet 7 inches but she had a pituitary gland operation to inhibit further growth.'

He pointed to a small wax figure of a woman in full Victorian bustle and frill at the neck who just about reached the giant's shin.

'That's Pauline Musters, known as Princess Pauline. She was a Dutch midget who had a drink problem. It's not very sensible to imbibe too much when you're only 23.2 inches tall.'

'No, I imagine not. Did the booze kill her?'

He waved his hand dismissively through the air. 'She died at nineteen years old. It was recorded as pneumonia and meningitis but alcohol was the real reason. It finished off her heart.'

I scrutinised a photograph of an elderly Japanese man, his face withered with age. According to the caption at its side his name was Shigechiyo Izumi of Asan who died at 120 years old, the world's oldest authenticated centenarian.

'Did you ever get to meet him?'

Norris nodded. 'Yes, back in 1980 in Tokyo when he was a hundred and sixteen. Poor old boy wasn't too well at the time.'

We walked on through the long curving labyrinth of corridors, studying exhibits under the strong spotlights.

'Ah, now this is Birger Pellas who had the longest recorded moustache at 9 feet and 1 inch.'

The thin and fair hairy extensions jutting from either side of the model's mouth coiled down to the ground like a pair of giant beaver tails.

'It wasn't very practical, was it?'

'No, not really, unless I suppose he plaited both sides and attached them to his head. Now, although he isn't featured here, Karna Ram Bheel was quite interesting. He had a moustache that measured just over 7 feet and when he was given a life sentence – not for having a long moustache, something else – the New Delhi prison governor allowed him to keep his whiskers in mint condition by using a combination of cream, butter, mustard and oil.'

'Revolting.'

He laughed. 'At least he didn't consume it. I once went on a promotional tour of Austria with a whole plane-load of record-breakers, including John Roy.'

'Who was he?'

'He had the longest moustache in Great Britain at 74 and a half inches but then in 1984 he accidentally sat on it in the bath and lost two feet from one side. Of course he couldn't look lopsided so he had to cut two feet off the other to balance it up.'

'That must have been a real bummer.'

He suddenly turned to me. 'Talking of things falling off, what happened about your ear?'

Reluctantly I pulled back my hair, revealing the badly stitched left lobe.

He peered at it in wonderment. 'You might have been better going to Savile Row and finding a proper tailor to sort it out.'

'Does it look awful?'

'Put it this way, I think you've dashed any chance of modelling earrings. Similarly with those bitten nails, you'll never land a job as a hand model either – although I suppose you could model gloves.'

He steered me towards a pair of wax hands in a showcase from which long and curling fingernails unfurled. I stepped back.

'Horrible.'

Norris tutted. 'Quite to the contrary. They're fascinating. Shridhar Chillal lived in Poona and he managed to grow his thumbnail to 37 inches. The aggregate measurement for just five nails was 158 inches.'

'Why would anyone want to do that?'

He regarded me with narrowed eyes and a grin. 'To enter *The Guinness Book of Records*, perhaps?'

'But how long would it take to grow a nail to that length?'

He considered this. 'Given that fingernails grow four times faster than toenails, about 0.02 inches per week, it would probably take almost a lifetime.'

I stuck my nose to the showcase. 'Imagine trying to type.'

'I doubt that was a priority for him,' he said dryly.

We entered the tallest structures section. A craggy under-lit model of Mount Everest faced us.

'Take Mount Everest,' said Norris. 'The world's highest peak at just over 29,000 feet. Few people appreciate that it was named by the British after the former Surveyor General of India, Sir George Everest, in 1865. Do you know how it should be pronounced?'

I shrugged. 'Ever-est?'

He rubbed his hands together. 'No! Eve-rest. All these years people have got it wrong. Pathetic!'

There came the sound of clicking heels and Maxine, the *Guinness World of Records* manager arrived.

'I've been looking for you two. What do you think of the new exhibits?'

Norris frowned. 'Where are they?'

She looked at her watch. 'Haven't you even got as far as the natural world? There's a new exhibit of the largest fungi and we've got a replica of the most expensive shoe.'

'Is that the mink-lined golf shoe from Norwich?' I piped up.

Norris tapped his chin. 'Odd the sort of things you remember, AN. How much is it worth then, Miss Clever Clogs?'

'I seem to recall it costing about eight grand.'

'£8,580 to be precise.'

Maxine shook her head. 'Look, you've only got thirty minutes before you leave for the BBC. I've arranged a snack for you both in the office. You'll have to come back and see the rest another day.'

We followed her back into the harsh light of the entrance hall.

'It's a shame you haven't got more time,' she said, tossing her mane of dark hair behind her as she bent to unlock her office door.

'I can pay another visit soon. It'll give me more time to absorb it all.'

Norris agreed. 'Always better not to rush things. Anyway, AN's suffering from a touch of elephantiasis today so she's a bit off colour.'

'Sorry to hear that,' says Maxine with a concerned expression.

We sat at a round table on which sandwiches had been laid out on plates. In the centre stood a rich chocolate cake. Norris's eyes lit up.

'Shall we start with the cake first?'

Maxine shook her head sternly. 'Watch him. He's a chocoholic. Mars Bars, Kit Kats and Cadbury's Fruit and Nut. One day it'll get him into trouble.'

Never had words been more prophetic, as I was to discover one day soon.

★ ★ ★

The BBC official behind the reception desk pushed passes in our direction and instructed us to follow his colleague out of the building. Under a grey cloudy sky, Zeus stood with a grumpy expression stamped on his huge face. According to Frank, his owner, he didn't like waiting and grew fidgety if left unoccupied for too long. Norris gave him a friendly pat, somewhat amused that with a shoulder height of nearly three feet, the creature reached as high as his waist. Although the dog seemed friendly enough Norris kept a beady eye on his enormous, salivating jaw.

'You're a big chap, aren't you?' he smiled, sneaking a slither of a smile in my direction.

'Woof!' The giant mastiff boomed and fixed him with large penetrating eyes.

I had never seen such a large dog in my life. His deep, thundering bark seemed to rise up from his enormous belly and reverberated around the room striking fear in the heart. At 8 feet 3 inches from nose to tail and 35 inches in height he seemed more like a young horse. Despite his 22 stone bulk, he was a docile and friendly creature and happily followed his master across the large quad towards the studio building. A concierge interrupted our path suddenly and demanded to see our passes. He didn't seem keen to let such a large dribbling beast into the building. 'We're here for a slot on *Blue Peter*,' the BBC reception clerk said.

Warily the man examined our passes and accompanied us to the studio, where he stood uneasily by the main door.

'That thing should be on a lead!' he moaned. 'He could rip someone's throat out.'

As we entered, the crew and presenters converged on us and Zeus seemed delighted to be the centre of attention. He wagged his tail and barked loudly, the sound leaping out of his immense belly and momentarily deafening us all. Biddy Baxter came bustling over and began briefing Norris on the show's various guests and his interview with Caron Keating and Zeus. The dog cocked an ear as if understanding every word and began sniffing at her big-shouldered jacket. She spun round to face him.

'My, you are an enormous creature! Our viewers are going to love you.'

Zeus began panting heavily and his big tongue unravelled from his colossal jaw like a roll of scarlet wallpaper, dripping saliva all over the floor. Someone fetched a bowl of water which he hoovered up at alarming speed.

'Now just one delicate point,' said Biddy to Zeus's owner. 'As you know we do have Goldie, our own Labrador, on the show, so we'd be grateful if you could remain here and keep Zeus firmly on a lead until he's due to appear and when he leaves the set.'

She turned to the fretful concierge. 'Can I ask you to keep an eye on things?'

He nodded unhappily and glared at Zeus. 'As soon as he's done his bit, I'd like him off BBC premises. It's dangerous having a ferocious beast in the studio.'

'He's hardly ferocious,' laughed Norris. 'He's a bit of a pussycat really.'

The dog, now firmly attached to a chain-link lead, jumped up at Norris excitedly. Frank, his owner, pulled the lead hard.

'Best not to mention the word C.A.T. He goes a little crazy!'

The concierge shook his head in disapproval and muttered, 'What did I say?'

Fifteen minutes later, the well-behaved Zeus was sitting between Norris and Frank and being filmed and feted. Caron Keating, dressed in a wide, open-necked white shirt and black bolero and jeans, stroked Zeus during the interview and showed complete nonchalance when he leaned forward to lick her hand. The piece ended and Zeus and Frank came bounding towards me, while Norris chatted with Biddy before joining us all.

I patted the dog's head. 'That was great! Well done, Zeus. It went like clockwork.'

Frank smiled. 'Yes, he's quite a star.'

As we headed for the door, Goldie appeared on set with Mark Curry, one of the presenters, and Zeus began whimpering loudly in anticipation as he looked up at her with longing. The concierge had evidently had quite enough of us all and began ushering us out of the studio, making the mistake of giving Zeus a quick prod on the neck. The big dog spun round and, before Frank could intervene, gave the concierge a quick nip on the backside. The man jumped in the air and gripped his derrière in anguish. It was all I could do to keep from bursting into laughter, but seeing the expression on his face I somehow managed to stifle my mirth. Obviously in some discomfort, he icily guided us towards the reception, limping awkwardly yet refusing to accept help. Once there he was bundled away to the medical suite where no doubt some BBC nurse would tend to him, hopefully without breaking into giggles. We hung around the reception discussing the incident. Frank was very upset and sighed deeply. 'He's such a gentle dog. I don't know why that man hassled him so much. I hope it's not too bad.'

Later on, Norris made enquiries at the reception desk and after a few quick phone calls, the operator grinned and told us that the man was apparently suffering from little more than a graze but a big dollop of wounded pride. We waved goodbye to Zeus and his owner in the reception area and went our separate ways. Norris and I shared a taxi back to Enfield.

'Poor man, he'll never live that one down. There can't be more humiliating incidents than being nipped on the rump by the largest dog in the world.'

Norris shook with laughter. 'Yes, he'll maybe not want to dine out on that story. Still, it proved one thing.'

I looked at him in some puzzlement. 'What's that?'

'That Zeus's bark really was much worse than his bite.'

★ ★ ★

I was sitting in Alan's office talking about the Little Buddy phenomenon. For the last few weeks our office had been plagued by calls about this fictitious character, dreamed up by his creators to front a chain letter campaign. We did not have such a category but this didn't stop the perpetrators creating a sorry tale about a little boy named Buddy, ill with cancer, who was trying to gain entry into *The Guinness Book of Records* by collecting letters from well-wishers. It was hard to know whether it was a mischievous con to get trusting members of the public to send postal orders and cash or whether it was done as a rather sick joke. Either way, it was thoroughly misleading and abused the kindness of strangers who sent letters and money to an address in Glasgow. While the case was being investigated, we did our best to warn callers not to participate.

'Have these sorts of things happened before?' I asked Alan.

He swivelled round in his chair to face me. 'You have to be on your toes in this job. Most of the public are trustworthy but there'll always be someone who tries to push the boundaries or even cheat.'

'But how come? We have such a strict authentication procedure.'

He laughed. 'We certainly do but some people try to bend the rules. Norris once told me about a guy who wrote in claiming to have balanced fourteen of the old twelve-sided threepenny pieces edge to edge which meant he'd broken the existing record by two.'

'And hadn't he?'

'Well, the photograph seemed in order but Norris found it suspicious that he'd broken the record by two coins rather than by one. Surely if you were trying to break the existing record, you'd create a pile of thirteen coins first before making an attempt using fourteen?'

'Fair enough.'

'So Norris asked the guy to send him a photograph showing him balancing thirteen of the coins.'

'And did he?'

'No because he was a cheat. He confessed that he'd used a strong adhesive to stick a large piece of carpet, a card table and a chair, to the ceiling. He'd then taped fourteen coins together, and suspended them from the card table. He then took a photo upside down and hey presto, the ceiling became the floor!'

'What on earth would drive someone to such lengths?'

He gave me a grin. 'Some people would do anything to gain immortality through the pages of the book.'

I shook my head. 'Now I understand why we have such strict rules.'

He yawned. 'Exactly. And when you're out there authenticating records at events always check on every detail. Don't be fooled.'

I nodded. Good advice.

'I thought we might all pop out for a beer tomorrow night. Be good for the team to have some time out together. Are you on for that?'

I smiled. 'Great. Thanks.'

He got up and smacked his hands together. 'Let me know if you need any help with anything.'

'Of course.' I hesitated at the door. 'Roy Castle was telling me that the *Record Breakers* TV show was your concept.'

He put his hands on his hips. 'Yes, that's right. We kicked it off in 1972 and it's still going strong.'

'I'd love to hear all about the history of the show and the record-breakers you used to feature.'

He winked. 'We can discuss it over a beer tomorrow night. You'll wish you never asked. I could go on all night.'

I pottered back to my desk, happy that at last I had been accepted as a fully fledged member of the editorial team.

FIVE

★ ★ ★

STRANGE ENCOUNTERS UP NORTH

Anxiously pacing up and down in the departures hall of Heathrow airport, I wondered where on earth Norris could be. We were due to take a flight to Leeds from where we would begin our Christmas promotional tour, visiting new record-breakers and carrying out book signings. He was supposed to have been meeting me thirty minutes earlier at the check-in desk. I bent to glimpse my watch and became vaguely aware of something hurtling towards me at speed. It was Norris wielding a luggage trolley rather like a chariot. I leaped out of the way as he stopped within a few inches of me.

'Have you lost your mind?'

He chortled happily to himself. 'Thought that would wake you up. Ah, plenty of time for check-in.'

I grabbed his suitcase from the trolley and nearly keeled over. 'What have you got in here? A body?'

He rubbed his eyes and gave a small yawn. 'I've got a few reference works with me and a partial manuscript for the book on islands I'm trying to find time to write. There might be a spare moment or two when I can do a little research.'

I gave a snort of laughter. 'With the itinerary I've set up for you? Dream on.'

He took the case from my hand. 'Let me do that. Now, how long have we got before take-off? I was rather hoping to find a confectioner's here.'

'We have to board immediately so you can forget about buying any chocolate.'

The impeccably attired check-in assistant attempted to mask a smile as she handed Norris his boarding pass. He pushed it into the pocket of his heavy coat. 'Sir, if you could make your way urgently to the departure gate I'd be grateful.'

We jogged across the hall and through security which was fortunately deserted at such an early hour of the morning. As Norris walked jauntily through the scanner machine, a smiling security guard approached and asked Norris if he could have a quick check of his coat pocket. Instantly he pulled out a large bar of Cadbury's chocolate wedged inside.

'Sweet tooth, sir?' laughed the guard, waving it in the air.

Norris looked mystified. 'But that's not mine.'

I tutted loudly. 'I'm afraid he's a chocoholic. It's very sad the lengths to which people will go to hide their addictions.'

Several amused staff looked over and gave Norris the thumbs up.

The security guard winked and handed the bar back to him. 'Good for you, sir. Your secret's safe with me.'

Norris nodded and in some bafflement followed me at speed to the gate. As we neared the cabin crew with our boarding cards extended, he yanked at my coat sleeve.

'You little devil. You planted that chocolate bar in my coat pocket, didn't you?'

I shrugged. 'Well I might have anticipated that you'd want a chocolate fix.'

'Were you a pickpocket in your last life?'

'Probably.'

It was fairly obvious that we were the last to board but Norris strode briskly down the central aisle, seemingly unconcerned that everyone else was already seated and strapped in. We found our row and within a short time the doors were secured and we were speeding along the runway and up into the pallid sky. Norris pulled some newspapers from his briefcase and passed a broadsheet to me.

'Absurd! Poor Margaret's barely been back in the driving seat six months and already the knives are out. I'd like to see one of those chumps trying to run the country.'

I pulled the newspaper towards me and met the steely gaze of Margaret Thatcher, her perfectly coiffed sandy hair sitting like a stiff meringue on her head.

'She'll no doubt ride the storm,' I said, trying desperately to hide the ennui in my voice.

'Did you not read Peter Riddell's interview with her in the FT last month?'

'Sadly I missed it.'

He gave me a reproachful look.

'More importantly, do you think they'll bring us some breakfast soon?' I asked wearily.

He ruffled another paper. 'There's a lot of controversy about the proposed Clause 28 but I doubt that's crossed your radar.'

He gave me a sly grin and we both giggled.

'Actually I do know about Clause 28. It's about local councils promoting homosexuality.'

He gave a cough. 'So you do bother to read the papers occasionally. What's your view?'

I yawned. 'I haven't really had time to think about it, to be honest.'

He gave an impatient tut. 'You don't necessarily need time to form an opinion.'

An air hostess with big, permed hair loomed over us with a toothy smile.

'Would you like some breakfast?'

'Absolutely,' I said, 'we both would.'

Norris acquiesced with a cursory nod while battling to fold up his newspapers.

I examined the little china bowl on my tray filled with apple and grapefruit slices. A single strawberry rested on the top of the pile. Among the items in front of me were a white cotton napkin containing metal cutlery and a dinky china cruet set.

'They do present things well, don't they?'

Norris peered at his tray. 'Well these airlines charge enough. How much did these flights cost?'

I shrugged. 'Ted sorts everything out directly with Guinness's travel agency so I've no idea.'

'You do wonder if we really need to go business class for such a short flight.'

I looked at him in shock. 'But everyone flies business at Guinness. Besides, you couldn't use economy.'

'Why ever not?'

'Because you're the star of the show. Guinness could hardly stick you in steerage.'

Norris took the lid of his china dish and steam rose up. 'Jolly hot! Scrambled egg and sausages. Not bad,' he said brightly. 'Let's hope she brings some coffee.'

He frowned suddenly. 'A bad affair in Pakistan last week. Did you read about it?'

'I presume we're talking cricket?'

He looked pleased. 'Indeed. Who knows what went on between Mike Gatting and that umpire, Shakoor Rana, but it will have repercussions for the game in the future.'

'I haven't followed the whole brouhaha, but wasn't Gatting accused of cheating?'

Norris chewed thoughtfully on a piece of sausage. 'Yes but he denied it. All the same, he was forced to issue an apology. To think of the whole series being lost just like that.'

'I've never understood cricket. It's so complicated.'

He remonstrated. 'Complicated? Not at all! I'll teach you the game one day.'

The air hostess reappeared, her crisp blue blazer and skirt now protected by a rather unflattering regulation overall, and handed us both coffees. She removed the debris in front of us and laughed as Norris dropped his metal fork under the seat.

'Just leave it, sir, we'll pick it up later.'

She set off along the aisle with her clanking trolley.

'You wonder how many of those knives and forks get nicked each year.'

'Not that many, surely?' I answered.

He took a sip of coffee and stared pensively out of the window into a colourless sky. 'I think you'd be surprised at human nature. If something's freely available, there will always be those who resort to base instincts.'

I stuck my head out in the aisle, aware of the smell of smoke and saw a man a few seats behind puffing furiously on a cigarette.

'I wish we'd sat further forward. We're surrounded by smokers.'

Norris turned to me. 'Are we? I hadn't noticed.'

I yanked a newspaper on to my lap. 'You know the BBC will be showing the last *Old Grey Whistle Test* on New Year's Eve?'

'What's that? Some confounded pop music show?'

I clapped my hands together in triumph. 'Hurrah! At last I've found something you know nothing about.'

Then I noticed a gleam in his eye. 'Bob Harris is the presenter, I believe. Must be in, what, it's fifteenth year?'

'Sixteenth,' I replied grumpily.

'Ah, yes,' he said with a lofty tilt of the head.

The seatbelt signs came on and soon we were descending at speed.

'We haven't discussed anything about arrangements for today,' I sighed.

'Why ever should we? If it's all done and dusted, why waste time discussing it?'

He had a point. The itinerary was set. All we had to do was keep with the plan but with Norris that was never simple.

★ ★ ★

We were sitting on the worn floral sofa in Mrs Brown's ill-lit sitting room. On the coffee table sat a rather sad and withered little plant in a brown plastic pot. Having for many months lovingly nurtured what was to be the smallest sunflower in the world, it had apparently come as a bitter blow to Mrs Brown to find her prized plant dead one morning. The smallest sunflower ever recorded measured 2.2 inches in height and was grown by a Michael Lenke in Oregon using a patented Bonsai technique. Mrs Brown's bloom purportedly had measured a fraction of an inch more, but where was the proof? She had posted an image of it to the editorial offices when it was hail and hearty but that alone didn't prove its dimensions. Many elderly friends in her village had passed by to admire it but no one had thought to write down the plant's exact measurements and have them authenticated by a local authority and reliable witnesses. Nor had an image been taken clearly indicating with a ruler its exact size. But Mrs

Brown was pushing 85 years old so could be forgiven for not having adhered to the book's strict regulations and guidelines. When her sorry tale emerged, Norris suggested we pop by her terraced home just outside Leeds to commiserate or at least offer some encouragement for another attempt. After all, we were in the area to meet new record-breakers and it wouldn't represent much of a detour. Rather thoughtfully Norris had brought her a Guinness pin badge and signed a copy of the new book. Our hostess went pink with delight and seemed thrilled that we had dropped by.

'The trouble is, Mr McWhirter, it's like losing a friend,' she muttered sorrowfully.

'Quite,' said Norris, blinking hard as he finished off the last powerful dregs of his tea. 'Perhaps you can grow another one?'

She shook her head and folded her plump hands on her apron. 'I couldn't do that. I loved that little sunflower. I kept it warm and fed and watered it every day. It was better than a dog.'

I felt my lip tremble. I had a ludicrous image of the little sunflower barking and waggling its petals as she fed it fertiliser and water.

'You'll think me potty but I used to talk to it all the time.'

Norris regarded her sharply. 'Of course you're not. Prince Charles famously declared last year that he talked to his plants.'

'They thought he was barmy, though,' she said laughingly in her broad Yorkshire tones.

Norris clattered his teacup down on the table. 'Well, a German professor by the name of Gustav Fechner published *Nanna, or The Soul Life of Plants* in 1848 and also claimed that they responded to sounds and words.'

She smiled happily. 'There, then, I'm in good company.'

'Indeed you are,' said Norris reassuringly, rising to his feet. I took my cue and stood up, thanking her profusely for her hospitality.

'It's made my day meeting you, Mr McWhirter,' she said, suddenly turning to me. 'Aren't you a lucky girl to work with such a brilliant man?'

Norris savoured the moment. 'Yes, but of course young people today don't always realise how fortunate they are. One can but try to pass on pearls of wisdom.'

I narrowed my eyes as he swiftly headed for the gloomy corridor which led to the front door. We waved from the street and jumped into the hire car.

'Oh great master, what pearls will you be shedding for me today?'

Norris started the ignition and smiled at the road ahead. 'I'm going to enjoy this jolly.'

'Jolly? I take my job rather seriously actually.'

'Not nearly enough, AN, otherwise you would have known about Gustav Fechner.'

'Don't be absurd. He wasn't a record-breaker. Besides, I can't possibly know everything.'

'True,' he said mischievously as he pulled out from the kerb, 'but you could at least try.'

★ ★ ★

Norris glanced over at the outstretched map on my lap. It had been a long day. Aside from meeting Mrs Brown, we had dashed to Leeds town hall for a meeting with the lady mayor and a group of elderly ladies who'd crocheted an enormous blanket for charity. It was 100 feet long and 68 inches wide and stood a good chance of making it into the next edition, although one could never say for certain. Often a last-minute rival attempt could pip an existing record to the post, and the largest blanket category was popular. We had then jumped in the car and headed to Manchester where Norris handed over a certificate to an eleven-year-old prodigy who'd just passed a maths A level. He would be appearing in the next edition for certain. We quickly gobbled down ham and salad sandwiches before greeting hordes of *The Guinness Book of Records*' fans at Manchester's main branch of WHSmith's. A little boy ran out in front of Norris as we battled to reach the store's entrance.

'Mr McWhirter, what's the largest spider in the world?'

'*Theraphosa blondi*,' replied Norris without hesitation.

'And the most poisonous snake?' piped up a young girl nearby.

'The sea snake off the coast of north-west Australia but the most poisonous land snake is the Australian inland taipan which is more than 6 feet long.'

A group of children shrieked in horror.

'I hate snakes so I'm never going to Australia!' announced the girl who'd asked him the question.

'Well if you don't like snakes, I'd avoid Sri Lanka too because more people die of snake bites there than anywhere else in the world.'

'What's the largest toad?' yelled out a teenage boy as we attempted to enter the store.

He hesitated. 'Hmm, that has to be the marine toad in South America.'

The young manager appeared and guided Norris to a table inside the shop where he would be signing books. His hair was gelled back into loose flicks that lolled on his white collar and he wore a lean-fitting dark suit with narrow black tie. He could have auditioned for Spandau Ballet.

'Do you get a bit fed up being bombarded with questions all the time?' he asked.

Norris shook his head. 'Not at all. It keeps me on my toes.'

'Have you ever got an answer wrong?'

'Not that I can recall but people rarely ask difficult questions.'

A moment later the doors were officially opened and a queue formed by the signing table.

Norris beckoned the first child over.

'What's your name?'

'Henry. Have you ever seen the world's largest fire engine?'

'I have indeed seen the world's most powerful fire engine, which is the Oshkosh fire truck in Oshkosh, Wisconsin. You know it can shoot 41,600 gallons of foam in just 150 seconds.'

An elderly woman appeared before us. 'Hello Mr McWhirter, now tell me – what is the oldest record in the book?'

He smiled. 'I think that honour would have to go to St Simeon the Younger who in AD 597 had squatted on a pillar for 45 years.'

'You're having me on!' she wheezed.

'It's all true. He was from the Stylites sect of monks who did a great deal of pillar-squatting.'

'Well I never,' she laughed and thrust a copy of the book into his hands. 'Can you write "for Splodge and Tinkle with love"?'

Norris faltered. 'Er, are they children?'

'No, they're my cats. They love your book.'

Norris gave a limp smile. 'That's good to know.'

The store manager returned with tea and biscuits and Norris continued to sign books and answer questions for another hour. Then his signing was interrupted for media interviews.

By the time everyone had departed we were both ready to hit the road.

A young female television reporter approached the table. 'One final thing, Norris. How do you remember so much?'

'I find that if I'm interested in something, I never forget it.'

'That must mean you're interested in everything!' she exclaimed cheerfully to camera.

Norris paused. 'Yes, I suppose I am.'

He heaved on his thick woollen coat and picked up his briefcase. We thanked the store manager and headed for the car. It was just as we were about to drive off that there was a tap at the window. Norris peered out at the crinkled face of an elderly man.

'Sorry to catch you on the off, but just a quick question, Mr McWhirter, would you happen to know the longest fight time with a fish?'

I thought I'd misheard him but Norris tapped the steering wheel thoughtfully and suddenly chuckled. 'Aha! I remember, in 1968 a man named Donal Heatley struggled with a black marlin off North Island in New Zealand for 32 hours and 5 minutes.'

The man beamed and shuffled off as Norris revved the car. He turned to me.

'You'll never believe it, AN, but for a moment there, I had a total blank. Such an obvious record too!'

I stared at him in disbelief. Sometimes with Norris, words genuinely failed me.

Now as we drove into a dark and fairly quiet Stalybridge and I observed Norris yawning heavily, I wondered whether I had created too onerous an itinerary for him.

'Are you exhausted?' I asked.

He shook his head. 'No, this is the last stop for today so we'll give it our best.'

'It won't take long. I invited local media but it's already nearly seven o'clock so probably it'll just be one local reporter. Don't expect too much.'

'That's fine by me.'

We parked in the forecourt of the Old Thirteenth Cheshire Astley Volunteer Rifleman Corps Inn and looked across at the modest brick building. Norris got out and stood stretching on the tarmac. A December chill had settled on the air and we both shivered involuntarily with the cold.

'When this pub was built in 1857 it was called the New Inn but because it was frequented by soldiers from the Cheshire regiment, the name changed.'

'Interesting. Well it all seems very quiet tonight,' I muttered, worrying that my press release had failed to rally the troops.

Norris shrugged and together we walked over to the entrance. Almost immediately garish buttery light flooded the doorway. The place was crawling with camera crews, photographers and customers.

Norris observed me wryly. 'So, AN, is this one of your little jokes? Just the local paper, indeed!'

I stood transfixed. Of course I had alerted all the media but I hadn't honestly reckoned on such a mass response so late in the evening. Stifling giggles, I walked with Norris towards the assembled throng whom he regarded with total composure and a winning smile. Peter Lawlor, the pub's landlord, came over to greet us.

'We've got you a hearty pint of Guinness!' he cried, passing a brimming glass to Norris. I was handed a flute of champagne. With perfect poise, Norris took a long draught of the dark brew and smiled for the cameras, licking his lips and raising the glass to Peter. We then all trotted outside whereupon

Norris presented Peter with a copy of the latest book and a Guinness certificate under the pub's fifty-five-lettered sign.

'You know I was born in Stalybridge and have always loved this pub, Norris. I've given it all I've got,' Peter said with emotion.

'And it's a jolly fine public house too,' replied Norris kindly.

'You've got to love what you're doing to make something a success.'

Norris nodded encouragingly.

'Move in a bit gov!' called a photographer.

'Mr McWhirter, can you give us a shot pointing up at the pub's name?' yelled another.

Norris blinked as camera bulbs flashed in the gathering gloom. At one point he caught my eye and mouthed 'You wait' which again had me in peels of adolescent laughter.

'Your colleague's quite a giggler,' observed Peter cheerily.

'Yes, she finds a lot to laugh about. And a great practical joker too.'

'Really? Fancy that!'

I knew Norris was referring to the silly prank I'd played on him earlier at Heathrow.

★ ★ ★

As the last reporters and pub guests took their leave of The Old Thirteenth Cheshire Astley Volunteer Rifleman Corps Inn, Norris and I said our goodbyes and headed back to the car.

'That was a success,' I said with a wink.

'Yes, thanks for calling up every paper from here to New York.'

I laughed. 'Who would have thought it at this time of night? So thoughtful of Peter to invite the whole of Stalybridge too.'

Norris shook his head. 'You are the limit. Now, any chance of my getting back to our hotel for a kip? They are expecting us, I hope?'

'Of course, I explained that we'd arrive late. Look, why don't you let me drive?'

He sniffed loudly. 'AN, do you think I'd trust you behind a wheel?'

'Why ever not?'

'I can think of too many reasons. I fancy you'd be a speed hog.'

'Not at all. Anyway, I'm better driving than map reading.'

'Thank heavens for that,' he said crisply and put his foot down hard on the accelerator.

★ ★ ★

We were on the M6 motorway heading for the hotel I had booked in the centre of Manchester. Heavy rain had started to fall and the beams of the headlights were harsh on the eye. Norris yawned.

'We should stop for petrol.'

Ten minutes later we pulled into a service station where we filled up the car. Norris looked longingly at the kiosk.

'You couldn't just pop in and get me some chocolate? A few Mars Bars and Kit Kats would do.'

I hesitated. 'I won't let you eat them now. Not just before you go to bed. They're bad for your teeth.'

He tutted. 'They'll give me energy for the next onslaught of press tomorrow.'

I took my handbag from the passenger seat and walked slowly over to the kiosk. Inside a fan heater was blowing out lukewarm air which sent my wild hair into a frenzy.

'Cold out there,' muttered the woman behind the counter.

'Freezing.'

'Where you heading?'

'Manchester.'

She nodded slowly and began ringing up my chocolate purchases on the till. I passed over some coins and took the plastic bag from her.

'That's funny,' she said, peering out of the window. 'Didn't you arrive here with your dad?'

I found the assumption amusing although, in truth, it was an easy enough mistake to make. 'What about it?'

'Well, he's just driven off.'

'WHAT?'

I rushed over to the door and sure enough, Norris and the car were gone.

'What is he playing at!'

'Oh dear. What d'you think he's done that for?'

'I'm not sure. I'll just go and see.'

I felt her razor-like eyes following me across the rainy forecourt. Either this was Norris's payback or he'd seriously lost his marbles. After fifteen minutes I genuinely became concerned. Maybe he'd had a memory lapse? Forgotten I was in the shop in his exhaustion? I heard an engine roaring and Norris appeared with headlights blazing at my side. He was giggling uncontrollably.

'How amusing,' I growled. 'Touché. Now, can we get out of here?'

I turned towards the kiosk to see the woman shaking her head in disbelief, her mouth gaping like that of a stranded fish. Thankfully she hadn't registered who Norris was. It wasn't the sort of diary story I wanted appearing in the nationals the next day.

The rain thudded on the roof of the car as we pulled out onto the M6. Few cars were on the road and in the darkness and warmth I began to feel drowsy. I worried that Norris might too and so pulled down the window a few inches. Cold air streamed into the car.

'Heavens, don't overdo it,' said Norris. 'We're both getting splattered by rain.' He gave a little yawn and grew fidgety.

'Any chance of one of those Mars Bars? The thing is I only had a few sandwiches at the pub and I'm starving. It'll do me the power of good.'

Doubtfully, I began searching the plastic bag for his booty. The wind rocked the car and the sound of hissing rain filled our ears. I rolled up the window and in the dark passed him a Mars Bar. The road unfurled before us like a black tongue, dark and slick with the relentless rain. Norris finished his chocolate bar and asked for another.

'I think one's enough.'

His eyes darted reproachfully towards me and then back at the road. 'Uh oh. What on earth's that coming up?'

It was too late. Before we could determine what the arrows and signs were indicating in the rain and darkness, we found ourselves hurtling through a labyrinth of orange traffic cones into a closed off area of the fast lane. Norris stopped the car abruptly by a flashing barrier and peered out of the window.

'How odd. That took me by surprise. Looks as if they're doing road works here.'

I was astounded by his calmness.

'This is serious, No,' I said, using my nickname for him. 'If the police find us here we could be in trouble.'

'Well they should have better temporary signs on the road. I'll just have to back out.'

'We can't reverse on a motorway!' I cried. 'Maybe I can move those barriers up ahead and guide you back out on to the road? Thank heavens there's hardly any traffic.'

We didn't have to mull the problem for long. A Panda car was approaching slowly from behind.

'Oh no!' I yelped. 'Just what we don't need!'

Norris wound down his window just as an officer approached the car.

'Got a little confused, did we, sir? Didn't see the barrier and the flashing lights?'

I bit my lip but Norris seemed unperturbed.

'Yes, I'm afraid so, officer. With this pounding rain and the darkness, it was awfully hard to see what was happening. One of the signs appeared to have blown over.'

The officer frowned. 'Can I have your driving licence, sir?'

Norris fumbled in his jacket pocket and handed over the licence. The officer, clad in a heavy black rainproof jacket, took it from him and returned to the Panda.

'Now what?' I said.

Norris shrugged. 'One good thing – it looks as if the rain's stopping.'

The windscreen wipers began to whine as they flipped monotonously from side to side. Norris switched them off and tapped his fingers on the driving wheel. A moment later, the man walked briskly back to our car and leaned in at Norris's window.

'You're Mr McWhirter from *The Guinness Book of Records*?'

'That's right.'

'Stone the crows! What were you trying to do, sir, create a new category for worst driver?'

Norris chuckled. 'Actually, one already exists. That honour was bestowed on a seventy-five-year-old male driver from Texas, who managed ten traffic tickets, four hit and run offences, and six accidents all in the space of twenty minutes.'

The officer smirked. 'You're kidding me?'

'No. Mind you, the most appalling driver in Britain has forty-one bans equating to seventy-one and a half years plus two life bans.'

The officer laughed loudly. 'Dear oh dear. You couldn't make it up. In fact, I've just bought the latest Guinness edition as a Christmas present for my son. I couldn't get you to sign a little message that I can stick into his book?'

'Of course,' said Norris.

The man smiled and plodded back to the Panda. I slid Norris a glance.

'Don't say a word, AN,' Norris said quietly.

The officer returned with some paper. 'His name's Steven.'

Norris scribbled a message by the central light in the car and handed it to the policeman.

'Well now, let's say no more about this little traffic incident. It was an easy enough mistake to make in that torrential rain. And right enough, a sign had blown down.'

'That's good of you,' said Norris.

'The thing is,' said the man. 'It's a bit tricky getting back on to the functioning lane. You'll have to follow me.'

He thrust his arm through the window and shook Norris's hand. Dutifully, we followed his Panda past the barriers and traffic cones until we were back on to a moving lane. He flashed his lights as I waved gratefully from my window.

I gave a big sigh. 'You were lucky.'

'Lucky? It had nothing to do with luck and everything to do with using one's loaf.'

I studied the map. 'Hopefully we'll reach the hotel in half an hour or so.'

Norris frowned. 'That long, you think? Well in that case, could you pass me another chocolate bar?'

★ ★ ★

After an early start the next morning, Norris and I visited a local primary school in the heart of Manchester offering the children an opportunity to quiz Norris on all manner of records. The press attended the event, amazed as ever by Norris's encyclopaedic memory. During the afternoon, we drove to Leeds for the flight back to London, fortunately encountering no maverick roadworks along the way. At the airport we left the hire car and trudged through the sudden flurry of snow into the warm terminal building. There were no delays and before we knew it we were back at Heathrow and climbing into Norris's grey BMW for the journey into London.

'I'm ravenous,' I announced as we neared Kensington. 'Do you fancy a free dinner?'

Norris laughed. 'I'm feeling peckish too. What had you in mind?'

I opened my handbag and took out a sheaf of invitation cards.

'What are those?'

'Oh, I get loads of invitations at this time of the year. They're all press or PR cocktail parties but some are pretty good. This one, for example, is an invitation for two to dine at a City wine bar.'

'It's all free?' asked Norris incredulously.

'Absolutely. Drinks included.'

He gave me a smile. 'Let's go there then. Are you sure your flatmate won't miss you?'

'Good heavens no. Jane has Christmas dinners in the City every night this week.'

Half an hour later we arrived at the plush wine bar near Shoreditch and were shown politely to a table. Music pounded from the bar but the dining room was located in a quiet area and the seats were comfortable.

'Do you do this sort of thing often?' asked Norris.

'Dine for free? On a Guinness salary, you bet.'

He laughed. 'It's a jolly good Christmas menu and look, they've even given us Christmas crackers. A waitress came over to take our orders and discreetly asked for the invitation I had received. She offered us a bottle of wine on the house in addition to the three course menu. Norris looked bemused.

'You must have Scottish blood.'

I nodded. 'Yep. Irish, Scottish and Welsh. A lethal cocktail.'

I held out my cracker. He snapped it and out popped a Groucho Marx pair of plastic glasses and black moustache. His cracker contained a pair of cheap clip earrings.

'Let's do a swap,' he said. 'Mind you, with your torn lobe, earrings probably aren't the best idea.'

The waitress returned with plates of smoked salmon and poured our wine, at which point a large group of young men walked in and took their seats at a reserved table.

'City traders,' I whispered across the table to Norris.

He nodded. 'Very possibly, or maybe insurance brokers?'

We tucked into our food, both hungry after a frantic day in which we had barely had time to snatch a bite after only a quick breakfast. I began laughing.

'I still can't get over that incident on the motorway last night.'

'Yes, a bit of a close shave. Of course if you'd given me the second chocolate bar I wouldn't have been distracted.'

'Oh that's ridiculous!'

'It's true, AN. I hold you fully responsible,' he said with mock gravitas.

A roar went up from the table of boisterous young men as they clinked glasses for the umpteenth time.

'I wish they'd keep the noise down.'

Norris gave a little grunt. 'Youthful exuberance.'

It was while we were finishing our main course that one of them began theatrically and loudly hissing at the others, 'It's Norris McWhirter!' The young men gawped at our table and in excitement began a low half-drunken chant of 'Norris! Norris!'

I sneaked a glance at Norris who observed them coolly. 'One of the hazards of the job,' he sighed.

In some irritation I rose to my feet and approached their table. A hush descended.

'I'm afraid you've made a big mistake. My uncle John has nothing to do with Norris McWhirter. He gets sick and tired of being confused with him. He's just a retired teacher down from Norfolk for the evening. He's never even possessed a copy of *The Guinness Book of Records*.'

With embarrassment they mumbled apologies and nodded in the direction of Norris, raising their glasses. I thanked them and returned to the table. Norris could barely conceal his amusement about his new persona. He picked up his plastic glasses and false moustache, deciding to don them for the rest of the meal.

'I'm not sure if that's such a good idea,' I laughed. 'You're drawing even more attention to yourself.'

'Yes, but poor old uncle John probably doesn't come down from the country very much so let him have some fun.'

Norris's face lit up when the dessert menu arrived. He chose chocolate fudge cake and having finished the last mouthful, sat back in his chair, replete and contented.

'So what are your plans for Christmas?' I asked.

'Oh this and that. My son, Alasdair, and daughter, Jane, will be with me and other family members. We'll have a busy Christmas, I imagine. I have a lot of work to do on my islands book among other things.'

I nodded and raised my wine glass. 'Well, Happy Christmas and thank you for such a fun trip.'

We clinked glasses.

'Yes, it was certainly unforgettable,' he said dryly. 'There's never a dull moment with you. I'll need a good rest over Christmas to recover.'

I laughed. 'By the way, there's something I wanted to ask you. How did the book really begin? I know the PR story I trot out about the managing director of Guinness, Sir Hugh Beaver, wanting to create a book to settle pub arguments, but is that the true story?'

'Pretty much. As you know, Ross and I were running a fact-finding agency in Fleet Street and already had a fascination for record facts and feats. One day, we received a call from Chris Chataway, an old chum from Oxford who was employed at Guinness's brewery. He was rather secretive and asked us whether we could meet Sir Hugh to discuss a "project".'

'And so you both went?'

'Of course. It was 12 September 1954. We drove over to the Guinness Brewery at Park Royal and had a relaxed lunch with Sir Hugh Beaver and his fellow directors. Mind you, they tested our mettle.'

'How?'

'They asked us all sorts of record facts such as how to find out which was the widest river ever frozen.'

He paused when he saw puzzlement etched on my face. 'Well, AN, think about it, obviously it could only be one of three Russian rivers: the Ob', Yenisey or Lena which all flow into the Arctic.'

'But did they actually tell you why they'd invited you to lunch?'

He laughed. 'That was the curious thing. It was only when I correctly identified the language with fewest irregular verbs that Sir Hugh decided we were up for the challenge. At that point he invited us to create a book of records for use by the eighty-one thousand pubs across the country.'

'So, what is the language with fewest irregular verbs?'

'Turkish, of course, AN. Don't be a dolt. It only has one irregular verb; *imek*, to be.'

A waitress strolled over with coffee, a small jug of milk and a plate of chocolate mints and placed them on the table. She smiled and sauntered off. I steered a cup of coffee in Norris's direction, amused to see him wolf down one of the chocolates.

'And how did you know Roger Bannister, the athlete?'

He sipped at his coffee and placed his serviette on the table. 'Ah, we go back a long way. Roger and Chris were good friends and fellow athletes at Oxford, which is why I was commentating for the BBC on 6 May 1954, the day that Roger made history with the first four-minute mile.'

'It must have been a spectacular moment.'

'It was quite extraordinary because the night before I had sat in the bath in my parent's house in Winchmore Hill imagining how I might announce such a feat. It was actually touch and go that Roger raced at all on the day because there was quite a strong wind.'

'So what persuaded him to go ahead?'

'Well, Chris Chataway and another chap, Chris Brasher, who in fact years later co-founded the London Marathon, were his pacemakers and were keen for him to have a go. When the wind dropped Roger agreed. It was supposed to be just an ordinary race meeting at the Iffley Road race track in Oxford so there were only about two thousand spectators. At 6 p.m. Roger set off in race number nine and came in with a record 3 minutes 59.4 seconds.'

'And you announced it?'

'Absolutely. I strung it out as long as possible to whet the crowds appetite,' he laughed. 'I've subsequently met so many fibbers who claimed to have been there that momentous day but in reality it was a modest affair.'

'And you and Roger Bannister are still close friends?'

He finished his coffee. 'Yes, Roger and I have been lifelong friends.'

A clock chimed. 'Gosh, No, it's eleven o'clock.'

As we rose to leave, he propped his briefcase against the table and pulled out a slim green volume. 'By the way, this is for you.'

It was a 1955 first edition of *The Guinness Book of Records* in good condition. I opened it at the title page where in tiny black ink Norris had written the date and the message: 'For the one and only Anna, Happy Christmas. Norris.'

'But this is such a wonderful gift. Thank you.'

I leafed through the creamy pages and examined the old black and white images. I pointed to one. 'Imagine! You've got the Empire State Building as the tallest building. Now it's the Sears Tower. Another record for Illinois.'

'Indeed. Many records have changed but some stand the test of time.' He showed me a photo of a tiny thatched building. 'The smallest pub is still the Smith's Arms at Godmanstone, Dorset.'

'Well, I shall treasure this. Thank you again.'

He gave me a poignant smile. 'It's good to treasure books, but one should always treasure memories more.'

Thanking the restaurant staff, we stepped out into the chilly night. At his car he gave me a peck on the cheek and drove off. I waved until his tail lights disappeared into the night, and, clutching my precious book, hailed myself a cab.

SIX

★ ★ ★

THE FORGETFUL MEMORY MAN

It was an icy day in February. My birthday, to be exact. Eric swayed down the aisle of the 121 bus and leaned against the metal pole in front of my seat. He was chewing gum, I presumed to stop him from thinking about smoking. He'd given up the weed some weeks back and was finding it a drag (or not!).

'See that guy in *The Sun* yesterday?' he asked.

'Which one?'

'The geezer who ate a pound of eels in 13 seconds.'

My brow crumpled. 'If you're talking about Peter Dowdeswell, that's an old record. He swallowed a pound of eels in 13.7 seconds back in 1978.'

Eric was adamant. 'I'm sure it was the same geezer. He ate a load of prunes too. Horrible picture!'

I pulled *The Guinness Book of Records* from my bag and scanned the gluttony record section. 'Yes, you're right, he ate one hundred and forty-four prunes in 31.27 seconds but that's not a new record either. Was it a general feature about him?'

Eric shrugged. 'Dunno. I was on me tea break and just had a quick butchers at the driver's paper. Anyway, it's your stop coming up so you better get moving, girl.'

I pushed the book back in my bag and walked slowly down the aisle to the platform, where the freezing air hit my face. I held tightly to the central metal pole, scrunched my eyes shut and leaned out into the wind. I loved the feeling of speed combined with cool air. Eric gave a series of disapproving clucks.

'Wish you wouldn't do that. One day you'll lose your grip and find yourself under a car. And I'll be the one that cops it.'

Opening my eyes, I gave him an apologetic smile as the bus drew to a halt.

'You know it's my birthday today?'

Eric reared back. 'You should have said something earlier!'

'Why?'

'I'd have given you a free fare.'

'Liar!'

He gave a cackle of laughter and winked. 'Happy Birthday, my darling!'

I arrived at the office deep in thought. Gluttony records which guzzled up a whole page of the Human Achievements section of the book would soon be a thing of the past and I was feeling inexplicably sad about that. Some big changes had been happening at the book of late. For one thing, Alan our editor had decided to leave to pursue television interests and Donald, a new editor, had arrived. Having built up a very good relationship with Alan and come to appreciate his boundless energy and enthusiasm, I was sad to see him go. Donald was a thoughtful Scot, academic and mild-mannered, but fortunately did possess a good sense of humour and irony. In time, I knew that the editorial team would adapt to his management style and we would rumble along as before, but for now everything seemed a little uncertain.

The idea to remove the gluttony section of the book lay with Donald and in fairness he was under quite a bit of pressure to do so. For some time there had been rumblings in the media about the health and safety risks involved and the legal ramifications if, God forbid, someone died during a record attempt. Guinness was careful to cover its back and issued stern warnings in the book, refusing to list potentially dangerous attempts such as the gobbling of ants, chewing gum, raw eggs with shells or marshmallows, which could potentially cause choking. The editor maintained that gluttony records should aim to improve the rate of consumption rather than the volume, but of course there were those who would always want to go one step further and it was those individuals to whom the new rules would apply. Now, of course there was one exception to the rule, and that was Michel Lotito of Grenoble in France, better known as Mr Mangetout, the world's greatest omnivore. We did list his extraordinary guzzling feats because they rarely involved food. He had in his time eaten ten bicycles, seven TV sets, six chandeliers, an entire coffin and a Cessna light aircraft, all of them ground down into small components to aid digestion. He was a medical phenomenon having baffled gastroenterologists worldwide with his ability to eat two pounds of metal and also glass every day to no ill effect. We were all very fond of Mr Mangetout and although Guinness Publishing would never have encouraged others to follow in his footsteps, the concept of excluding his achievements from the book was out of the question. They were more of a medical feat than anything else.

Alex, clad in a V-neck patterned sweater over his shirt and tie, was hovering by the door as I entered, clutching a folder of photographic slides and munching on a biscuit. It amazed me that he could eat so much and yet maintain a lean and athletic physique. He ushered me into the open-plan office.

'Now listen, are you likely to get any good shots when you're in Paris?'

I paused. 'Can I take my coat off?'

He grinned broadly. 'Well come on, we haven't got all day. What time do you call this? It's 8.15 already.'

I followed him to the kitchen where I flung my coat over a chair. 'It's my birthday.'

He paused while filling the kettle. 'Is it? All right, I'll make your coffee this morning. So tell me about Paris.'

I sat on one of the plastic chairs at the white kitchen table. I noticed it had grubby brown ring marks from old coffee cups. 'Who else is in?'

Alex turned to face me while busying himself by the kettle. 'Oh, two of the secretaries came down for some coffee earlier. They've run out upstairs.'

'They could have cleaned the table after them.'

Alex raised his eyebrows and grabbing a cleaning cloth ran it over the table. 'There. Happy?'

'Yes, much better. OK, now regarding Paris, I'm going with Creighton Carvello, the memory man, and with any luck we're meeting up with Mr Mangetout.'

'Excellent. Can you get some good shots of him eating something interesting while you're there?'

'I can hardly guarantee that. We're just meeting for a friendly drink.'

'Get him to nibble a table leg or something. You're in PR for heaven's sake. Use your imagination a bit.'

'What are these shots for anyway?'

'I just need some decent file shots. What about Creighton, is his record visual?'

'Hardly. He memorises whole packs of cards and then recites them all in order.'

'Hmm. Still, a shot or two with him holding one or two suits would do.'

The door banged open and Lisa walked in. 'The usual suspects!'

She took off her coat and rubbed her hands together. 'Happy Birthday! Mum's made a cake for elevenses. We can all pig out.'

'What a pair of stars! Thanks, Lisa.'

'Eileen's made a cake? Why can't we have it now?' said Alex.

Lisa gave him a shove. 'I don't remember inviting the picture department.'

He gave her one of his disarming smiles. 'Let me make you a coffee?'

She wrinkled her forehead. 'No way, I like to do my own. Now, Alex, can you help me move my new filing cabinet and then we'll negotiate the cake situation.'

He nodded and stalked off along the corridor towards her desk. Putty in her hands.

The phone rang. It was Ted, my hero. If there was one man in the building who deserved sainthood it was probably Ted, the accountant. It was rare to find him without a benign smile and he was forever getting me out of financial scrapes when I was sent to meet press or invigilate a record in some obscure part of the country and had already squandered my salary. The normal procedure was for staff to claim back expenses but I was such a cheapskate that I often had to go cap in hand in advance of a trip. My flatmate Jane and I had decided to buy a flat together now that the government was allowing separate mortgages on the same property, and so I was trying hard to save enough for the deposit.

Ted gave a little cough. 'Just me. I was wondering about the Paris trip. Do you need an advance of cash? And what about French francs?'

'I'm not leaving until next week but yes, please. I'm skint as usual.'

A long indulgent sigh. 'I've got your flight tickets whenever you want to collect them.'

'Bless you, Ted. I'll be up in a while.'

Lisa observed me from her desk. Her hands were cupped around her mug and she was blowing elegantly on the rising steam. 'He's lovely, Ted. Wish everyone could be like him.'

I nodded. 'Yes, he's a paragon of virtue.'

'You are lucky going to Paris. Wish I could come with you.'

'It's not a holiday.'

She sniffed. 'Yeah, but all the same, you're bound to have a fun time. What's your itinerary?'

I pulled a file off the top of my bulging in tray and began scanning it. 'Philippe Scali, the editor of the French edition, has organised interviews on some of the main French TV channels. We arrive in time for the main evening television news and then spend the next day at various TV and radio stations.'

'Cor, you'll be busy. So what'll Creighton be doing?'

I studied one of the sheets in my hand. 'Philippe wants him to memorise a random sequence of several packs of cards on live TV. It's part of a record-breaking celebration in Paris he's organising.'

'Blimey, that sounds like a tall order,' she replied.

'Water off a duck's back for Creighton. I watched him memorise a random sequence of three packs of cards in Middlesborough once without making one error.'

Her mouth dropped. 'Flipping heck!'

'I've only met him once but he seemed such a quiet, modest chap.'

'So you're off to Scotland with Norris this afternoon and then flying to Paris the day after tomorrow with Creighton?'

I nodded slowly. The next day, Norris and I would be meeting with editors from various Scottish newspapers and had also agreed to drop by Mr and Mrs Macdonald of the Gleniffer Press in Paisley, the creators of the smallest book, a tiny edition of Old King Cole. We'd also be looking in on a gluttony record attempt happening in Pizzaland in Glasgow.

'I don't envy you both judging the pizza-eating record. Bet that's going to be messy!'

Lisa was right; watching individuals stuffing their faces with one kind of food in a limited period wasn't my idea of fun. I turned round to see Donald by my desk. He pushed the bridge of his metal-rimmed spectacles back against his nose and offered me a tentative smile.

'Any chance of a quick word about the gluttony section?'

I followed him into his office, still finding it odd to see him ensconced at Alan's desk. He pushed his mop of light grey hair back from his face and politely offered me a seat.

'We've got to handle this gluttony business carefully but I've decided that we will remove the records from the book.'

I bit my lip and sighed. 'I know it's a bit of a revolting category but people love them.'

He eyed me steadily. 'Not the press.'

'Actually, a lot of the press feed off them – excuse the pun. It's just a few of the more po-faced journalists who don't like them.'

'What does your friend, Geoff Smith, at the Press Association think?'

I shrugged. 'He thinks we should act cautiously and maybe ease some of them out, rather than get rid of them in one fell swoop.'

He straightened his yellow polka dot tie and tapped his chin thoughtfully. 'I'm not sure about that. In some ways I think it's better just to put an end to them all and move on. They sit uncomfortably in what is in reality a fairly academic title.'

He had a point. Despite its many eccentricities and quite frankly daft records such as bed pushing, apple peeling, bubblegum blowing or custard pie throwing, *The Guinness Book of Records* was essentially a cerebral tome. In fact, the light-hearted and zany records were mostly confined to the human endeavours section, a mere ten per cent of the overall content, which meant that the book appealed to all ages and tastes. Had Guinness resorted to all-out silliness or vulgarity, the book would have instantly lost its quite unique appeal of balancing weighty facts against the more trivial ones.

'The press will accuse us of being killjoys.'

He shrugged. 'Better that than killers. We're lucky no one's died during one of these gluttony attempts.'

'But surely people should be responsible for their own actions?'

Donald threw out his hands. 'As you and I know, sense rarely enters into the debate. By including the category we could be accused of encouraging those sorts of people who like to take extreme risks.'

'What about Mr Mangetout?'

He raised an eyebrow. 'Hmm. He should go in theory. What if some copycat decided to emulate him and began tucking into a car or train?'

I stood up and stretched my arms. 'It's your decision but when are we talking about implementing it?'

He got up and wandered over to the broad window, his hands on his hips. 'Not for the next edition. It's too late for that because we've already accepted submissions. We need a run in, wouldn't you say?'

'Absolutely.'

I wandered back to my desk and puffed out my cheeks.

'Now what?' asked Lisa.

'Donald says the gluttony section has to go. I daren't say anything to John Kenmuir when I see him in Glasgow tomorrow. At least if he sets a new record it'll get into the next edition. There's going to be a phasing out period.'

'Thank heavens for that. We'd have riots on our hands.'

'Talking of which, we'll have to orchestrate a careful media campaign around it, nothing alarmist.'

Lisa clicked her teeth. 'I'm not sure Fred upstairs is going to like it. He'll worry that it'll affect sales.'

I sat brooding at my desk. Fred, Guinness's sales director, lived and breathed the book and was fond of the fun records which, as anyone knew, attracted the lucrative youth market. He and his book reps wouldn't be too happy about losing some of them. I wondered whether Donald had broached the subject with him, and with Norris for that matter. As founder and editorial advisor he acted as a sounding board for the editor and always offered intelligent ideas and more often than not, solutions. Eileen appeared jingling her trolley.

'Cup of tea?'

'Please.'

Lisa took a cup and saucer from her mother and passed it to me. She held out her own gaudy mug for filling.

'What on earth is illustrated on your mug?' I asked her.

She blushed. 'My Little Pony. You know, the kids toy. It's all the rage.'

I shook my head in mock despair. 'Oh Lisa! And look at all those trolls and knick-knacks on your desk.'

'She's got a nodding dog, too,' her mother declared. 'She's a big kid at heart.'

Lisa rolled her eyes. 'So what? Anyway have you got any custard creams, Mum?'

She delved under the top shelf of her trolley and emerged with a packet of biscuits.

'Don't put on weight now after all that dieting you've done.'

Lisa gave a cry. 'It's not for me! It's for her! Give me a break, will you?'

Eileen gave her an old-fashioned look and pushed her chariot off.

The phone rang. It was Creighton. He was worrying about the kind of food we'd be eating in Paris.

I frowned. 'Food? We'll be eating at the hotel most of the time.'

He sounded anxious. 'I'm not sure about French food. All those funny things they eat like frogs' legs and horse.'

'We'll avoid them, I promise.'

'And snails?'

'Don't worry. I'm sure the hotel will cater for every taste.'

He sounded very anxious. 'Do I need to take my passport?'

'Yes, you do.'

After reassuring him as best I could I replaced the receiver and re-examined Creighton's punishing media schedule. I hoped for both our sakes that he was going to be up for the job.

★ ★ ★

John Kenmuir, a rosy-cheeked, stocky man in his thirties with wavy dark hair, was wearing a large white bib, sitting in front of an empty table in Pizzaland, Glasgow. The restaurant was packed with excited onlookers and an impressive gathering of local press and photographers. I noticed everyone was giving the table a wide berth – and for good reason. At the sound of a bell, and with great ceremony, a chef appeared from the kitchens bearing a silver platter the size of a small coffee table on which sat a massive tomato and cheese pizza. John smelled it, a smile of satisfaction on his lips, while the throng murmured excitedly. The restaurant manager watched eagerly as Norris and I stood examining a stopwatch. With great aplomb Norris lifted his arm high in the air. There was a hush. He observed the attentive faces around the room and then lowered his arm quickly, his eyes fixed on the stopwatch.

'Go!' shouted Norris.

There was a collective cheer and frenzied clapping and whistling.

On Norris's command, John immediately dived into his 2 lb pizza and wolfed it down in exactly 55.28 seconds, shaving more than four minutes off the existing record. What seemed like a bloodbath lay before us as splattered tomato sauce trickled down the table legs and covered John's face and bib. Norris and I went over and congratulated him. 'Well done,' said Norris as the press gathered round. 'You have effortlessly superseded the previous existing record set in 1984 by Geir Storvann of Drammen in Norway of 5 minutes and 23 seconds for a 1.8 lb pizza. This is a new record for Scotland. Congratulations from all of us at Guinness!'

Wild whooping and clapping broke out as John leaped to his feet and punched the air. In the ensuing mayhem Norris and I were able to quietly slip away into an awaiting taxi and head off to the Gleniffer Press in Paisley.

'That's put me off pizza for life,' I exclaimed.

Norris smirked. 'Still, it was fascinating to see the way he hoovered it up. Imagine inviting him round for dinner?'

I laughed. 'At least nothing would go to waste.'

He yawned. 'It'll be good to see the Gleniffer Press. I've always enjoyed visiting publishing houses and print shops.'

'Why's that?'

'My Scottish father, William Allan McWhirter, fired my passion for books and newspaper printing.'

'Didn't he edit the *Daily Mail*?'

'In the thirties, that's right. In fact, he was the first man ever to become editor of three national newspapers, the *Daily Mail*, *Sunday Pictorial* and *Sunday Dispatch*.'

'Golly, so that's where you get your record-breaking streak from?'

'Maybe.'

'Were you close to him?'

'It was different in those days. I suppose I was rather in awe of him. He worked for Lord Rothermere, a bit of a taskmaster, so was constantly at the office. What I do remember is that his staff called him Squire and Mac and that he was well loved by one and all.'

'I thought you had to be ruthless to be the editor of a national newspaper?'

'That's probably true but my father wasn't born with a silver spoon. He understood hard graft. Apparently his favourite line was, "If you cannot say good of someone, say nothing at all." He was a fair and kind employer.'

'Gosh, how times change.'

'Why do you say that? Hasn't Guinness been pretty good to you?' he said with a glimmer of a smile.

'Oh yes, but I'm one of the lucky ones. I don't think there's much of a code of honour in the workplace anymore. My flatmate's an insurance broker and what she tells me goes on in office life in the City astounds me. '

'You're too cynical for your own good, AN.'

'Am I?'

He sighed deeply. 'Then again, maybe not. The world isn't what it used to be.'

We sat in awkward silence.

'So. What are our plans afterwards?'

'We've got meetings with *The Scotsman*, *Edinburgh Evening News* and *The Glasgow Herald*. That'll keep you busy until evening.'

He rested his head on the back of the seat and shut his eyes. 'Never a dull moment, AN. Never a dull moment.'

★ ★ ★

A day later, I stood at the British Airways desk at Heathrow, anxiously craning my neck for any sighting of Creighton. It was three thirty in the afternoon and I was worried that his flight from Newcastle might have been delayed or that he'd met with some other obstacle. It was therefore with some relief that I saw him ambling towards me with an enormous suitcase and duffel bag. He was sweating profusely and was out of breath; and, bizarrely, wearing bright red shoes.

'Everything all right, Creighton?' I called as I rushed to greet him.

He grabbed my hand and shook it vigorously. 'Boy, am I pleased to see you. I forgot my passport and had to go back home, then at the airport I forgot the gate number and I've been in a pickle all day.'

That didn't bode well coming from the world's greatest memory man.

'Well, everything is going to be fine now. We can have a relaxing flight and a catch up about the schedule.'

He collected his boarding card from the check-in staff and ran a fretful hand through his wiry black hair.

'What time do I appear with my cards on the French television show tonight?'

'Eight o'clock. So we've got plenty of time.'

He nodded and walked briskly beside me as we headed for the gate. We found our seats on board and chatted about his itinerary until I noticed Creighton's eyes closing.

'I might just have a bit of shut eye,' he yawned.

I let him sleep while I finished off some work. The sky was dark and impenetrable. Occasionally a light from another plane would wink at us in the distance and then nothing. Just blackness. I tried to doze but the sound of the plane's engine kept me awake. I drank a black coffee while Creighton slumbered peacefully in his seat.

We touched down at Charles de Gaulle and headed for the taxi rank in blinding rain. Creighton was on great form, chatting and full of good cheer. On the way to our hotel, he memorised two packs of cards that I had carefully shuffled and seemed rather nonchalant about his debut on the French national news. Philippe, the French editor, had booked us in to a plush and understated Parisian boutique hotel with white walls, antiques and ornate upholstery.

'Welcome to Paris,' said the reception clerk as he handed over our large gilt keys decorated with petrol blue silk tassels.

'Blimey, it's really posh,' giggled Creighton in his strong Middlesbrough tones.

Soon after, we left for the TV studios. The traffic was heavy and it was seven thirty before we arrived at the modern building in a quiet suburb of Paris. After mumbling in French to the reception staff, I was sufficiently understood to be directed to the third floor.

'Hey, you speak French!' cried Creighton as we stepped into the empty lift.

'Well, some might dispute that, particularly the French.'

'It sounded really great. You're right clever, aren't you?'

'No Creighton, I am not and I have a memory like a sieve so I can't even conceive of how you remember all those cards.'

He shrugged modestly. 'It's all about concentration.'

'I believe you,' I replied doubtfully.

Bing. The lift doors opened and we stepped out practically into the Gallic embrace of a garlicky news editor. He wore tight, high-waisted jeans from which billowed an open-necked white shirt.

'Well, how nice to see you both! Please follow me. I am Serge LeBoeuf, the show's editor. My colleague, Céline, will look after you.'

I turned to see a young woman standing demurely by his side dressed in a navy blazer and pencil skirt. A red paisley silk scarf peeped out from the inside of her pinstriped shirt and her raven hair was pulled back into a tight chignon bun. She hung back for a second and then with a prim nod gestured for us to follow. Serge swept down the corridor in great haste and threw open the door of what turned out to be a large newsroom full of computers, television screens and gabbling French people. Like the White Rabbit, he scuttled down a flight of stairs in the centre of the room followed by the taciturn Céline. In some bewilderment we followed suit.

Serge paused at the bottom of the steps, fondling his hair which cascaded in waves to the brim of his shoulders. 'This is the studio gallery. Mr Carvello, you will now have a quick make-up session and a chat wiz ze producer before we take you into ze studio. You have your playing cards with you, *n'est-ce pas?*'

'Yes, of course,' puffed Creighton. 'I just need to get them out of my bag.'

'No hurry. You can just give zem to Céline before you go into ze studio.'

Creighton eyed me anxiously.

'I'd like to get the cards out now really. I don't like panic and last-minute problems,' he stuttered.

I turned to the editor. 'Actually can Creighton have some time to catch his breath and locate his card packs? He needs a few moments' peace and maybe a cup of coffee?'

'OK,' shrugged Serge. *'Pas de problème.'*

'What time is his slot on the news tonight?'

'Hopefully eight fifteen.'

'We have some time then.'

He flicked back his mane of dark glossy hair, nibbled impatiently on a nail and gave a few quick instructions to Céline. She beckoned us over.

'Can you follow me and I'll get you a drink and organise make-up?'

Serge smiled manically and dashed off. Some minutes later we found ourselves ensconced in a make-up studio, sipping at dark coffee. Creighton pulled out a few sets of cards and turned the packs over in his hands somewhat shakily.

'Feeling nervous?' I asked gently.

'A bit. It's all these bright lights and the noise that gets to me.'

'Well, when this is over, we can go back to the hotel and have a calming supper and a relatively early night. We have a ten o'clock show in the morning so it's not too early a start.'

Creighton swallowed hard and closed his eyes. He seemed to be reciting something to himself. Maybe a winning mantra or comforting verse. Who could say?

Fifteen minutes elapsed and the large and sandy-haired news producer arrived. He was puffing on a cigarette and seemed to be clinging for dear life to a pack of *Gitanes*. He introduced himself as Bernard and shook our hands.

'*Enchanté*. OK, my friends, remember this is a big programme. It has millions of viewers across France so we don't want any mistakes. *Pas du tout*. It is, how you say, alive.'

'Live,' I corrected.

'*Précisément*,' he replied. 'Now Mr Carvello, we will only have time to demonstrate your brilliant memory skills with part of a pack of cards. We will announce you as having flown over to be part of a *Livre de Guinness* celebration. OK?'

'Fine,' nodded Creighton. 'What's a *livre*?'

'He just means the French edition of the book, Creighton.'

'Oh right you are.'

Bernard turned to me with a brisk smile. 'If you do not mind, mademoiselle, please come with me to the viewing gallery while I take Mr Carvello to the studio to agree final details before he goes on air.'

I gave Creighton an encouraging squeeze of the arm. 'Go and sock it to them.'

He smiled weakly. 'I'll do my best.'

Moments later I found myself in a gallery sitting next to a group of weird-looking news staff, all peering hard at wide television screens. A voice bellowed over a tannoy, indicating in French that Creighton would be on next. I watched as he was settled in a chair in the studio, in front of him a pile of playing cards. A minute later and the languid female presenter strolled over to him, and began speaking to camera.

She was giving background information about Creighton, describing him as the world's greatest memory man, capable of memorising six separate packs of cards – 312 in total – on a single sighting and only making four errors. *Zut alors!* She then smiled winningly and coquettishly at the camera and sat in a chair opposite him. I felt my stomach churn. Quickly and efficiently she commenced shuffling the cards, her long tapered fingers working their way through the pile. I briefly pondered whether she'd ever been a croupier or had been practising for nights before the show. Sitting opposite Creighton she began slowly showing him each card in turn, replacing them face down on the table in front of him. He nodded after studying each card. Seconds later she picked up the cards on the table and asked him to start reciting them back to her in the order he had been shown them.

A translator stood by to translate his words. At first everything seemed to be going well, but not for long. There came a strange sound, a cross between a howl and a shriek, from somewhere in the newsroom. I turned to see a raging Serge stomping towards me, a scowl on his stubbly visage.

'*Merde*! What is going on? He is getting ze sequences all wrong! *C'est un cauchemar!*' It's a nightmare, he was saying. I stood up to face him. 'What on earth is the matter?'

He pointed a grubby, nail-bitten finger at a television screen.

'He has not got one right! We are having to improvise and ze translator is having to give a different interpretation of what he is saying!'

I peered at the screen and to my horror noticed that the camera was no longer resting on the face of each card that Creighton was being shown. The presenter merely showed the card to him but the audience was blanked out. Obviously it was because Creighton was getting them all wrong. I sank my head in my hands for a moment and then approached Serge. 'Look, the stress and fast pace of the studio have obviously unsettled Creighton. He has never had a problem remembering cards before.'

He regarded me furiously. 'Thank God we are switching to the next item. It was a disaster! Horrible. The poor presenter was in shock. He is a fool! A fraud!'

My composure slipped. 'He is neither a fool nor a fraud. I am astounded at your rudeness. These things happen. It is called human error.'

'I never want to see him again. Please, go and collect him and leave.'

He stormed off towards the corridor and the lifts, slamming the door behind him.

'Charming manners,' I muttered to myself.

Céline appeared with a shaken looking Creighton. He pulled a face.

'I don't know what happened back there. I was OK for the first five cards but then I had a kind of blank and...'

I helped him on with his coat. 'Never mind, Creighton. Let's just get out of here. I need to make some calls back at the hotel.'

Céline accompanied us in the lift and down into the street. She gave me a sheepish smile as she crept back into the building. I hailed a cab and sat miserably in the back wondering how I was going to explain what had taken place to Philippe, and also Norris and Donald. As we neared the hotel, Creighton suddenly beamed at me and slapped his knee.

'I know what I did wrong! I was just one card out of sequence all the way.'

I tried to smile.

'I'll be fine tomorrow now, don't you worry.'

We shared a chicken casserole in the restaurant and discussed the timetable for the next day. Should I cancel everything? It was Friday evening and it was unlikely I'd be able to reach Philippe given that he'd told me he would be spending the weekend out of town. I saw Creighton to his bedroom along my corridor and rang Norris. He listened patiently and gave a long sigh.

'Not a good start to the weekend but there's still time to save the day.'

'How?'

'It seems to me that it was just a bad case of nerves and now that he's worked out what went wrong on the show I'm sure he'll not slip up tomorrow. Sleep on it and if you're in any real doubt, pull out of all the shows. I'll call Philippe and calm the waves.'

I thanked him and then mentioned Creighton's fear of unusual French food, even garlic. He gave a little cough. 'A man after my own heart. What did you feed him this evening?'

'Just a chicken casserole.'

'Thank goodness. If you'd fed him frogs' legs, I'd have told you to call it a day and to get on the next plane home.'

I laughed loudly. Norris had the final word.

'Always remember, AN, that things are never as bad as they seem, and that is a fact.'

★ ★ ★

The next morning Creighton was on sparkling form. He ate a huge breakfast of toast, eggs and bacon and set off down the icy street with a spring in his step. At the television studio where he was to take part in a morning chat show, he smiled confidently and chatted with the producer as if they were old friends. I was astounded. What miracle had taken place in the night? As he was shown into the studio, I crossed my fingers and would have crossed my toes given the chance but it wasn't necessary. Creighton was a triumph. He memorised a whole pack of cards accurately and without hesitation. The producer came up and shook my hand.

'This man is a consummate professional. A genius! How does he do this?'

With relief I led Creighton from the studio and out into the rainy street. 'Well done! The producer said you were brilliant.'

He lapped up the praise. 'I can't wait for the next show!'

We had a few hours to kill so I took him up the Eiffel Tower, a short walk from the studio we would be visiting next. Creighton was like a big kid. He revelled in every minute up the tower, pointing excitedly at all the miniature buildings below and asking me to identify them from my guide book. We arrived for the next show, a current affairs chat show, and once again, Creighton performed magnificently. After scoffing a cheese baguette in the hospitality suite of Antenne 2, Creighton went on air for his final performance. Everything went like clockwork and it was then over to a local Paris radio station to give a joint interview. Thankfully, it was conducted partly in English.

★ ★ ★

I had arranged for Michel Lotito, Mr Mangetout himself, to join us for a drink of champagne since he was appearing on a radio show only a short distance from our hotel. He arrived on time and greeted me warmly as we took our seats in the cosy bar. For a man who ate planes and bikes I was surprised to see he was of modest build with a friendly face and twinkling eyes and no signs of metal fatigue.

'It's lovely to meet you!' he exclaimed. 'You speak with people on the phone and wonder what they're like. I didn't expect you to have such curly hair and you are even younger than I imagined.'

Creighton sat star-struck. 'I can't believe I'm meeting the world's greatest omnivore. It's such a privilege.'

'But no! It is I who am privileged to meet the world's greatest memory man!' cried Michel Lotito.

Our champagne arrived and I took a long sip. Delicious. Creighton was wringing his hands together.

'Er, Michel, can I ask you a daft question?'

'Of course.'

'How is it that you are able to eat metal and glass?'

Michel placed his champagne flute on the table and sighed. 'It is like this. The medical experts discovered that I have an unusual stomach lining and also a method of digestion that helps to break down difficult materials.'

'Amazing!' said Creighton.

'But when did you discover your extraordinary abilities?' I asked.

'When I was just a boy back in the fifties in Grenoble, I started eating wood and crockery, things like that. It went from there really. I became an entertainer and the idea of breaking records appealed to me. It has been my living.'

I raised my glass to them both. 'How fantastic it is for me to be sitting with two phenomena. That must be a record in itself.'

They both laughed. We chatted for another hour until Michel rose to leave.

'One day I hope we'll meet again,' I said.

'Yes, and next time perhaps you'll show us one of your omnivore feats in action,' giggled a slightly tipsy Creighton.

'No need to wait,' smiled Michel and without a moment's hesitation, he picked up the champagne flute and bit a huge chunk out of it.

★ ★ ★

Early the next morning I tapped on Creighton's bedroom door.

'Are you awake, Creighton?'

A muffled grunt. I heard stumbling and then the door opened a crack.

'Shall we just order breakfast in our rooms? It'll be faster.'

He nodded. 'How do we do that?'

I pulled the card hanging from his doorknob and passed it to him. 'Just fill this in and hang it outside your room.'

I looked at my watch. 'Do it soon because they stop collecting them in fifteen minutes.'

I returned to my room, packed my case and suddenly heard a knock at the door. Thinking it was my breakfast arriving very promptly, I swung open the door. Creighton was staring back at me in some panic.

'Whatever's wrong, Creighton?'

'I've had a bit of an accident in my room.'

I rushed in to the corridor and followed him to his bedroom where, on first inspection, I thought he'd slashed at himself with a razor. What looked like dark red blood was smeared on the white bed covers and sat in globules on the wooden floor. I raised a hand to my mouth. He gave a nervous giggle.

'It's only red shoe polish, don't worry.'

'What?'

'You told me to fill in that breakfast order but I didn't have a pen so I luckily remembered I'd brought my jar of liquid red shoe polish with me and so I dipped my finger in it and tried to use it to mark the items on the menu.'

I shook my head in disbelief. How could someone with such a brilliant mind do something so unutterably mad?

He nibbled on his lip. 'Well, it was going fine until I accidentally knocked over the pot and it went everywhere. I tried to wash the sheet but it seems to have made it worse.'

I stood surveying the mess, wondering how on earth I was going to explain myself to the reception staff and to David, my managing director, when I returned to London. Creighton stared at me with mournful eyes. 'I'm really, really sorry.'

It was no good. The ludicrousness of the situation was just too much. I burst into fits of giggles. I laughed so hard I thought I might never stop. Creighton at first seemed startled but then began laughing himself.

I patted his back. 'Come on Creighton, just pack up and let's get to the airport. We'll have breakfast there.'

'You're not angry then?'

'No, Creighton, I'm not. After all, things are never, ever as bad as they seem.'

SEVEN

★ ★ ★

BRIDGE AND BRAINS

It was a crisp, bright spring day as I strode into the office, feeling rather smug that I appeared to be the very first person in the department. How virtuous was that? It was barely seven thirty and yet there was so much to do before the big event. I was wearing a suit, the smartest I could find. As it happened it was a rather petite men's slate-grey suit from an Oxfam store that my enterprising elder sister had fashioned into a jacket and pencil skirt. For the bargain price of three pounds, one could hardly complain.

It had never crossed my mind that I should ever rub shoulders with the Right Honourable Margaret Thatcher, prime minister of the United Kingdom and possibly the only woman in the world who could induce fear, admiration, fierce loyalty and at times loathing in those around her, sometimes all at the same time. At the age of eighteen when I was eligible to vote, it just so happened to be the year of the general election and, along with the majority of my girl friends, I voted for Margaret Thatcher. Did we do it because we were staunch Conservatives? No. We were women. We wanted a woman in power; to give a thumbs up to sisterhood and a nod to those heroic bustle-clad feisty belles from a bygone era who had fought for our right to vote. What would those suffragettes have felt the day Margaret Thatcher took her seat as the prime minister in parliament? Would they have shed a tear of joy to see that their hard-fought battle had not been in vain? And today, some years on, I would be meeting the woman who had put us girls on the political map.

I stood at my desk and pulled the photocall schedule towards me. Norris, Alex and I, accompanied by Chrissie and Ron who often carried out photography work for Guinness Publishing, would be meeting at the House of Commons at 10.00 a.m. At 10.30, Margaret Thatcher, together with 31 re-elected British women MPs, would be converging on the building's terrace for a formal group photograph. This shot would be included in the new edition of *The Guinness Book of Records* under the title of Lady Legislators – the largest assemblage of British women MPs ever taken in one shot. I rubbed my hands together. The media interest in the event had been huge and I was looking forward to widespread coverage across the national press. It was time for a strong coffee. I was about to enter the kitchen when I heard a strange gnawing sound. Was it a mouse? I walked gingerly along the corridor, peering under desks and bobbing my head over partitions until I became aware of a pair of legs jutting out from under a desk. They were long legs and the feet sported a pair of shiny black shoes. It could only be one person.

'David, what are you doing?'

A head poked out. 'Ah, hello. I'm just trying to saw off some of this old carpet. I don't think it was ever fitted properly. It looks rather untidy. Look at these loose threads.'

'But presumably you can't see it unless you're behind the desk?'

'That's the point. I am behind the desk and I can see it.'

'Would you like a coffee?'

He lapsed into deep thought. 'Thank you very much but no, I think I'll finish off here and return to my office.'

'We're seeing Margaret Thatcher today.'

He smiled. 'Yes, that should be interesting. Of course Norris and Margaret have been close friends for years. I doubt she'd have agreed to do this photo for anyone else.'

'Is there anyone Norris doesn't know?'

He laughed. 'If there are people he doesn't know, they'll most certainly know of him.'

He unearthed himself from the desk, put a mini saw and chisel back in his toolbox and sauntered off. I caught sight of Alex dashing into the kitchen. I popped my head round the door.

'Excited?'

'Not sure about being excited. I'm feeling slightly anxious. Let's hope everyone turns up, most importantly MT herself.'

'I don't think she'd let Norris down, and as for the women MPs – they'd be far too terrified not to show up, wouldn't they?'

He laughed. 'You're right. I wouldn't want to cross her.'

With steaming coffee, we trundled back to my desk and talked through the minutiae of the event.

'We will have very limited time to perform these shots so every minute will count,' he said.

'Come on, Alex. Chrissie and Ron won't let us down. They're real troopers.'

'Yes, but if any MPs turn up late it could blow everything. We want this to go smoothly and I need one very good group shot. As it is, ten MPs are abroad and so couldn't make it.'

'They'll probably be for the chop when they return,' I grinned.

Lisa appeared. 'Got here early to help out. D'you want me to do anything?'

'Maybe you could put all the press packs in a bag and just make sure that we have all the telephone numbers of the key players.'

She nodded and strolled over to her desk and picked up a notebook. She called to me.

'By the way, can you call back that brainy woman when you have a sec? You know, Marilyn Vos whatsit.'

'Or possibly even Marilyn Vos Savant, the woman with the highest IQ in the world?'

'That's the one,' she said distractedly, copying down phone numbers from her Rolodex.

'She's really nice on the phone. I like her American accent.'

'Isn't she being inducted into the *Record Breakers* Hall of Fame?' asked Alex.

'Yes, I imagine that's why she's calling me but she really needs to speak with David Frost and the BBC TV team. It's their event.'

Lisa grinned. 'I'm really looking forward to the party after the show. There'll be loads of celebrities and record-breakers. It's only next week so I'll have to polish my tiara!'

Alex raised his eyebrows and laughed. 'Come on, let's get going. I want to be there early to fix up the shots.'

Donald arrived. 'All set?'

'I think so,' said Alex. 'It's a daunting prospect coming face to face with the great Mrs T.'

Donald gave a chuckle. 'I'm sure you'll cope. Just get a shot with them all looking directly at the camera.'

'We'll do our best.'

Alex and I arrived at the House of Commons in good time and after security checks were shown along one of the sweeping corridors and up to the Terrace Pavilion. The natural light flooding in from windows on the south side of the building seemed to please Alex who walked around the room in ponderous mode, evidently trying to decide the best place for the historic photo shoot.

'It'll probably be best to do it right in the centre,' I suggested.

He tapped his chin. 'Yes, but Chrissie and Ron might prefer them with their backs to the light. What's that plastic stuff on the windows?'

'Some kind of candy-stripe sunblind, I think. It's odd that they don't have a carpet on the floor. It's not very cosy up here.'

'It's probably to show that they don't flagrantly waste taxpayers' money on baubles and internal decoration,' he muttered.

I walked over to the windows and looked out over the Thames. It was sludgy and grey and dotted with small vessels and pleasure cruisers. My eyes scanned the clutter of docks and dilapidated flats that glowered back at me from the other side of Westminster Bridge. A moment later Norris bounded into the room, hotly pursed by Chrissie and Ron.

'Thank heavens. We're all here,' I said.

Norris gave a puzzled smile. 'Why ever shouldn't we be? Anyone seen Margaret?'

It seemed odd to me that anyone should call Margaret Thatcher so chummily by her first name. I was already secretly quaking in my boots at the thought of being introduced to her. In fact, I was rather hoping I could avoid the experience altogether in case a bad wave of nerves hit me or I had one of my giggling fits at the wrong moment. A gaggle of women MPs rolled up.

'When are we kicking off?' asked one, rather robustly.

She noticed Norris and broke into a smile. 'Why, if it isn't dear Norris. How are you? So good to see you. Tell us what you want us to do.'

Norris shook hands with the woman who, it transpired, was Dame Jill Knight, and beckoned Alex and me over.

'Dame Jill should sit in the front row. Can you place her by MT?'

Alex nodded. 'Of course. We'll get everyone into position in a few minutes.'

'I have to be out of here by eleven,' muttered a dumpy woman in a floral dress.

'That won't be a problem,' Norris said quietly.

More female MPs began trickling into the room and soon there was a general hubbub as the women began chatting and calling vociferously to one another. They wouldn't have been out of place at a Women's Institute meeting of the fifties with their twinsets and pearls and coiffed hair.

'They've all dressed up for the occasion,' I whispered to Chrissie.

She smiled. 'Yes, they've certainly made an effort. Now hopefully it'll work if we arrange them in chairs in the centre of the room.'

She took her eye away from her lens and pushed her fair hair back. 'Ron reckons we have one lot seated around the PM in the first row, and form two rows behind where it'll be standing only.'

I looked across at Alex and Ron who were putting out chairs and discussing shots. Norris was surrounded by a group of women MPs who seemed to be hanging on his every word. As for the PM herself, she had not as yet arrived. Perhaps her intention was to make a dramatic entrance or more likely to ensure that she didn't waste time hanging around while the shots were being set up.

Alex and I politely ushered the ladies to their seats, leaving the central one absent for the great leader herself. There was a gentle vying for places in the front row and a few haughty expressions from those relegated to the back row. Diane Abbott arrived breathless and whispered to a fellow MP, 'Is she here yet?' And then, a hush fell as Margaret Thatcher walked slowly and assuredly into the room. She surveyed her troops with penetrating eyes and serenely walked over to Norris who offered her a peck on the cheek. Her golden hair was perfectly groomed and she wore a black suit with white trimmings. Large pearls sat in her ears coordinating with the single short string of pearls around her neck. In her pocket stood a perky white hankie and she gripped one of her famous black handbags by its handle. There was a flurry of movement and in rushed the MP Emma Nicholson. Margaret Thatcher's eyes fixed on her for a few moments, rather like a crocodile's might when in line with passing prey.

I turned to Alex. 'She's probably copped it.'

He smothered a smirk with his hand. We stood stiff as ramrods ready for the moment when the Prime Minister would take her seat. Chrissie and her older companion, Ron, appeared composed but I imagined they were probably in a state of some anxiety as they stood poised for action. Meanwhile, Norris proffered the PM an arm and led her over to the chair that sat plumb in the middle of the front row. On one side of her sat the smiley and relaxed Conservative Dame Jill Knight and on the other was the Labour MP Joan Lestor in a vibrant green suit and canary-yellow blouse. On her left sat Dame Elaine Kellett-Bowman, a rather gentle soul wearing a loud patterned dress and an enigmatic smile. Betty Boothroyd and Lynda Chalker occupied the end seats. I trained my eyes past Dame Jill to the three occupants on her right. Janet Fookes, a vision in white, sat to her side even sporting white tights and shoes, and next to her were Dame Peggy Fenner in a floral dress and blazer, and

Jo Richardson in an understated pinstripe suit. I surveyed the back row and in some relief saw that Emma Nicholson had found a place next to the stylishly dressed Diane Abbott. All seemed to be in order.

With a nod from Norris, our photographers got ready to take the photograph. Ron asked everybody to face the front as Chrissie huddled close to the camera. Just as the shot was about to be taken, Margaret Thatcher caught Norris's attention and in a steely voice she said to him, 'Norris, make sure that in the image used in the book, my eyes are open.'

Norris gave a bemused smile and a tilt of the head. Three shots were taken in total. The women were growing restless. The party broke up and gathered around a table where teacups had been laid out. Norris called me over. 'I think it would be nice for you to meet Margaret.'

'I'm not sure. She looks awfully busy with all those women around her.'

He gave a little whinny. 'Nonsense.'

I followed behind him, feeling extremely silly in my £3 suit, and wondering what on earth I would find to say of any consequence to a personage of such importance. Before my nerves completely got the better of me, Norris gently pulled the PM to the side. 'Can I introduce you to Anna who has helped to organise the event today. She handles all the press and also judges records with me.'

Her intelligent blue eyes didn't waver from my face while Norris spoke. Up close her face seemed softer and her manner gentle. She shook my hand and smiled. 'Well done. I think it's all gone off rather well, don't you? Now, come and join us for some tea.'

She led me into the throng of lively female MPs. I felt myself cringe as a few motherly women gave me indulgent smiles, probably sensing my unease. The Prime Minister passed me a cup of tea as I stood in a huddle of women that now formed a crescent around her. At one point she made an observation about the problem of certain brands of tights that rode down the legs and caused Nora Batty-type wrinkles at the ankles.

'It's so annoying, isn't it?' she said to us all.

I heartily agreed along with the others, although secretly shocked that a PM could even broach such a topic in public. And yet why not? Hadn't all of us girls had that awful moment when a pair of tights began to ride down the legs, forming ugly crinkles and wrinkles just where one didn't want them? I realised too that Margaret Thatcher in her own way was trying to put all of us at ease. She kept firmly to topics of everyday conversation in a light and breezy manner. When I thought no one would notice, I attracted a waiter's attention and asked for a cube of sugar. Margaret Thatcher beamed and looked approvingly at me. 'There's nothing wrong with a bit of sugar.'

I mumbled a thank you and gulped down my tea.

'So what did you study at university?' she suddenly asked me.

'English and Classics,' I replied.

'A sound choice. Do you enjoy your job?'

I laughed. 'Of course, it's the best job in the world.'

Norris strode over and spent some quiet moments in private discussion with the Prime Minister after which she surveyed her watch and announced her departure. Her two besuited silent male watchdogs followed at her heels. The room sighed in palpable relief. Alex tapped my arm.

'All seemed to go off OK, didn't it?'

'Yes, I think so. She was rather nice and, dare I say it, normal.'

He scrunched up his nose. 'You're right. It wasn't what I'd expected. She was extremely approachable. Who would have thought it?'

The photographers had packed up and were waiting to take their leave.

Chrissie stepped forward. 'I'm afraid one of the women in the front row blinked a lot so I can't guarantee we'll have a clear shot of her. They were quite a fidgety bunch.'

'As long as it wasn't the PM,' rejoined Norris as he approached the door.

'No,' she laughed. 'We made sure of that.'

We waited until all the women had cleared the room, and slowly walked together down the corridor and back out into the central lobby.

Norris smiled. 'Well done. That'll make a cracker of a shot. I loved the way Margaret kept all of the troops in order. So, what did you make of the PM?'

I shrugged. 'She seemed extremely nice and friendly. If you judged her by reports in the media you'd imagine she was some kind of ogress.'

Strolling out of the building and standing in a patch of sunlight, he looked across at Parliament Square.

'That's the thing, isn't it? People make hasty judgments about those they've never met or are ever likely to meet. It can be destructive and above all grossly unfair. I'm glad you liked her. She's a very decent person.'

I watched as he set off at a brisk pace along the road and hailed himself a cab.

★ ★ ★

I darted into the Carlton Tower Hotel in Knightsbridge and was directed to the Rib Room restaurant on the ground floor where I found Rixi Markus waiting for me.

'Darling, you are a little late but don't worry.'

I was breathless, having rushed directly from the BBC studios where I was meeting with the *Record Breakers* production team.

'Sorry, Rixi, the traffic was horrendous in White City,' I gasped.

She took my arm and with her faltering walk led me into an elegant room adjacent to the restaurant where a small group of guests were chatting together. She pointed to a man whose face was immediately recognisable to me. It was Bernard Levin. His hair, a controlled series of grey corkscrew curls, rolled back from a wide brow, and his doleful brown eyes took refuge behind heavy, black-rimmed spectacles with enormous lenses. He smiled as we approached and shook my hand.

'Don't tell me, you're the mystery guest? The only non bridge player present.'

I raised my eyebrows. 'I'm afraid so but Rixi insisted I joined you all so I shall just nod and try to look intelligent during lunch.'

'Oh don't do that. There are only five of us here and not one of us is very bright.'

Rixi reared back. 'Speak for yourself, my friend.'

I glimpsed the other guests, an elegantly attired lady and two suited older men.

'So do you bridge players often meet here for lunch?'

'Only when time permits,' said Rixi, 'I dine here alone most days but occasionally it's nice to have some stimulating company. I have little time for stupid people and everyone here is exceptionally intelligent.'

I wasn't sure whether this was an attempt at humour but given Rixi's razor-sharp intellect and Bernard Levin's reputation as a brilliant political commentator, I didn't doubt her. How we had become friends was puzzling in itself. Since the very first time she had telephoned me at the office, I grew used to her calling for a chat. Despite my loathing for any kind of card game, let alone bridge, we got on famously. We often met at the Carlton Tower Hotel, her home from home, which was only a couple of minutes' walk from her fortress-like flat in Cadogan Gardens, although sometimes I would pop round to her home for a drink after work. I was always unnerved by the number of bolts and locks on her steel-lined front door, once commenting that it could prove a serious handicap in a fire. She had laughed and told me that she had faced far worse hazards in life. And she had. On her many glass and ornate tables in the apartment were photos of her Austrian Jewish family. Many had died in Nazi concentration camps and her own at times tormented life read like a novel. As a child she had lived in Vienna but had been forced to flee to London to escape the Nazis during World War Two. As the son of Ukrainian Jewish emigrants, I imagined Bernard Levin would have related to Rixi and understood how her past, like his own, had defined her.

I was introduced to the other guests and soon we were enjoying a delicious and relaxed lunch in the hotel's private boardroom suite. The conversation ranged from literature and music to politics and hardly touched, to my relief, on bridge.

'So what do you enjoy doing?' asked Levin at one point.

'Writing. One day I may try my hand at journalism but I don't think it pays terribly well.'

That made him laugh. 'You are absolutely spot on. Mind you, publishing isn't much better.'

'No, but working for *The Guinness Book of Records* is a wholly unique experience even if one doesn't earn very much.'

'So give me a few of your favourite records.'

I sat and thought for a little while. 'I rather like the most indisciplined football match on record in which all twenty-two players were booked – including the one who went to hospital along with an injured linesman!'

'Where did that take place?'

'Hampshire, of all places. My other favourite is the world's worst singer, Florence Foster Jenkins, a soprano who had a sell-out concert at Carnegie Hall in 1944 and performed a high F that apparently induced tears in the audience. Norris told me that her high F had been made higher as a result of an injury sustained in a crash in a New York taxi.'

He roared with laughter.

I had often read Bernard Levin's articles in *The Times* and had always fancied him a true socialist and yet when we touched on Norris, whose conservative political views were well known, he was full of praise.

'We might not always see eye to eye politically, but Norris McWhirter believes in the freedom of the individual and I applaud him for that. You see, so do I.'

David had once told me that Norris's brother Ross had formed a political entity known as The Freedom Association, and that after Ross's murder it had been left to him to take up the reins. I decided to ask him about it. There was still much to know about Norris. For now, I enjoyed my lunch, basking in the witty banter of the various guests. At the end of the meal, Bernard Levin patted my arm.

'Remember Norris started out as a journalist. You could do a lot worse.'

169

Like a modern-day Cinderella I waved goodbye to my sophisticated fellow diners as they dashed into taxis while I took a bus back to the office. Maybe I was wrong about bridge. If bridge players could be such good fun perhaps the game might, after all, have some merit.

★ ★ ★

A week later, I found myself once again back at BBC Television Centre but this time it had nothing to do with the *Record Breakers* programme. Earlier in the evening David Frost had presented a wholly new annual show called *The Guinness Book of Records Hall of Fame*, in which six formidable record-breakers were presented with awards. This time they were Steve Davis, the champion snooker player, Edwin Moses, the unbeatable hurdler, Bob Geldof, who had raised £35 million for famine relief, Dick Rutan and Jeana Yeager, the first pair to fly an aircraft around the world without refuelling, and last but not least, Marilyn Vos Savant with the highest IQ and her dashing husband, Dr Robert Jarvik, inventor of the artificial heart. How one couple could combine such enormous brainpower was mind-boggling enough, but they were also, bizarrely, two of the most glamorous and attractive people in the room. Lisa and I swam through the guests, chatting to record-breakers and journalists and scoffing the canapés whenever we had the chance. My assistant had been full of excitement about the party and although not wearing the promised tiara, did wear a short, off-the-shoulder sequinned dress and lots of kohl round her eyes.

Geoff Smith, my friend from the Press Association, tapped me on the shoulder. 'Great do. A nice story for the regional press. Now are there going to be any speeches?'

I looked at my watch. 'David Frost and Norris will say a few words any time now.'

'Excellent. In that case I'll get myself a refill.'

He hopped off in the direction of a waiter and was soon lost from view. I looked around the room. There was quite an impressive group of well-known faces including actors, musicians and writers. Tim Rice, who penned a whole raft of Guinness Publishing pop music titles, known as British Top Singles, glided by talking animatedly with Bob Geldof and Don Black, the lyricist. Andrew Lloyd Webber was talking with Norris a few feet away. Meanwhile, Gyles Brandreth was in animated conversation with Nicholas Parsons. Both lay claim to the record for longest after dinner speech, albeit in different editions of the book. The event was undoubtedly a big hit and had attracted an A-list crowd of guests. A moment later David Frost stood up on the stage and greeted the assembled throng. 'I'd like to pay a special tribute to our fantastic award winners tonight...' I crept to the side of the room where Lisa was leaning against a wall. She stifled a yawn. 'It's been a long day.'

'We can leave after the speeches.'

She baulked at the suggestion. 'Are you mad? When do we get a chance to hang out at such a swanky event? No, I'm staying until the end!'

Norris had now stepped up on the stage and was delivering a brief speech. I heard him referring to Marilyn Vos Savant, and her phenomenal IQ: '... and of course we shouldn't forget that other high IQ scorer, Andragone Eastwood Demello of California, who has a score of between 225 and 250 and is purported to have uttered the word "hello" at barely seven weeks old.'

General laughter and applause followed and soon Norris was bobbing down the steps of the stage and into the crowded room. He caught my eye and came over.

'That was another brilliant speech.'

'We aim to please,' he said with an ironic grin. 'So where have you been hiding out? I haven't seen you for almost a week.'

'Well, you're the one who's been busy flying off to New York and France.'

He sighed. 'Yes, both productive trips but it's good to be back.'

'I meant to tell you that I had lunch with Bernard Levin and Rixi Markus.'

He chuckled. 'An interesting combination. I imagine bridge was the missing link.'

'Yes, but as you know I don't play.'

'Did it matter?'

'As it happened, no.'

He laughed. 'I'm sure Bernard Levin talked on a number of interesting subjects.'

'He did and he also said that you and he had something in common.'

'Really?'

'The freedom of the individual.'

He seemed amused. 'Indeed. He's an interesting chap. He had a tough childhood and when he was a baby his tailor father hopped off and they didn't meet again until he was a young man.'

'Well, despite such adversity both he and Rixi have done pretty well for themselves.'

Norris tutted. 'I must say you seem to be keeping very rarefied company these days, although before you get too big for your boots can I make one suggestion?'

'If you must.'

He shot me a mischievous smile. 'Perhaps it's time to up your IQ and, better still, to take up bridge?'

★ ★ ★

Alex was pacing around the kitchen clutching three photographs.

'I mean how could all of those women have been blinking so much?'

'A bad case of St Vitus Dance?'

He gave a grunt. 'Do you think some of them were snoozing when we were taking the shots?' he replied in some exasperation.

I pushed a coffee into his hand and took the images from him.

He was right. In all three shots one female MP or another had her eyes firmly shut as if dozing. I peered at the one he had ringed in red pen.

'Ah, this one seems OK and Margaret Thatcher's eyes are open. Mind you the lady on the far right of MT seems to be having a kip.'

Fretfully Alex grabbed it from me.

'Exactly. That's Dame Elaine Kellett-Bowman.'

'At least she has a smile on her face.'

He looked up at the ceiling in despair. 'Well, we have no choice but to go with this one.'

'I think that's a wise decision and after all Margaret Thatcher looks good in it. That's the critical thing.'

He flung himself in a chair. 'They were quite a fidgety bunch. Poor Ron and Chrissie had a difficult job on their hands and in a limited timeframe.'

'Yes, but don't you remember what it was like having school photos done? We used to fidget about and I can't recall one picture taken of my classmates in which we all had our eyes open.'

He laughed. 'That's very true. Anyway, the important thing is that we captured an important historic moment in time.'

'Precisely, let's drink to that.'

Norris popped his head round the door. 'I'm just heading back to Wiltshire. I hear the images have come back from the House of Commons shoot?'

Alex eyed him a tad gloomily. 'They're very good except one woman has her eyes closed in all of them.'

Norris gave a start. 'Not Margaret I hope?'

Alex shook his head. 'Oh no, she's wide awake in every shot. It's a dame in the front row.'

Norris shrugged. 'As long as Margaret looks good, I don't think we need to worry what anyone else is doing in the photo. They could be doing handstands for all I care.'

And with a wink he pottered out of the kitchen.

EIGHT

★ ★ ★

JACKSON THE RECORD KING

It was a sizzling July day. The piazza of Covent Garden was awash with people, drawn by the booming music emanating from gigantic speakers placed at either side of the square. While a Capital Radio DJ cracked jokes and yelled out to the gathering crowds, a huddle of sultry and ultra-cool rap artists stood nearby, clicking their fingers and gyrating to the music. Norris and I wandered upon this scene in some bemusement.

I tapped his sleeve. 'Right, we've got an hour here and then we've got to shoot over to the Trocadero Centre to see the new exhibits.'

Norris turned to me. 'So we just judge these musicians and head off?'

'Exactly. This event has been set up by Capital Radio to find the fastest rapper ever. It's not a record we would normally have in the book but Shelley thinks it's quite fun.'

Norris looked at the crowds and then at the DJ jabbering into the microphone.

'You have to wonder what all these spectators are doing here on a weekday morning. Presumably the youngsters should be at school?'

I sighed impatiently. 'Probably, but that's not our problem. All I care about is getting you on *Thames News* and Capital Radio and featured in the *Standard*.'

He narrowed his eyes. 'You're shameless.'

I laughed. 'Why else are we here if not to milk the media?'

A tall and youthful figure bounded over to us. 'Hi! I'm Julian from Lynne Franks PR. So great that you could join us.'

'That's all right,' mumbled Norris, distracted by the sound of drums.

'We don't have a lot of time so can we get started soon?' I asked.

Julian browsed a clip folder in his hand. 'We're due to start in fifteen minutes. Can I introduce you guys to the DJ and the rap artists?'

We followed him over to the stage, shook hands with the DJ and then headed off to meet the competitors. Norris proffered a hand as we approached the group and was given a series of high fives. He took it in good grace and smiled cheerily at them all.

'So, presumably you are carrying on the traditions of the likes of Big Daddy Kane and LL Cool J?'

They stared at him in some shock. As did I.

'Hey man, you know about rap?' said an older man wearing shades and a reversed baseball cap.

Norris pushed out his lower lip. 'Not as much as I probably should but I'm aware of its historical roots. It's also known as emceeing or spitting, I think?'

There were nods of approval all round. A young man came over and, smiling broadly, punched his shoulder.

'I'm called Fly. I always loved your book. Now I know why. You're a really happening guy.'

Norris stole me a glance. I concentrated hard on a distant gull.

'So today there are five of you pitching for the fastest rapper title?' asked Norris.

Fly nodded. 'That's right, man. We are the finalists. There have been several heats on live radio and now we're the final ones.'

'Excellent. Well, perhaps before we get started, you can give me a little demonstration?'

They all clapped their hands and laughed.

A young man stepped forward and introduced himself to Norris as KK. 'Sure, but then you gotta have a go yourself. That's the deal.'

I looked across encouragingly at Norris. 'Oh I think that's a brilliant idea. I think you'll get the hang of it very quickly.'

He raised an eyebrow and picked up a small drum on the ground. 'So my understanding is that you chant rhyming lyrics in time to a beat?'

'That's right,' said KK. 'You have to kind of coordinate breathing, vocal presence and make your words have impact. Here – have a go.'

Norris was offered a chair. He sat down with the drum between his legs and began tapping.

Fly scratched his chin. 'So, maybe you say something like, I dunno, "I'm Norris McWhirter, the Guinness record king. In my book there's hip hop, jive and every cool thing".'

I stifled a guffaw.

Norris nodded. 'Very good. Well, let's have a go.'

KK took a seat next to him and began beating on the drum and saying the words. Norris repeated them in the same way. There was a kerfuffle and a news reporter and cameraman from *Thames News* arrived at quite a turn of speed.

'This is great, guys. Are you going to do some rap, Norris?'

I bit my lip. I hoped this wasn't going to be one of those embarrassing media moments when, in the vein of Prince Charles trying to dance with Maori dancers, Norris would be made to look extremely silly. I walked over.

'Are you sure about this, No?'

He grinned. 'Yes, I'd like a go.'

A moment later he was tapping away at the drum and doing a line of rap. The rappers began whistling and clapping, followed by others in the crowd who in some surprise watched Norris in his woollen tweed suit sitting happily among them. The DJ called everyone up on to the stage and Norris performed a rap duet with KK to the delight of the crowd. The competition followed. To hear the rappers talking at breakneck speed and yet able to articulate their words and keep to a rhythm made me realise that it really was quite an art. KK was declared the overall winner and Norris presented him with a Guinness book and a certificate. The *Standard* appeared.

'So what's your favourite kind of music?' the young reporter asked him.

Norris paused. 'Well, I was invited on to *Desert Island Discs* recently and I chose some golden oldies that I particularly like, record-breakers, as it happens, and also a few current hits.'

'Such as?' the girl enquired.

'*Thriller* by Michael Jackson, the best-selling album of all time.'

'What oldie did you choose?'

'*Livery Stable Blues*, the first jazz record released. Oh, and the Indian singer, Lata Mangeshkar, who made thirty thousand solo recordings.'

'And your favourite?'

'Probably Florence Foster Jenkins, purported to be the world's worst singer.'

I watched as she scribbled down his words.

'Time to go,' I whispered.

Norris waved to his new rapper chums and we set off. When we'd at last managed to hail a taxi I turned to him in the back of the cab. 'By the way, how on earth did you know the names of those famous rappers?'

He gave me a superior smile. 'That would be telling. As you are constantly discovering, AN, there is more to me than meets the eye.'

★ ★ ★

The *Guinness World of Records* exhibition in Piccadilly was throbbing with visitors. Much as I often popped by the museum for meetings with Maxine, the general manager, I rarely had time to take a proper tour of the place. Besides, I much preferred to do this with Norris because he always filled me in on fascinating historical details about record-holders, information that only he seemed to really know.

Norris and I now stood in the music section examining a cut-out of Michael Jackson.

'He's a very enterprising young man. His Victory Tour in the United States brought in a tour gross revenue of $81 million.'

'Have you ever met him?'

'Oh yes. I presented him with a first edition of the 1984 *Guinness Book of Records* in which he gained the record for best-selling album. He sold twenty-five million copies of *Thriller* worldwide. It was a rather nice event at New York's

American Museum of Natural History. Funnily enough, his manager has just written to me asking if I'd attend his Bad concert at Wembley later this month.'

'Wow!'

'Fancy calling it "Bad" before the audience has even had a chance to make an assessment!'

'You must know the "Bad" track?'

'As it happens I don't.'

'I wonder why he's inviting you there.'

He regarded me in mock surprise. 'You don't think I'm an obvious candidate for a loud pop concert at Wembley Stadium?'

I sniggered. 'I think it might have more to do with the fact that he admires you. I hope you'll go?'

He gave a sniff. 'I thought he was a very nice chap when I met him before. I'm not a great fan of loud music but I'll make the effort.'

Norris pointed at a replica of the world's most expensive violin, a Stradivarius which sold for a purported $1.2 million to a private buyer. He turned to me.

'I once met an underwater violinist. He managed to play Handel's *Water Music* submerged in a swimming bath in Washington State.'

'Impossible!'

'Not at all, AN. Where there's a will, there's always a way.'

We moved on. 'Ah, Placido Domingo. He once received eighty-three curtain calls and was applauded for one hour and thirty minutes after singing the lead in *La Bohème*. Mind you, Luciano Pavarotti trumped him a few years later with a hundred and fifteen curtain calls.'

'That seems a little excessive.'

He slid me a grin. 'Music has been known to induce pathological behaviour.'

Maxine, the exhibition manager, approached us from the sports section.

'Lisa just called to remind you about this afternoon's sales and marketing meeting.'

I thanked her and groaned. 'More meetings. I'd better head off to Enfield.'

Norris tutted. 'I always think meetings are an unnecessary waste of one's time. There are so many more important things to do.'

'I totally agree.'

Maxine rolled her eyes and laughed. 'Yes, well, back in the real world meetings are a necessary evil.'

'But why are they?' probed Norris.

She shrugged. 'I suppose if you get everyone in a room and they can all agree certain strategies, it can save on time and confusion later.'

Norris didn't look convinced. We tripped after her into the private office.

'I love the new exhibits,' I said.

She threw her security pass and keys on her desk. 'Yes but we need more. I'm hoping we might get funding for some updated models for the Human Being section. The current ones are getting a bit tatty.'

'Is it a big expense?' I asked.

She gave a sharp intake of breath. 'You wouldn't believe it! Those exhibits cost a fortune but we've got to be current. People won't keep coming back if we don't keep up to date.'

Norris accompanied me to the exhibition's reception area.

'There's one thing, No, you simply mustn't forget when you go to Wembley Stadium.'

'Really, what's that?'

'Earplugs.'

I stepped onto the downward escalator which led from the Trocadero Centre into the hustle and bustle of Piccadilly. The thought of Norris taking his seat amidst screaming fans at the Jackson concert in Wembley made me laugh. I only hoped that someone would be taking photos for posterity.

★ ★ ★

I was sitting in the sales and marketing meeting, listening to Fred, our cheery northern sales director, talking about the latest sales figures for the book. He turned to me.

'The overseas editions have been performing very well too. I hear you're planning a get-together with the foreign editors, love?'

Fred used the word 'love' when addressing most of the women in the office. If he hadn't been a diehard northerner, he might have been accused of chauvinism, but having studied in Leeds where the term was a constant, I never found it offensive.

'We're thinking of holding an editorial conference in London, that's if we can find the budget.'

Chris laughed. 'Sneaky. You see how she just slipped that in.'

Fred grinned. 'I think it's a good use of money, don't you Chris?'

He blinked. 'If it makes everyone feel warm and fluffy, I suppose so. Anyway, they'll be footing their own fares and accommodation, won't they? We'll just be paying out for the venue and sarnies.'

'He's a generous soul,' said Fred.

'I was thinking we could tie it all up with Red Nose Day. They'll be over just when Red Nose fever's breaking out. We could get some silly pics for the trade press.'

Fred nodded. 'Nice one, love. I like that. Shows we're all team players.'

Chris snorted. 'I suppose you'll want money for the plastic noses as well.'

I laughed. 'Maybe we can cut out Eileen's biscuit round for a week and use the money to fund them?'

'Now you're talking,' said Chris, a twitch of a smile on his lips.

'What's all this about Michael Jackson?' Fred suddenly asked, scratching his shiny pate.

'Norris told me that he's been invited to the Bad concert by the big man himself,' I replied.

Chris seemed miraculously impressed. 'Interesting. Jackson must be a big fan of the book.'

'I suppose it helps if you're actually in it,' I replied.

Fred nodded. 'He's doing seven concerts and if it's true that they're all sold out, he'll probably end up with some kind of record. Surely there must be some press mileage in all this?'

'Of course,' I replied. 'Once I know the score, I'll tip the nationals the wink. On the other hand, we'd better tread cautiously until we know the full story.'

'What d'you mean?' asked Fred.

'Well, maybe Norris will want to play down his part in it all. If he gets to meet Michael Jackson, he might prefer to keep it out of the press.'

Fred looked thoughtful. 'OK. Talk to Norris nearer the time and see what he thinks.'

Chris coughed. 'I can't see those two having much in common.'

Fred straightened his tie and tapped his desk. 'Oh I don't know. Norris usually pulls a rabbit out of the hat that surprises us all. We'll probably find he's an authority on moonwalking.'

I gathered up my files. Fred was right. I'd never seen Norris thrown by any situation or anyone. On the other hand, perhaps meeting Jackson, the king of pop, might genuinely leave him lost for words. We'd find out soon enough.

★ ★ ★

Ken, manager of the *Guinness World of Records* exhibition in the Empire State Building in New York, was practically yelling at me down the phone line. He was beyond excited. I could almost hear his heart beating faster than the wings of a hummingbird.

'You gotta believe it!' he was saying in his pronounced American twang. 'Michael Jackson just walked into the building without a by your leave. I mean, honest to God, the girls at the reception could not believe their eyes. They ran into the back office and hauled me out and I. Just. Stood. There.' He paused for breath.

'Hang on Ken, you're telling me that Michael Jackson just walked off the street unannounced and visited the exhibition?'

'Exactly,' he said, exhaling deeply. 'I mean that guy is something else. I was shaking. I went up and introduced myself and told him that it was one heck of a pleasure that he should pass by and he was just like – you know – nice.'

'Did he say why he didn't call in advance?'

He laughed. 'Anna, these guys don't need to call in advance. Wow, was he cool. I showed him round the exhibition. Thank God it was fairly early so it was pretty empty. I then took him to the showcase where we've got an image of him and some fake memorabilia, and his *Thriller* album; and he is so like, really happy.'

'Didn't you get him to sign something or…'

'Wait up! I'm coming to the best part. Oh my God, you're going to love this. OK so I get one of the assistants to go get the key to the exhibit to open it so we can get out some stuff for him to sign but guess what?'

'WHAT?'

'They can't find the key!'

I let out an, 'OH NO!'

Lisa and Muriel who were in deep conversation nearby, stopped in their tracks and regarded me with concern.

'So, wait for it, we look everywhere and MJ is so calm and polite. He and his people just smile and hang around and finally I'm so desperate I get a hammer and smash the glass of the exhibit.'

I burst out laughing. 'You're mad.'

'No, I'm not. I needed those exhibits signed. Then I get the girls to go fetch a camera. Guess what?'

'Don't tell me, you couldn't find one.'

'Correct. So I get one of the staff to run like a possessed coyote round to the local grocery store to get me a disposable camera and all the time MJ is just standing there politely discussing world records with me.'

I shook my head in disbelief. 'You know he's invited Norris to attend his Bad concert?'

He gave a shriek. 'You're kidding me? This just gets better and better. I tell you it's been a roller coaster of a day.'

I laughed. 'It could only happen to you. So you got the picture in the end?'

'You bet. I got a picture of him standing by the cabinet although not by the smashed door and he signed all the memorabilia. Such a great guy. Then he says he's sorry but he's gotta go, smiles and thanks me, and he just walks out.'

When he'd rung off I regaled everyone in the department with the story. Shelley, who handled the music section, was visibly awed.

'He must be such a nice person to have waited patiently like that. No prima donna antics or tantrums,' she said.

'He seems to be becoming our new best friend,' I replied. 'It'll be interesting to see what Norris makes of him.'

Muriel gave a giggle.

'What's funny?'

She put a hand to her mouth.

'Oh dear, I'm just wondering what on earth Norris will wear?'

Shelley and I exchanged looks.

'I can't see him going for a spangly number,' laughed Shelley.

I smiled. 'I think Norris will go just as himself in his same old suit. Probably exactly how Mr Jackson would like him to be.'

★ ★ ★

Lisa and I were sitting in Guinness's library surrounded by press releases. A couple of teacups sat discarded and unloved on a sideboard, a few telltale tea leaves lurking in their depths.

'I quite like folding and sticking things in envelopes. It's mindless but strangely satisfying.'

Lisa stared at me. 'Oh don't get all philosophical on me. It's a chore, nothing more.'

'I don't agree. Sometimes I like doing simple tasks. It's so less stressful than having to engage the brain.'

'Talking about engaging the brain, have you sorted out your trip to New York and Miami next month?'

'Damn it. Ted asked me to pop up earlier to order the currency for it and I forgot.'

The lucky charms on Lisa's wrist jangled in disapproval. 'You see, your brain's atrophying. Go on. You'd better go and sort it out.'

I rose and made my way through the department and up to the next floor. David peeped from behind his office door.

'Did you want to see me?'

'No, I'm on a mission to sort out my flight tickets and currency for the States.'

'Poor Ted,' he snorted, and disappeared into the depths of his office.

Ted looked up from behind his partition wearing a Cheshire cat smile.

'Alms for the poor!' I cooed at him.

He sunk his head in his hands. 'I was hoping to have a problem-free day.'

'Oh come on, Ted, I'm not that bad. I just need you to order me some dollars.'

'What about your flights to Miami?'

'The sponsor of the world's longest conga attempt is sorting them out. I've got to hop off to see Ken in New York en route but I can book a flight with our travel agency.'

'OK. If you're away five days I suppose I'll need to raise you a few hundred dollars.'

'You're a lifesaver.'

He pulled a face and told me to scarper. When I returned downstairs I found Norris at my desk. The day of the Michael Jackson concert had finally arrived. As always Norris was dressed in one of his Gieves & Hawkes woollen suits. He was sporting what looked like an old school tie.

'They're certainly not going to mistake you for a teenage fan.'

He raised an eyebrow. 'Thank heavens for that. Anyway, I shall reveal all in the morning.'

'Have a good time and remember to ask him about the Neverland Ranch and Bubbles his monkey,' I said.

He closed his eyes for a second. 'Good heavens. I hope the conversation won't plummet to such murky depths.'

With a bemused smile, he picked up his old scuffed briefcase and sauntered off along the corridor.

★ ★ ★

It was eleven o'clock in the morning and I was expectantly listening out for the familiar jingle of Eileen's tea trolley when Norris appeared soundlessly in front of my desk.

'Well I never. I imagined you'd be sleeping off the effects of last night.'

He cast me a scornful look.

'It was quite an extraordinary night. I arrived at Wembley Stadium and a young chap with one of those earpieces led me to a room backstage. A few minutes later Michael Jackson came in. He was slightly built and very diffident but he seemed pleased to meet me again.'

'Was he nervous about going on stage?'

'If he was, he didn't show it. Anyway, he asked whether I'd join him later for a chat at his hotel.'

'Then what?'

'I was taken out to the front row, next to some interesting guests. A very nice woman introduced herself as the singer Shirley Bassey, and I noticed Frank Bruno and there was that American actor, Jack Nicholson. Of course the film he starred in, *One Flew Over the Cuckoo's Nest*, is the longest-running film in Stockholm. It's been playing continuously there for more than eleven years.'

'I bet he was interested to learn that.'

'Of course. It was an impressive gathering.'

'And what did you make of the concert?'

He faltered. 'It was probably rather loud for my taste but some of the music was very catchy. Of course with any of these sorts of events, there's inherent hysteria in the crowds.'

'Did you wear earplugs?'

'No I decided to grin and bear it. There were people flinging themselves about in their seats. It was quite a sight.'

'Mind-boggling.'

'Quite. Anyway, I told Michael before the show that, quite apart from his Victory tour record, and having the best-selling album of all time with *Thriller*, that he had broken a UK record with the Bad concert. He seemed very happy about that.'

'What were the costumes like?'

'He seemed to be wearing a lot of heavy chains and constantly changed outfits. He did this very clever step that seemed as though he was gliding. The American actress next to me told me it was called moonwalking. Very skilful.'

'And what happened after the show?'

'I joined Michael backstage. Incredibly he didn't seem remotely exhausted after all that singing and dancing.'

'Did you travel in his famous battle bus to The Mayfair Hotel?'

'Yes, it was a white coach with blacked out windows. It was complete bedlam at the stage door. I did wonder if many of those gyrating and screaming fans had been drinking or even taking drugs.'

I giggled. 'Never?'

'It was peculiar. Michael got in the vehicle holding hands with a timorous young boy. He was rather like a little brother to him. They whispered a lot and it made me realise how childlike Michael was. His young companion was very bright and knew a great many records.'

'The press have nicknamed MJ "Peter Pan".'

'Very appropriate. So we had a very absorbing discussion about records, which we continued in his suite at The Mayfair Hotel. You know he has every edition of *The Guinness Book of Records*, even the original from 1955.'

'That's incredible. What's his knowledge of records like?'

'Most impressive. He seemed to like the human dimensions section of the book and obviously he was interested in the music section.'

'Did you like him?'

'Yes. I found him a considered young man and extremely courteous and intelligent.'

He drained his cup and perused his watch. 'I have to make a move.'

'Where are you off to now?'

'Oh, Michael's offered to teach me how to moondance over at his hotel.'

I gulped. 'I don't believe it!'

'Good, because if you did you'd be a fool.'

I watched as he ambled along the corridor, happy in the knowledge that even a private audience with the king of pop was not enough to turn the head of the world's greatest record-keeper.

NINE

★ ★ ★

DANCING IN THE STREETS

It was a mellow summer's day and a light breeze skipped across the waves, ruffling our hair and the stripy canvas seats of the 6,500 deckchairs laid out on Weymouth's long and sandy beach. Lisa and I walked with John, the director of Weymouth Tourist Board, along the sweeping Georgian esplanade, enjoying the sunshine and discussing logistics for the record attempt shortly to take place.

John turned to me, squinting in the bright sunshine. 'As you'll probably know it was King George III who put Weymouth on the map. Thanks to him it became one of England's most popular seaside resorts back in the 1790s.'

'Was that before or after he went potty?' I asked.

He smiled. 'Who can say, but I'm sure the sea air probably did him the world of good if he was becoming a bit unhinged.'

'Actually King George III holds British records for being the longest living king and for having the longest reign.'

'Is that so?'

Lisa gave a little cough. 'Going back to the musical chairs event, do you reckon all the punters will turn up?'

John gave a confident nod. 'Absolutely. It's been publicised for weeks across all the local media and we've had huge interest. As long as we beat the current record of 5,151, we'll be OK.'

I glanced at my watch. 'So they'll be arriving soon?'

'Any minute.'

He pointed towards a series of ropes festooned with brightly coloured ribbons. 'That's where they'll start queuing up and receiving their numbers.'

I searched the beach for evidence of a tannoy system and spied large speakers set up on a makeshift stage facing seemingly endless rows of deckchairs. The record attempt would involve all participants rising from their chairs when the music started and walking in an orderly fashion along their particular row of deckchairs until the music stopped. At that stage, a batch of twenty chairs would be taken away and people would have to scrabble for a seat. Those without one would have to leave the game. This routine would continue until just one person was left.

'Thank heavens the weather's looking good,' I said, peering up into the bright blue sky. A pair of gulls swooped low and then circled back towards the harbour, cawing furiously.

'Now, what about the judging of the largest trifle?'

He rubbed his hands together. 'I reckon that'll be finished by about four o'clock. So we can judge it straight after the deckchair event.'

'It's going to be a busy day,' said Lisa with a sigh.

We set off along the promenade and down on to the beach. I thought briefly about Donald who was up in Scotland witnessing the world's largest tap dance and wondered how he was getting on.

Half an hour later things were hotting up on the beach. Hundreds of people in beachwear began to arrive and were immediately directed to deckchairs. There was a festive spirit and entertainers were keeping the crowds amused and handing out sweets and goodie bags to the children. While waiting for the event to begin, I spoke with the local press.

'What's the current trifle record?' asked a reporter.

'One was made in Humberside that weighed 300 pounds and contained 11 gallons of sherry.'

'Whoa!' said one of the radio presenters. 'If ours contains that much sherry there are going to be a lot of happy people on the beach tonight.'

'Ah, but remember the sherry is just one of many ingredients in a trifle,' I replied.

'We're going to thrash that record today,' yelled John from the stage. 'We're going for a trifle weighing 1,954 pounds, and containing 18 gallons of sherry.'

A cheer went up. A mass of people in deckchairs began chanting, 'Weymouth, Weymouth!'

Record fever often broke out during mass participation events, something Norris always described in one word: 'hysteria'.

'Do you judge every big record attempt?' a young journalist asked.

'We try to support charity record attempts like these but there's a limit. We receive nearly fifty thousand enquiries every year and hundreds of requests to attend events worldwide. For a team of about ten people, that's a tough call.'

I surveyed the look of utter surprise on the faces of the press. Few realised what a modest enterprise *The Guinness Book of Records* was and how much work was carried out by so few.

'How many languages is the book published in?' someone shouted.

'Thirty-one,' I called back.

'Flipping heck!' mumbled a man in front of me.

'What percentage of the book is given over to daft records like the trifle and musical chairs attempts?' asked a young woman.

I paused for a few seconds. 'I take it you're referring to what we call "Chapter ten" records? The baked bean guzzlers, pogo stick bouncers, fastest bed-makers?'

She nodded. 'Exactly.'

'Well, believe it or not, they constitute only about ten per cent of the entire book.'

A collective sigh went up. I sneaked a look at my watch and saw John giving me a surreptitious wink.

He faced them all. 'Well ladies and gentlemen, take your seats, the game is about to begin!'

His announcement was greeted with excited clapping. I looked across the beach and saw row upon row of people dutifully sitting in deckchairs, waiting for the music to start. Where else but in England could one find such a scene?

The musical chairs attempt was now underway but keeping the ranks in order wasn't as easy as it at first appeared. Rather like trained sheep dogs, the stewards pounded the sand, rounding up participants who had stopped moving, preferring instead to dance wildly by their deckchairs to the strains of Janet Jackson's current hit song 'Control' as it crashed through the speakers. They were firmly encouraged to walk along their rows to keep within the game's rules, which required people to vacate their seats and to keep moving while the music played. There was much hysterical giggling and excitement whenever the music stopped, with those unable to find a seat good-naturedly ambling off to the side of the beach to join the many spectators. After what seemed like hours Lisa and I found ourselves joining in the frantic clapping and wolf whistling as the last two people in deckchairs rose for the final game. A steward removed one of the chairs and the two young women skipped gingerly around the only deckchair remaining on the acres of sand. Prince was in mid flow with 'U Got the Look' when the music stopped abruptly. Both women made a dash for the single deckchair but only one managed it. She raised her arms triumphantly as the crowds yelled their approval. With great solemnity I took her name and announced, 'Weymouth has created a brand new musical chairs record with a total of six thousand five hundred participants. The last person in the chair was Christine!'

I invited her up on the stage whereupon she received a certificate and current edition of the book.

'And now,' announced John, 'We are about to weigh the giant trifle, which has been made by our very own Weymouth Catering College.'

A huge cheer rose up as people began clapping and whistling. John joined me and we marched together across the hot sand to where a huge trifle in a metal container was receiving the finishing touches in the form of cake decorations, slices of fruit and glacé cherries. I stared up as it was lowered carefully from a large open-top lorry by a hoist. I estimated that it must have been about 6 feet in diameter and at least 5 feet deep. A tempestuous sea of thick white cream rested on its surface, sullied by multicoloured sugar decorations, chocolate shavings and all kinds of fruit. I felt perspiration coursing down my neck. John was looking equally hot, his wavy dark hair damp and his skin glistening with sweat. I checked the original weight of each ingredient with the official witnesses and added up the final weight in pounds. As predicted, the trifle weighed exactly 1,954 pounds. As the press gathered, John and I again took to the microphone for our double act, announcing the record and standing for press photos.

Balloons were released and the strains of 'Dancing in the Street' flooded the beach as people queued up to receive their spoonful of trifle. Lisa began joggling about, clapping her hands together.

'I love this track. Bowie and Jagger are the best.'

John beckoned to me.

'I don't know about you and Lisa, but I could do with a cool pint.'

We gathered up our few remaining press packs and headed after him up the beach and on to the esplanade. The sun was gradually beginning to disappear behind a fat white cloud and when I looked back it seemed such a strange sight. Several thousand people forming an enormous basilisk of a queue, as they waited ever so patiently for their portion of sherry-kissed record-breaking cherry trifle.

★ ★ ★

New York was warm and sultry and the traffic crazy, but somehow, cocooned in the belly of the Empire State Building, I couldn't hear a thing and even felt a slight chill in the air-conditioned room. Norris and I were visiting New York's very own *Guinness World of Records* exhibition and Ken, the general manager who'd in the last year become a good buddy and ally across the pond, was delighted to show us around.

'It's a shame you guys aren't going up to our exhibition in Niagara Falls. You'd have met Sandy Allen who works over there.'

Norris gave him a kindly smile. 'I did visit the exhibition when it first opened and Sandy and I have met several times before.'

As it happened I too had met Sandy, the tallest living woman at 7 feet, 7 and a quarter inches. When I met her she told me that she took a 16 triple E American shoe size or 14 and a half in UK sizing, and weighed 33 stone, although it hardly showed because of her height.

'So this is the famous cabinet that you smashed for Michael Jackson?' I asked.

Ken laughed. 'Did you hear about that, Norris?'

He chuckled. 'I most certainly did. I asked Michael about it when we met in London. He found it very entertaining.'

'That's what we're all about here.'

He beckoned us on. 'So, Norris, you're doing some radio shows while you're over?'

'I'm doing some media promotions for the American edition while madam here swans off to Miami.'

He nodded. 'The world's largest conga. It's been all over the media. That's going to be a blast.'

'Hard work,' I said with a smile.

'Ha! Hard work. She'll be lying on Miami Beach lapping up the sun while I have my sleeves rolled up here in New York.'

'You could have come,' I retorted.

'Gyrating with more than a hundred thousand people along Miami's Calle Ocho to deafening music doesn't hold too much appeal,' he replied dryly.

'Let's hope mass hysteria doesn't break out,' I sniggered.

Norris folded his arms. 'As I always maintain, marathon dancing should be distinguished from dancing mania which as anyone knows is a pathological condition.'

'Is that so?' asked Ken.

'Indeed. The worst outbreak of dancing mania was in Aachen in July 1374 when a swarm of people took to the streets and broke into a frenzied and compulsive choreomania which went on for hours.'

Ken giggled. 'What happened?'

'Well, they eventually succumbed to either injury or exhaustion.'

I barely concealed a snort of laughter. 'I can just imagine some po-faced fourteenth century scribe standing on the sidelines tutting in disapproval as he chronicled the event for posterity.'

'Thank goodness he did or we wouldn't know about it today,' sniffed Norris.

Ken punched my arm. 'Hey, just think, you'll be able to strut your stuff with all the great and the good of Miami. But with any luck Norris and I will catch the event on TV in New York.'

Norris's eyes glimmered. 'Now that will be enjoyable, AN, watching you cavorting around the streets dancing the conga. I shall never let you live it down.'

I poked my tongue out at him. 'Never did mockers waste more idle breath.'

Norris bit his lip. 'Interesting quote. Let me think. Was it Helena in *A Midsummer Night's Dream*?'

'Not bad for a non-literary person,' I replied.

Norris stopped to peer in at an exhibit showing tallest structures. 'To think that in Illinois they're working on what will be the tallest building in the world. It will have sixty-nine storeys and be 2,500 feet tall.'

'It had to be Illinois,' I groaned. 'Again.'

Norris laughed. 'Talking of tall buildings, back in the seventies I came here with Don Koehler, at the time the tallest living man at 8 feet and 2 inches. We took the lift to the very top floor and when we got out he nearly swooned. He forced me to go back down, confessing that he had a terrible head for heights!'

Ken and I laughed.

'Is that really true?' I asked.

'Of course,' Norris replied.

We made our way to the reception area where Ken had ordered a cab for Norris.

I gave him a hug. 'I'm off to Miami at the crack of dawn tomorrow so I'll see you back in London.'

Norris winked. 'I shall wait to hear all about it. Are you out with Ken tonight?'

He nodded. 'Yeah, don't worry. I'll look after her and make sure she's back at the hotel on time.'

Norris picked up his briefcase. 'I've got to attend some awards dinner tonight so I'm afraid I can't join you.'

'Who's being awarded?'

He gave an embarrassed cough. 'I believe I am. Have an early night.'

I waved as he headed for his taxi. Somewhat ruefully I would be remembering those last four words from Norris over the next few days.

★ ★ ★

Something loud and piercing was reverberating through my head. Groggily I sat up and surveyed the room. Where was I? I turned to see my small tormentor, a flashing digital alarm clock, blinking violently in the semi-darkness. I thumped it into submission, tore myself out of bed and stumbled over to the light switch, stubbing my toe on my suitcase on the way. It was four thirty in the morning, time to get dressed and ready for the taxi taking me to JFK airport where I'd be boarding a flight to Miami. So much for the early night Norris had suggested. Ken and I had spent a leisurely evening in a local restaurant discussing the weird and wacky world of records over some beers. The problem was that we made the decision to visit another bar for just one last beer. That was the killer. I got back to the hotel around 1.30 a.m. with what felt like a bag of rocks rolling around in my head. I had set the alarm and crashed out only to awaken as if never having slept. The rocks in my head now seemed to have grown heavier and more angular, my eyes had shrunk and my tongue felt like sandpaper. With as much energy as I could muster, I flung all my belongings in a suitcase, had a shower, brushed my teeth and took the lift to the hotel reception. My taxi driver was slumped in the car. He didn't speak a word of English although when I uttered the letters 'JFK' he took off like a rocket through New York's dark labyrinth of streets.

The flight to Miami International was a blur. I slumbered all the way until an air hostess shook my arm and asked me to belt up for the final descent. A cup of black coffee had failed to revive me and I narrowed my eyes in pain as I stared out at the piercing blue sky and heavy ball of fierce sun grinning at me through the clouds. Like an automaton, I followed the crowds through passport control and past the rows of sinister-looking police in shades clutching guns and occasionally breaking out into loud Spanish. Damn. I hadn't bought a Spanish dictionary. Before me stood the luggage carousel. Bleary-eyed, I grabbed my suitcase as it swam before my eyes and headed for the exit. The light emanating from the frantic, overcrowded arrivals area was enough to persuade me to find my sunglasses. As I grappled with my bag, a tall impeccably groomed man wearing black shades approached me. Warily I stepped back wondering whether he was a CIA agent or possibly a hit man. He was neither, though he seemed to know who I was. He spoke with a rich

Cuban accent, politely addressing himself as Carlos Gonzalez from the Kiwanis Club of Little Havana.

'We have a tight itinerary but first let me give you these.'

He handed me some gleaming keys on a gold fob. I stared at them for a few seconds, wondering if this was some kind of initiative test.

'*Venga!*' he said, scooping up my luggage. 'Let me show you to your car.'

Dazzling sunlight flooded the busy forecourt of the airport as he hurried me along past crowds of excitable Latinos to what looked like the glossiest, sleekest cherry-red convertible car I had ever set eyes on.

He smiled. 'Like it? It's a Ford Mustang. All yours for the next few days.'

I opened my mouth to speak but couldn't think of anything appropriate to say. The idea of my getting into this highly polished, brand new convertible with a stinking hangover combined with a complete naivety about how to handle an American car on American roads seemed all wrong. Now, if Donald, the book's editor had been with me, that would have been fine. The man was a walking car bible, although he only really bothered with the sleek and elite of the motor world. What would his advice have been now?

'It's a beautiful car but I really do think I'll have to decline your kind offer.' I passed the keys back to him.

He frowned. 'What's the problem?'

'Me. You see I couldn't bear it if something happened to the car while I was driving it and just think of the ensuing bad publicity for Guinness. I just have to say no.'

He examined his perfectly polished Gucci loafers. 'We drive very slowly around here you know.'

'I'm sure but all the same...'

He sighed. 'OK. I'll drive you back to your hotel in it and then we'll go straight off for lunch.'

I smiled weakly. 'We have a lunch now?'

'Yeah, in about an hour, an early lunch at one of Miami's top Cuban fish restaurants. You choose your own live fish to eat.'

'And who else is going to be joining us?'

'Oh, about twenty of the Cuban guys from the Kiwanis Club who've made the conga possible. They're all the key sponsors so it'll be great for you to meet them.'

We got into the car, MY car, and drove off to the hotel, a huge steel tower winking seductively at me in the sun.

'See you down here in twenty minutes or so. OK?'

I practically threw myself into the bedroom and lay flat on the bed. Why did I have that last beer? Ding dong. A bellboy was standing beaming at me.

'Wanna see how everything works?'

'Oh I'll find out in time, don't worry.'

'Sure?' he asked. 'Well let me at least turn on the TV.'

Before I could object he pushed a knob on the huge television set facing my bed and walked briskly from the room. There was a loud screeching of brakes as Don Johnson skidded across the screen and leaped out of a huge Cadillac in an eye-wincing white suit and black T-shirt. Much as I liked *Miami Vice* and as fitting as it seemed given my current location, this wasn't quite the time to laze around watching TV. I fumbled with the buttons of the TV until I'd managed to turn it off. It took me a further five minutes to work out how to open the curtains and the sunblinds and another five to crack opening the veranda door. Sun and sea air flooded the room. I was staring out at Miami Beach. Ah how I could have just taken a towel and flung myself in a bikini down on the sand. I breathed in the briny air and decided that a mini-makeover was necessary. I changed out of my jeans into a formal shirt and pencil skirt, slapped on some make-up and perfume and pulled my one decent handbag out of my suitcase. Next, I threw on some pearls and slung a fake Hermes scarf around my neck. The internal line was bleeping. It was Carlos.

'Ready?'

Sure I was ready, even for a fishy lunch on a queasy stomach. We Guinness folk could take all that life threw at us.

Juan, Gerardo, Pedro, Jesus, and the gang were already ensconced at an enormous table in the dark cool interiors of the restaurant. Carlos ran his hands through his immaculately coiffed and gelled hair, and opened the door for me.

'You'll love the Kiwanis. They are a welcoming bunch.'

'Are you all Cuban American businessmen?' I asked him.

He stroked his neat beard. 'I have a legal practice like many. Some are doctors, entrepreneurs, that sort of thing. We believe in working hard and ploughing money back into the community.'

He led me over to the large table where I went around the guests shaking hands and introducing myself. The president gave me a warm welcome and then everyone got up to choose their fish. I was led over to a long counter.

'Can I recommend the snapper? Done spicy it's beautiful.'

'Great. I'll take that.'

I returned to my seat where a large glass of white wine smiled back at me. 'I think I'll just stick to water,' I said to one of my Hispanic hosts.

He laughed. 'Had a late night?'

'You could say that. We live and learn.'

'Have a glass and I promise you'll feel better.'

I did as I was told and he was right. Within half an hour I was feeling bright and chipper. My spiced Caribbean snapper was beyond delicious and the Kiwanis members were hugely entertaining.

'So how did the Kiwanis Club of Little Havana begin?' I asked.

The president patted my arm. 'A group of twenty-five Cuban friends got together and decided to start a non-profit making club which would benefit the Hispanic population in Miami. We do all sorts of events and raise money for school projects mostly.'

Carlos nodded. 'We've been holding Carnival Miami for some years. It takes place in Calle Ocho, that means Eighth Street, which is in the heart of Little Havana, where most of the Cuban community live.'

Pedro, a large jolly man on my right interrupted. 'You like tamarind ice cream?'

'Sounds delicious.'

'Great.' He looked towards the counter. 'Hey Manuel, get her a *tamarindo* and a coconut ice cream.'

I raised my eyebrows. 'I can see this is going to be a slimming few days.'

Everyone laughed.

'So if my limited history serves me right, the majority of the Cuban American community settled here post the Cuban revolution in 1959?'

Carlos drained his glass. 'Actually my family came here much earlier, around the time of the 1929 depression. It was the first wave of emigration from Cuba. Of course, 1959 was a time of great flux. Fidel Castro saw to that.'

There was a sombre silence until the waiter arrived bearing all manner of delicious desserts. Everyone cheered up.

'So tonight we have the opening ceremony on Miami Beach and tomorrow is the big event,' said Carlos.

'Great – and who'll be attending the event tonight?'

'Everybody who's anybody,' laughed the president. 'It'll be full of music and fun and we'll be doing a conga along Miami Beach.'

My enormous combo ice cream arrived. Somehow wine, fish and coconut and tamarind ice cream had done the trick. I felt ready to take on the world. Carlos dropped me back at the hotel where I had a few hours to unwind and get ready for the night ahead. At seven o'clock I arrived in the lobby as agreed to find the diminutive singer Gloria Estefan checking in. She was surrounded by suitcases and various members of her band and was wearing clingy black trousers and a wide-necked white shirt. Her russet hair tumbled in ringlets to her shoulders. Carlos strolled over to me.

'Gloria will be leading the conga tomorrow afternoon so you'll be up on the roof of the Bank of America Tower together.'

She caught his eye and wandered over, shaking my hand and giving me a radiant smile.

'So you're from London? Have you ever met Princess Diana?'

Of all the most unlikely people for me to have met it was the people's princess and yet curiously I had encountered her several times during my time as a press officer at Help the Aged.

'I have had the privilege of meeting her a few times.'

Her eyes lit up. 'Wow, that's amazing. And what is she like? Is she as beautiful in the flesh?'

'She is, maybe more so.'

She shook her head. 'Unbelievable.'

A moment later and a fleet of limos arrived at the front of the hotel.

'Anna, we must leave,' said Carlos. 'Gloria, we'll see you on the beach. Remember to bring your dancing shoes!'

★ ★ ★

It was a sweltering day. The previous evening we had danced the night away on Miami Beach, doing the conga along the golden sands, and enjoying Cuban cuisine. The great and the good of Miami turned out for the event, which was held on the terrace of a palatial beachside hotel. It was well after midnight before I had been dropped back at the hotel so I valued sleeping in until eight o'clock. The morning was spent discussing last-minute details for the conga event and meeting key members from the sponsorship and support team. Now I was standing on the wide rooftop of an enormous skyscraper staring down at Calle Ocho far below me. Thousands of people were milling about and the street seemed to stretch as far as the eye could see. Carlos grabbed my arm.

'You see down there?'

I followed his extended arm. 'The street starts there at the Florida Turnpike on the west and stretches to Highway 1 on the east. Our event runs from 27th to 4th Avenues and we'll have manned stations at each intersection and raised platforms every few metres. Everyone who takes part is given a number as they enter at one of the intersections.'

I craned my neck to see the stations set up along the street and was pleased to see the raised platforms in the zone directly in front of the tower.

'So the police will stand on the platforms and monitor the crowds in a five-metre radius?'

'That's right. According to the rules, everyone has to keep their hands on the hips of the person in front and dance the conga for exactly fifteen minutes.'

I nodded. 'It's critical that Gloria Estefan makes that clear to the crowds when she makes her address.'

He smoothed his beard. 'OK. We'll make sure to go through it again when Gloria arrives.'

The Miami Sound Machine band had already set up on the roof and was playing some numbers in the background. Within an hour, the VIPs had arrived, as had Gloria Estefan, and also a mountain of press. Seven television crews vied for space on one side of the roof while radio stations and press photographers crowded around us. At 2.45 p.m. Gloria and I got up on to the dais ready for the beginning of the event. It was to begin at exactly three o'clock. Below us people were streaming along the street, tiny black dots moving continuously while police officers stood high on the platforms, blowing whistles and controlling the crowds. Gloria yelled into the microphone and a wild cheer rose up from the street.

'People of Miami, can you hear me? Are you ready? We are going to do the world's longest conga and you've got to keep dancing for fifteen whole minutes. Now grab the hips of the person in front of you...'

Screaming, clapping and cheering rose from the crowd. Gloria winked at me and began laughing. 'You guys all having fun down there?'

More screaming, whistles and distant music. The Miami Sound Machine struck up the first chords of the conga and Gloria shouted out instructions to the excited crowds.

Carlos came over and whispered in my ear. 'You know every radio station in Florida will record the event live at precisely three o'clock. Imagine!'

The clock struck three and a cheer rose. The dance began. Gloria began singing, 'Come on shake your body, do the conga…'

I began grinning to myself imagining Norris up here. The music was pounding and the noise from the street below quite deafening despite its distance. The police on duty had to ensure that every single person within their individually allotted patch of Calle Ocho kept their hands firmly on the waist of the person in front and snaked around in a swaying hypnotic circle. If one person along the broad street broke the chain, the whole record attempt would be ruined. As I peered at the gyrating crowds below, a news reporter grabbed my hand and whirled me off the stage while other press couldn't resist the conga beat and began swaying to the music. I was only glad no one was taking pictures. I would never have lived it down in the office. The time seemed to go by in a flash and before we knew it, Gloria was doing a count down to the end. A huge cry went up as, exhausted, she announced that fifteen minutes had elapsed. A few tense moments elapsed and finally the police reports came in together with the final tally of numbers. I was stunned to learn that exactly 119,986 people had participated in the event. I took the mike.

'People of Miami, on behalf of *The Guinness Book of Records*, I'm delighted to announce a new world record. Thanks to your efforts Miami and the United States of America can feel proud. Together you have put Miami forever on the map by creating a new world record for mass conga dancing. Today you have smashed the existing record of 8,659 participants held by the Camping and Caravanning Club of Great Britain. I am now able to announce, officially, that the Calle Ocho 1988 Conga had a participation of 119,986 people. Well done Miami!'

A loud cry soared from the tightly packed street, practically drowning out my words. There was wild cheering, crying, screaming and euphoria as the music started up once more and the festivities continued. Gloria and I embraced and descended the stage to make press statements while the organising committee and volunteers shook hands and hugged one another, overcome with emotion after their months and months of meticulous planning. The press interviews went on for another hour in which time the crowds below slowly began to disperse. There would be huge celebrations in Miami tonight.

'What a fantastic event,' I said to Carlos. 'The Kiwanis deserve a medal or at least a Guinness certificate!'

'Of course and you will be expected to return here to present it to us,' he said with a wink.

'Like a shot,' I smiled. 'Next time I promise to have a very early night in advance of the trip.'

He flashed me a smile. 'In that case I'll have the Mustang at the airport on standby.'

I shook my head. 'That's maybe not such a good idea. Even Norris doesn't trust me behind the wheel. He thinks I'm a speed hog.'

'Is that so? Well no sweat, I'll just give Don Johnson a call and ask him to play chauffeur.'

I slipped into a sweet reverie imagining Mr Miami Vice and I dancing the conga together across Miami Beach under a silky moon. Some hope!

★ ★ ★

Later the next day I made my way to the airport. Throughout the departures lounge huge television screens replayed images from the big event with rather embarrassing shots of me trying to do an elegant conga along with Gloria and the Kiwanis on Miami Beach. Then they cut back to the tower, homing in on Gloria and me as we made our speeches. The Miami security guards greeted me with 'give me five's as I hugged Carlos, his wife and other club members goodbye. My new Cuban American family in Miami.

'Be sure to return with our certificate!' they called after me as I waved goodbye.

Everyone seemed to know what I'd been doing in Miami.

'Hey that's you on the screen!' shouted the passport control officer. 'Way to go! Miami got the record!'

On the British Airways flight I took refuge in a quiet business-class seat but was soon jolted out of my reverie when images flashed up on the television screens on board reliving the record attempt. Was I ever going to escape the embarrassment of my appalling attempt at the conga? An air hostess wandered along the aisle once the plane had lifted up into the sky. 'Here's a congratulatory glass of champagne,' she said. 'Fancy coming all the way to Miami to judge the conga!'

At Heathrow I made my way to one of the exits and could hardly believe my eyes. Norris was standing nonchalantly close to a group of limo drivers all of whom were holding name boards. To my amusement I noticed that Norris held one which underneath my name read in big black letters: 'World famous Conga dancer this way!'

'Oh very funny!' I said. 'What on earth are you doing here?'

'Well, I noticed that by complete fluke our flights touched down at roughly the same time so when mine got in from JFK I decided to have a coffee and wait for you. Given your startling dance performance in Miami, I felt I should welcome you in appropriate fashion.'

I groaned. 'Please don't tell me you got to see the event in New York?'

He giggled. 'Oh yes, it was hugely amusing. Ken and I loved watching your face, that prim and steely expression, as they got you to start off the conga on Miami Beach. And the heart-warming speech up in the skyscraper was an award-winning performance, worthy of RADA.'

'Oh stop it!'

He grabbed my case, overcome with mirth. 'Come on, Guinness arranged a car for me. It's just outside.'

'Well I'm glad I keep you amused.'

He opened the door for me. 'Rest assured, AN, you keep me endlessly amused. Now where shall we drop you off?'

TEN

★ ★ ★

THE LEANING TOWER OF BREAD

David was sitting at his desk with a sceptical look on his face.

'Are you partial to giant lizards?'

'Not hugely. Well, in truth I've never had many dealings with them.'

He took a sip of coffee. 'Rather you than me.'

'But I'm not going to have to touch one of these Komodo dragons, am I?'

He broke into a grin. 'I wouldn't advise it.'

Norris appeared in the doorway.

'What ho. I wondered where you were. When are you leaving for Jakarta?'

'In an hour or so,' I replied. 'David's advising me to keep a distance from the giant Komodo dragons.'

He wandered in and glanced thoughtfully at the ceiling. 'Very good advice too. They're pretty lethal creatures. If you're hoping to take a tape measure to one, be sure to wear leather gloves.'

'I hadn't been planning on it.'

David couldn't control his face and began giggling. Norris gave him a wink.

'I'm glad you find my trip so amusing. As it happens the Komodo dragons will be in a pit, according to the Indonesian tourist office, and will be measured by a reptile expert at Jakarta zoo.'

'That is a relief,' said Norris dryly. 'So apart from wrestling with Komodo dragons, what else are you doing in Jakarta?'

'I'm verifying the largest tower made of cake and toast. Apparently it's nearly 25 feet tall. It's part of a promotion for the Indonesian food festival.'

Norris took a seat opposite me. 'I don't know much about cake towers but I can tell you that the largest specimen of Komodo monitor measured accurately by an American zoologist was over 10 feet long. That was back in 1928, but some claim they can reach 30 feet in length.'

'Well, I shall keep out of their way. The tallest cake sounds more palatable in every sense.'

David interrupted. 'That all depends on what they want you to do with the cake tower.'

'What do you mean?'

'Well, how are you going to measure and authenticate it?'

'Our understanding is that they have witness statements and an army group took exact measurements with accompanying images.'

'Let's hope you don't have to walk inside it. The whole thing could collapse,' said Norris in exaggerated sober tone.

'I give up with you two.'

Norris stood up. 'I'm off to see Fred for a catch up on sales of the book so I probably won't see you until your return. Remember David's advice. Oh and take Mars Bars.'

'Why on earth would I do that?'

'You may thank me. You can't go far wrong with chocolate.'

I returned to my desk downstairs where Alex and Lisa were engrossed in a copy of *The National Enquirer*.

'It really is a marvel, isn't it?' announced Alex. 'A sort of American national treasure.'

'Yeah, right!' scoffed Lisa. 'I'm amazed people pay to read that stuff.'

'Well, we do,' I replied.

'But it's our job to read it,' she said rather primly.

'Anyway,' said Alex, 'are you going to make sure we have some great shots for the book? This tower of bread sounds interesting.'

I shrugged. 'Harvey is coming with me and he's an excellent photographer so we should have some good shots.'

'Is he the guy from *You* magazine?'

'The picture editor. He's going to run a double spread hopefully.'

'That's quite a coup,' sniffed Alex.

The telephone rang. It was Harvey agreeing the time we'd meet at the check-in desk for Jakarta.

'He's a laugh, isn't he?' said Lisa as I finished the call.

'Yes, he's got a good sense of irony,' I agreed.

'You might both need it,' sniggered Alex.

'You lot are a tower of strength,' I grumbled.

As I reached the reception, Norris came bustling towards me. 'These are for you, just in case.'

He thrust five Mars Bars into my hands.

★ ★ ★

Harvey, with sleeves rolled up and weighed down with an armoury of cameras, accompanied me from Jakarta's busy airport out into blazing sunshine. He was tall and stocky with a shock of curly hair the colour of granite and a neat moustache. We both stood basking in the sudden warmth, our legs stiff after the long flight, when an attentive chauffeur rushed up, brandishing our names on a cardboard sign.

'You Miss Guinness, yes?'

Was it that obvious? Maybe the sickly white skin was a giveaway. Our baggage was whipped up by an airport porter and a minute later we were whizzing along to our hotel, with air conditioning pumping into the back of the limo.

'This is the life,' said Harvey, a big grin slapped on his face. 'Nothing like travel to get you inspired. So, give me the heads up on our itinerary.'

'Tomorrow we're off to visit the Komodo dragons and the food festival.'

'That's cool, and what about the tower of bread?'

'Supposedly we see that tomorrow afternoon.'

He sank back in his seat and yawned. 'So, on Friday we're off to an island?'

'The chairman of the festival has organised an overnight stay on some tiny island in the Java Sea.'

'Great stuff.'

'Then we fly back on Sunday evening.'

As we got closer to the city I found myself glued to the window, absorbing the colours, sounds and chaotic traffic scenes. Dogs, chickens and random cows tottered into the road while scooters and noisy, brightly orange *bajaj*, the vehicle similar to the three-wheeled tuk-tuk in Thailand and Sri Lanka, hurtled around the streets, their drivers honking furiously. In the midst of the madness there were horse-drawn carriages and large-wheeled cycles with outward facing passenger seats on the back.

'What an extraordinary place.'

Harvey turned to me. 'Yeah, these cities in South East Asia are a photographer's dream ticket. That passenger cycle is a *becak*. They're thinking of banning them here because they're cluttering up the place.'

At the palatial and traditional five-star hotel we were taken to our suites. Harvey popped his head round my door just as I replaced my telephone receiver.

'That was the chairman of the food festival. Tonight he's taking us to a traditional Rijsttafel dinner at a restaurant called the Oasis.'

He clapped his hands together. 'You are going to love it. You know it's an amazing feast of God knows how many dishes. The Oasis is a well-known hang-out of the great and the good visiting Jakarta.'

'You're very well informed.'

'I make it my business, honey.'

★ ★ ★

At seven thirty we were picked up by limousine. Refreshed from our afternoon lounging by the pool, we were ready for the Rijsttafel experience.

'D'you eat out much?' asked Harvey.

'Not on my salary.'

He patted my shoulder. 'Life's tough when you're on the way up.'

'You know there's a guy in the States who's dined out forty-six thousand times in sixty nations.'

'Get away! Where's he from?'

'Ha! As always, Illinois. I tell you, there are more records in that place than anywhere else in the world.'

'That's odd.'

'Anyway this guy, Fred Magel, became a restaurant grader in 1928 and has been dining out ever since.'

He shrugged. 'Mind you, it could get you down eating out that much. I mean, where's the novelty?'

Our conversation was interrupted by our driver who excitedly informed us that we had arrived. The chairman of the food festival was waiting with an entourage on the front steps of what looked like a grand old mansion. He bowed.

'It is our honour to host your stay. Please come in to Oasis. This house once belonged to F. Brandenburg van Oltsende. You know of him?'

'I'm afraid not,' I replied.

'He was a millionaire and owned tea, rubber and cinchona estates. That was when the Dutch were our paymasters.'

A gong suddenly sounded and a traditionally dressed Indonesian waitress approached me with a corsage. Harvey gave me a wink and whispered. 'Things are hotting up. I wonder what they give the guys? One of the waitresses would be nice.'

I tutted and followed our host, who was already striding across a chequerboard entrance hall and heading for what appeared to be a private room.

'Here is where we'll eat our banquet. The word Rijsttafel means rice table. It's a very traditional feast. The Dutch coined the phrase from the Indonesian words *'nasi padang'*.

Harvey nodded knowledgably. 'I was explaining the origins to Anna earlier.'

I looked at him in surprise, noticing a small grin on his face.

The entourage that had been silently following us now fanned out and took their seats. We were seated on either side of the chairman on elaborate gilt chairs piled with silk cushions.

A stream of exotic waitresses arrived and bowed elegantly. Harvey could hardly contain his delight, smiling broadly, his dark eyes fixed on the heavenly visions before him. The chairman leaned towards me.

'You like *bapi kecap* and *bebek betutu*?'

I was about to explain that I'd never met either of them but came to the hasty conclusion that he might be talking about the food.

'Absolutely.'

Harvey was grinning from ear to ear, enjoying my moment of uncertainty.

'Anna loves spicy food, don't you? The spicier the better.'

The chairman smiled at me broadly and clapped. 'Excellent. Then spicy it will be. We have many, many courses tonight and we shall make sure they are as hot as you like.'

I gave Harvey a grimace, thinking of the five gooey Mars Bars back in my hotel room. Perhaps there might be call for them after all.

★ ★ ★

After a late night at the Oasis, Harvey and I awoke early to visit the Komodo dragons at Jakarta zoo.

Harvey was clicking frantically at his camera.

'They're big buggers, aren't they?'

I stared down into the huge pit of smudgy-coloured reptiles. If their claws weren't quite so long, sharp and quite frankly lethal, they'd probably make rather sweet domestic pets. I decided not to share these thoughts with Harvey who was always ribbing me.

'They're the world's largest reptile, right?' he suddenly asked.

'Yes, and they hang out mostly in Australia and Indonesia. The name must derive from the Indonesian islands of Komodo where they were discovered. Nowadays they're a protected species. The Latin name is *Varanus komodoensis*.'

He paused and fixed me with laughing eyes. 'Oh, the readers of *You* are really going to want to know that.'

'Well, you never know. Anyway, adult males normally grow up to 7 feet or more and weigh about 130 pounds. Don't you think it's fascinating that they're so prehistoric-looking? I always think the Komodo monitor looks like a dragon straight out of a fairytale.'

He shook his head. 'You are something else. Come on. I'd like to get a shot of that huge monster.'

He pointed to the other side of the vast pit where a gigantic scaly creature with long tail, sludgy skin and terrifying claws lurked in the shade by a pool of dark water. The sun smouldered, its bright, intrusive rays homing in on us like dazzling searchlights. Wincing, I pushed the floppy sun hat firmly over my eyes just as two elderly Indonesian gentlemen came into view holding heavy buckets and a long tape measure. They wore dark green caps emblazoned with the zoo's logo and beige short-sleeved shirts and shorts. Jakarta zoo wasn't very busy, although a group of curious local children had come over to observe Harvey changing the film of his bulky camera and now seemed excited when they saw the two officials. The men approached me and bowed low. They were thin and wiry with wizened skin the colour of coffee.

One stepped forward. 'Miss Guinness?'

I nodded.

'We park keepers. Now we measure our biggest dragon. Then you see that Komodo is king of all lizards.'

He showed me the contents of his bulging bucket. It contained copious dead chickens and a pair of thick leather gloves on the top. He and his colleague smiled cheerfully and donned gloves before making their way slowly to the gate of the enclosure. I heard a rattling as they inserted keys in the various locks.

'They're not going in there, are they?' Harvey asked aghast.

'Looks like it,' I replied.

A moment later and the diminutive and slightly built pensioners began walking nonchalantly among the Komodo dragons dishing out chickens and bits of what appeared to be flesh.

'Can you see what he's feeding them?' Harvey asked.

'Bits of human arm, a few heads, toes, that sort of thing.'

He tutted and looked through the lens. 'Mostly carrion, I bet.'

A moment later and to our utter astonishment, one of the keepers rolled on to the largest Komodo dragon and sat astride its large girth while his colleague began calmly measuring its bulky frame. I held my breath, waiting for the thin little man to be snapped up in one big gulp but the enormous Komodo, sandy brown in the sunlight, lay patiently in the dust, gnawing on some flesh until the job was done. The two men upturned their empty buckets and stood still while they conferred over the tape measure and scribbled in a little notepad. They locked up and returned to us, passing a piece of paper to me.

'Nine feet and two inches. Very big lizard. You know, they can run more than 13 miles per hour?'

I shook my head. 'That's extraordinary for such a heavy-looking creature. They gulped down that meat quickly enough.'

The older and more timorous zookeeper sucked his teeth. 'Very dangerous. They even eat their own babies.'

'Lovely,' muttered Harvey.

Someone was coughing politely at my shoulder. It was the chauffeur.

'We must leave for the food festival. The chairman would like you to visit the cake makers and then we will go to the record-breaking tower of bread.'

'Cool, let's go,' said Harvey a tad eagerly, evidently much relieved to be leaving the happy snappers behind in their well-secured pit.

★ ★ ★

Our limo turned into what appeared to be a large, rough patch of wasteland attached to a verdant park known as Taman Monas. Having spent some hours wandering around the food festival we were now at last visiting the *pièce de résistance*, the record-breaking tower of bread. We jumped out of the car and walked briskly across to where a gathering of local media stood waiting for us. The chairman's face crinkled into a smile as he led me over to meet VIPs and government officials standing nearby. High, high above us loomed an enormous, highly decorated baked edifice and next to it a towering Garuda bird, the national emblem of Indonesia, also made of bread.

The façade of the bread tower was made from what looked like brick-shaped cakes, all in various colours and decorated with Indonesian script and patterns, yet peering inside the open doors I noticed that pieces of toast seemed to line the interior. We walked slowly around the circumference of the tower. It was quite extraordinary to think that Nila Chandra, an elderly culinary expert and cake designer, had created such a solid and formidable edifice purely from cake and bread.

'So this is 24 feet and 7 inches tall and just over 18 feet wide?'

Nila Chandra nodded modestly. 'Yes, that is correct. Come and take a look inside.'

'Inside?' I squawked.

'Yes, it is quite safe if you walk carefully.'

Harvey followed up the rear, giving the odd nervous look skywards. Maybe he didn't want to tempt fate.

'It looks solid enough but I'm not sure about walking inside,' he whispered.

'Come, come,' smiled the chairman.

Harvey and I stepped gingerly into the house, a grown-up Hansel and Gretel.

'It smells wonderfully sweet. I could just break off a piece of this sugary bread and eat it.'

'Yeah, well don't get ideas while I'm still in here,' grumbled Harvey. We took tentative steps, eyeing each other warily as a strange cracking and clicking sound greeted us, rather like breaking ice. It was dark and shady inside and I rather appreciated having a break from the heat. From above there suddenly came a loud whirring sound.

We walked to the doorway and peered out. A helicopter was descending nearby. Dust whirled up like a hurricane from the dry muddy ground and the leaves of the trees trembled with the sudden blast of air.

'All aboard,' said the chairman. You can photograph the tower from the air now.'

Harvey grabbed my arm and whispered urgently in my ear. 'Listen, I'm not getting into that thing. I was once in a helicopter accident a long way back, broke my back and was laid up in a hospital for a year.'

'Crikey.'

'So count me out, darling.'

The chairman was frantically beckoning to us. For a moment I nearly chickened out and then decided that wasn't part of the Guinness creed. 'I shall be going up but Harvey would prefer to do some ground shots.'

'Are you sure? The view will be nice up high and we'll keep the door open so you can lean out and get good views.'

I felt my stomach churn.

'Then the pilot will circle all the way around and dip down so you can see the special designs carved on the icing at the top.'

'Oh don't go to any special trouble just for me!' I replied.

'No trouble.'

Harvey was chuckling into his camera. 'Any last words?'

'You know it's easy to go off people, Harvey.'

'Ah don't say that. This could be our first and last trip together.'

I followed the pilot over to the helicopter and clambered aboard. The sound of the whirring blades and engine were deafening as we rose, clouds of dust welling up around us like the ash from a mini-volcano. The door was wide open and I grabbed on to my seat for fear of being flung out. The pilot gave me the thumbs up and we were off, making a loop around the park and heading back, aiming seemingly straight at the tower of bread. I had visions of us crashing headfirst into its midst, icing and toast and jam exploding from its depths, but we didn't. Instead, the helicopter listed as we circled the tower, zooming in so close that I could almost touch the icing on the top. I held my camera steady and snapped away before the helicopter lunged forward. Next we circled the giant Garuda symbol, and then with what seemed like a never-ending turn, we banked left and finally began our descent. A little groggily I rose from my seat and with jelly legs stepped on to the ground. I'd read somewhere that it was always essential to lower one's head for fear of decapitation from the swivelling propeller blades, so rather like an upturned duck I scrambled across the muddy earth to the waiting crowd. Harvey was shaking with laughter.

'You've watched too many Vietnam movies. What was with all that head ducking?'

'At least I went up,' I sniffed.

To polite clapping I proclaimed the tower of bread and cake a world record, handed over the Guinness certificate to the chairman, and stood with all the officials in a line as photos were taken by the local press.

'Now the surprise!' smiled the chairman.

Oh no. I'd had more than enough surprises for one day. There was a roar and from across the park came the sound of heavy-duty motorbikes. Even Harvey stopped giggling and looked up.

'It's the Jakarta Harley Davidson Club, here to take you on a lap of honour around the town and back to your hotel,' said the chairman.

I looked down at my apparel, a cream linen shirt and flouncy skirt. Just the job for a motorbike ride across a muddy park.

I poked Harvey in the ribs. 'You're not getting out of this one!'

The gang of leather-clad easy riders slipped off their bikes. I counted about fifteen big shiny metal beasts, glinting in the sun. But uh-oh, what were attached to two of them? Surely not sidecars? Memories of the big and cumbersome Olive from the TV sitcom *On the Buses* came flooding back to me. Could I live this humiliation down?

'This is madness!' Harvey was yelling at me.

I giggled as Harvey crammed his huge frame into his own sidecar, his arms glued to his sides like a man in a straitjacket. I stepped gingerly into mine and stopped laughing when my voluminous skirt bunched up around my restricted thighs and was soon covered in ominous black stains that appeared to be motorcycle oil smeared all over the vehicle. Harvey's helmeted head was sticking out of his tiny sidecar like that of a giant insect and once again I found myself in peals of laughter. There was never a dull moment – and rarely dignity – in the world of record-breaking. Off we thundered at great speed, the mud and dust flying up into our faces. I pushed the goggles I'd been given closer to my eyes, and grabbed on to the door frame as we hurtled off around the park, bumping and jumping over small mounds of earth, puddles and rough soil.

An hour later we staggered into the hotel. My hair would have rivalled Medusa's and my now grey linen ensemble was crying for a washing machine. I licked the thick dust on my lips.

'That was fun, wasn't it?'

Harvey narrowed his eyes. 'I'm off for a shower and possibly a very large drink. Meet you in the bar in half an hour.'

I nodded trying to hide my mirth at his stiff gait. As if sensing it, he turned suddenly.

'That is,' he muttered, 'if I can still walk!'

★ ★ ★

Harvey and I stood by the landing stage of a tiny island in the Java Sea, waiting for the boat that would whisk us back to Jakarta. After our action-packed time in the city, it had been wonderful to have a few days to chill out in the sun with only the sound of lapping waves and voyeuristic lizards for company. In high spirits and with the beginnings of a tan we looked up into the sky.

'Can you believe it? A spot of rain,' said Harvey.

'Well at least the air's cooler. Is that our boat?'

We looked out to sea and, sure enough, what looked like an old fishing boat was heading our way. It had a broad and basic lower deck open to the elements and at one end a small flight of stairs that led up to a tiny, cramped upper level. It had a weary air about it and seemed to limp into the jetty.

'Not quite as luxurious as the way coming,' sniffed Harvey, referring to the smart yacht we'd travelled in on the outward journey.

A few minutes later the two barefooted Indonesians that comprised the crew were beckoning us on board. Neither spoke English and they seemed rather serious, pointing up at the sky in a gesture of concern.

'They're used to monsoons here so don't worry,' said Harvey, sensing my sudden unease.

We set off almost immediately, the engine chugging loudly and a puff of grey acrid smoke rising up into the still and bleak sky. On the open deck there was nowhere to sit so instead I remained standing and studied the emerald waves churning about us.

'It seems a bit choppy up ahead,' Harvey observed. 'Don't they have sharks in the Java Sea?'

'So I've heard,' I replied.

The two Indonesians were both on the small deck high above, hovering over the steering wheel.

'Talkative pair,' said Harvey dryly.

Twenty minutes into our journey there was a clap of thunder and heavy rain began to tumble from the sky. We looked at each other in silence. The boat began to rock violently and soon rolling waves began buffeting its sides. I flew across the deck when a ferocious wave crashed down on top of us.

'Blimey! That was a bit sudden.'

Harvey rushed over. 'You OK? Look, I'd better stash my cameras down below. For God's sake, hang on!'

I gripped the side of the boat as it suddenly began to swing from side to side, water sloshing on to the deck as Harvey, with difficulty, began to descend the steps to the dishevelled and pokey cabin. The wind howled and soon a maelstrom was upon us. In a matter of moments I was saturated in seawater, barely able to open my eyes, and terrified to lessen my grip on the wooden rail I clung to like a beleaguered limpet.

'Harvey! Are you there?'

The wind was so strong now that all I could hear was the sound of water smashing on to the deck and the rattling of imprisoned sails. I coughed and spluttered as seawater filled my mouth and nostrils. As the boat listed hard to the side I felt my feet lift in the air. Could I make it to the cabin steps? Where the hell was Harvey? God, he hadn't gone overboard, had he? Where was the damned crew?

'Harvey!' I screamed at the top of my voice.

Suddenly he was at my side, sodden, his wet hair moulded to his face.

'This isn't funny!' he shouted, grabbing my arm as I attempted to lower myself down on to the deck. 'I hope those guys know what they're doing.'

'Should we go downstairs?' I yelled above the wind.

'I'm not sure. It stinks of fish and is swelteringly hot. I have a feeling we might be safer up here.'

At one point a face full of fear looked down at us from the top deck and then disappeared.

'This isn't looking good,' said Harvey.

Were we going to perish here, tossed by the winds into the briny jaws of the Java Sea to be gobbled up ignominiously by sharks?

Hanging on for dear life, we managed to raise our heads from the deck to look out at the wild sea. To our joint horror, we saw what looked like upturned vessels. A family in a far-off boat were huddling inside their fishing boat, wild-eyed and dazed. At one point I imagined I saw the distinctive fin of a shark but decided not to share this with Harvey.

Miserably I hung on to a slimy wooden pole until my fingers stung with pain and numbness. We were frozen and shivering and raving at one another and passing sorrowful endearments as only people can on the brink of probable doom. Finally in defeat and misery, we huddled together in a corner of the deck, waiting for the inevitable moment when we would find ourselves tipped into the jaws of death. We coughed, we spluttered, we yelled, we prayed; well I did. And then after what seemed like an interminable cycle in a washing machine, the storm abated and the rain lessened. We both looked up at a dismal yet clearing sky. Stiff-legged and shaky, we rose to our feet only to see the dry shores of Jakarta in the distance.

'Oh my God! We're going to live!' I shrieked.

We both practically did a jig on the deck for joy. As the boat finally docked, the two crew members leaped down the steps and helped us from the boat. They gave us watery smiles, relief shining in their eyes as they padded off.

'There's a fishermen's bar over there. Come on, we need a brandy,' said Harvey.

'I thought I saw a shark,' I said.

We both got a bad case of the giggles, overcome with exhaustion and hysteria after our near-death experience. I sat on a bar stool and laughed until I ached. If Norris had been there he would probably have said that we were both suffering from a pathological condition. Not tarantism or compulsive choreomania, because neither of us had been dancing, but a form of hysteria nonetheless.

★ ★ ★

When Harvey and I arrived back at Heathrow his luggage appeared before mine so I told him to go on ahead. I knew he had an urgent meeting back at his office. As it happened, mine was the last suitcase to appear so I wearily collected it and headed for Customs. I had nearly made it through the green channel when a sharp-faced official hauled me back. He was shaking his head and viewing me with steely grey eyes.

'Can you open that box please, Miss?'

I groaned. 'Oh do I have to? It's only a bread tower.'

'A what, Miss?'

'It's a tower of bread. Well, not a real one obviously but a replica.'

In vain I tried to explain what I'd been doing the last few days and how I'd had a spin in a helicopter over an enormous edifice constructed entirely of bread and icing. He wasn't buying into any of it.

He folded his arms. 'Let me get this straight. You've been to Indonesia to judge the tallest tower of bread and watch giant lizards? Sounds a bit of a tall story.'

'Look, I've got nothing to hide.'

I wished Harvey was still with me. He'd no doubt have talked or joked his way out of this small diplomatic scene although, after a turbulent flight of the worst kind, he didn't seem to be on laughing form. Neither was I.

'Good, well if you've got nothing to hide, we'll open up the package and take a look.'

I groaned. The large box which the chairman of the food festival had given me was a gift for Norris and contained an exact replica of the bread tower. It had been carefully wrapped in sections and then bubble wrapped. I didn't want it ripped apart. The officer began cutting at the cardboard and string.

'They have a lot of drugs in these countries,' he sniffed. 'Did you know that?'

'I'm sure they do but I can't say I had much time to think about that during the trip.'

A colleague came over and began cutting at the box. I looked around me. I'd been taken off to a small grey room away from the main thoroughfare. Did I really look like a criminal?

As the sections of the tower were revealed, I noticed puzzlement on the faces of the officers.

'What the heck is this?' said the younger one.

'As I explained to your colleague, it is a replica of the tallest tower of bread. Now if I can possibly get going...'

They painstakingly erected it and searched the packaging. Nothing.

'You were telling the truth,' said the officer, chuckling. 'I thought I'd seen it all...'

They shoved everything back in the huge box but I could hardly carry it along with my case and handbag. They took pity on me.

'Come on, we'll help you to the exit.'

We progressed through to the departures lounge where a driver holding a Guinness sign was waiting for me.

The older officer was contrite. 'I'm sorry about that, love, but we get some odd things coming through Customs from that part of the world. I love *The Guinness Book of Records*. Do send my best to Mr McWhirter. I'm one of his biggest fans.'

I asked the driver to wait while I telephoned Norris from a public phone box.

'Arrested at Customs?' he snorted. 'That takes the biscuit.'

I told him about the fateful boat journey. That made him laugh even more.

'I'd have thought very badly of you if you'd been eaten by a shark. I'd never have got my replica tower of bread.'

I agreed to meet him later at the office.

'We can catch up over a sandwich,' he guffawed, 'or maybe not. Perhaps you've had more than enough bread for one day?'

ELEVEN

★ ★ ★

TRIFFID CHRYSANTHEMUMS, CHANTING AND CLAIRVOYANTS

Norris was sipping on a cup of weak, milky tea in the hotel's elegant foyer. His eyes followed the heavy traffic and the chic Parisians going about their business beyond the large glass windows.

'That tea looks revolting,' I said as I flicked through a copy of *Paris Match*.

'I prefer my tea very pale. I don't need extra adrenalin from an overdose of caffeine as you obviously do.'

I sighed and took a sip of the rich, velvety black coffee.

'Ah, but you can't beat real *café*. Why you can't get coffee like this in London, I'll never know.'

He gave a dismissive turn of the head and folded up his copy of the *Telegraph*.

'So, AN, when are you off to the Loire?'

I yawned. 'I'm meeting the organisers of the trip this afternoon. Apparently there'll be quite a few gardening journalists coming from the UK and a French TV crew.'

'What, they're all keen to see these gigantic chrysanthemums?'

'So it seems.'

He shrugged. 'I wouldn't have thought it would be that exciting. I mean, there are far more interesting record-breaking plants and trees around.'

'Yes, but this is a potentially new record and besides it's not in some obscure and inaccessible part of the globe.'

He sniffed. 'They could easily go to Newland in Gloucestershire to see the Newland Oak which has a girth of 44 feet and 9 inches, or better still, search out the *Amanita Phalloides* Death Cap which can be found in the UK.'

'Why on earth would anyone want to do that?'

'Because it's the world's most poisonous toadstool. Within six to fifteen hours of consumption, extreme sickness and delirium takes hold and then total collapse and death.'

'That would be a fun record to authenticate.'

'Poor old Cardinal Giulio de' Medici, Pope Clement VII, succumbed to it.'

'When was that?'

'Oh, 24 September 1534.' He scratched his head and frowned. 'No, that's wrong. It was 25 September.'

I rapped the table. 'Returning to the subject in hand, there's a press dinner tonight after which we'll be staying at a rather nice-sounding bijou hotel near the Pompidou Centre. In the morning we'll take the train to Château-Renault.'

'You do get around.'

'Well you're hardly standing still. Can you join us tonight?'

He shook his head. 'Philippe, our esteemed French editor, has organised a day of media interviews for me and then we have a dinner later.'

'Of course. Are you seeing Mr Mangetout at all?'

'He intends to pop by the hotel for a coffee tomorrow morning. Let's just hope he doesn't resort to demolishing the cup and saucer while he's at it.'

He pulled open a file and pushed the image of a frail, elderly woman towards me.

'That is Jeanne Calment who I shall be meeting in Arles tomorrow late afternoon. To think she's one hundred and thirteen years old and still able to walk about in her nursing home.'

'She looks like a feisty old bird.'

He grinned. 'There's a wonderful story about her. She had no living heirs, her daughter and grandson having died many years back, so at ninety she agreed to sell her apartment to a lawyer named André-François Raffray, on a contingency contract. The agreement was that he would pay her two thousand five hundred francs every month until her death and the flat would be his.'

'He presumably thought she'd be popping her clogs in a matter of years?'

'Precisely. And here she is still the picture of health at the age of one hundred and thirteen. Poor chap must be kicking himself.'

I laughed. 'Didn't she once meet Vincent Van Gogh?'

'She is the last living person to have met him but he didn't seem to have made a good impression on her. She described him as dirty, disagreeable and badly dressed.'

'I wonder how she's reached such an old age.'

He drained his cup. 'She puts it down to olive oil and port wine and, most important of all, chocolate. She eats a kilo every week!'

'Good grief! I suppose you think this gives you licence to eat several Mars Bars every day?'

He tapped his chin. 'Actually a Mars Bar weighs 62.5 grams so following Jeanne Calment's recommendation a kilo would be equivalent to sixteen Mars Bars. That means I could have two bars every day with two to spare.'

'What tosh!'

'She's smoked all her life too, at least a few every day.'

'It just goes to prove that good genes are everything.'

The door of the hotel swung open and Isabelle, a polite woman from the French editorial team, approached us.

Norris looked at his watch. 'Time for me to go.'

Isabelle gave us a cordial greeting. 'We have a car waiting outside.'

I accompanied them to the hotel's lavish forecourt. Norris gave me a wink as they drove off into thick traffic. I crossed the Champs-Elysées with its neat line of horse-chestnut trees running along both sides of the road. There were no record-breaking oaks in evidence or, for that matter, one single chrysanthemum.

★ ★ ★

It was late morning when we arrived in the Loire Valley. An hour earlier, in the company of the group of British gardening press I had met up with the night before in Paris, I had taken the fast TGV train from Paris Montparnasse station to Tours. Together we would be visiting the famed gigantic chrysanthemums in the area. The minibus that eventually collected us from the station in Tours hurtled through the country lanes at great speed and now, as we approached the final part of our journey, progressed at a more leisurely pace. We arrived in glorious spring sunshine in the picturesque town of Château-Renault with its cobbled streets and medieval, closely knit, dove-grey houses. I noted from my guide book that this little town which sat between Tours and Vendôme in the rural Indre-et-Loire district of France was known for its gentle and bucolic pastoral scenery and crumbling chateaux that harked back to 1066. In fact, that whole area was overrun with castles. Amboise, a few miles south of the town, boasted a rather fine castle overlooking the Loire and so did Blois, Vendôme, Tours, Chinon and – a bit of a giveaway – Château–la-Vallière. It seemed to be virtually impossible not to trip over a castle along the Loire so when I discovered that we would be staying in Château de Bauchant, a sixteenth-century castle converted into a hotel, I wasn't remotely surprised. Soon we rattled up a long sweeping drive and stopped outside a fairytale castle surrounded by undulating pastures and forests. It was of a soft grey hue with tiny leaded windows running along its facade and up and down two solid towers sandwiching the main body of the edifice. It had turrets and spires and patriotic French flags waving from the upper reaches and a collection of large, tail-wagging dogs that had gathered, presumably to greet or eat us, in the driveway.

The host of our chrysanthemum trip was Gerry Mayhew, sales director of Harris & Hubert, a seed and fertiliser supplier from Bristol. One of Gerry's French horticultural clients, a Monsieur Fontaine, was based in a small village near Château-Renault and had over the years perfected the growth of giant chrysanthemums using Bloomers, a fertiliser produced by Gerry's company. Once I'd set eyes on the flowers, I hoped to return to the UK with a new record for the natural world section while Gerry Mayhew had his sights set on global coverage for Bloomers.

The previous evening I had met Gerry and the party of eight British gardening correspondents in Paris and together we had spent a jolly evening at a local restaurant before setting off early the next morning for Tours. However there had been a strange occurrence at the hotel the night before we left Paris. Having collected our bedroom keys at around midnight from the reception desk, Gerry had suddenly called me back. Assuming that he had wanted to discuss some aspect of the trip, I was puzzled to be asked whether I kept a dog whose name began with N. I explained that not only did I not have a dog with the initial N, but that I didn't have a dog at all. He had looked disappointed and run a restless hand through his grey gelled hair. Just as I had turned to go he enquired as to the date and month of my birth.

'I thought as much!' he had exclaimed, his face lighting up like a glow-worm.

Making my excuses, I had quickly made haste to the lift, concluding that either the man was a nutter or that I was the subject of some strange wager. I had gone to bed wondering what it could all possibly mean.

We stood by the minivan admiring the chateau before us and stretching our limbs. To my unease I observed Gerry, tall and wooden, staring at me from a distance with dark and manic eyes. Fortunately Harris & Hubert had arranged for the company's PR consultant, a young woman named Roxanne, to accompany Gerry on the trip so we weren't left entirely at his mercy. Roxanne was a cheery soul, although given to wearing multicoloured hippy dresses and laughing loudly like a persistent hoopoe. As a team of staff arrived in white livery and gloves to wrestle with our luggage, Roxanne came bouncing over to me.

'It's so cool here, isn't it?'

'I don't find it that cold actually.'

She gave me a funny look. 'Anyway, I've been thinking about Château-Renault and it struck me that it must have got its name from Renault, the French car firm.'

I gaped at her. 'I think you'll find it comes from Renaud, the son of the chap who created the wooden tower where the present castle now stands.'

'Seriously?'

'Well, that's what it says in my guide book.'

She did her funny hoopoe single-note laugh and dashed off to inspire the rest of the party with her musings.

Sarah, a well-known freelance writer, sidled up to me.

'I don't want to unsettle you, but I've been noticing since the moment we all got together last night in Paris that Gerry has been eyeing you in a strange way.'

So it wasn't just my own paranoia.

'I have noticed,' I replied. 'He asked about my birth date and whether I had a dog with the initial N.'

She bit her lip. 'Oh dear. I hope he's not lost his marbles. We'll have to keep an eye on him.'

After settling into the hotel, we spent some time touring the lavish gardens and their own significant chrysanthemum borders.

'Are you all partial to chrysanthemums around here?' I asked the chateau's owner.

He shrugged in a rather laconic way. '*Non, pas du tout.* They are as good as any other flower but they seem to like the soil and climate here.'

'And the man who has grown the enormous chrysanthemums, do you know him?'

'*Bien sûr*, he is well known here. Monsieur Fontaine grows his flowers under glass in special conditions and in huge pots with special fertilisers.'

Gerry appeared like a jack-in-the-box in front of us.

'Of course, it's mainly due to Bloomers, our fantastic fertiliser.'

The hotel owner puffed out his cheeks. 'I'm not sure about that. All I do know is that he wins all the town's horticultural contests.'

Gerry fixed me with a wild smile. 'Perhaps the stars are on his side. What do you think?' 'I think Monsieur Fontaine just happens to be good at tending his plants,' I replied.

After lunch and a leisurely tour of the town, we met with the local mayor and during the late afternoon I gave an interview to Mike, one of the gardening press. He suddenly laughed.

'I always find press trips like this amusing. They remind me of those Agatha Christie stories set in country houses with a whole raft of peculiar characters.'

'Thanks a lot,' I said with a grin.

'I mean, take Gerry. I sat next to him on the plane and he was rabbiting on about how he goes to seances and has a soothsayer. People are very strange.'

I sat bolt upright. 'A soothsayer? That is peculiar.'

He tutted. 'I can't be doing with all that rubbish. And then one of the bar staff here told me the hotel was haunted. A likely story, but then I suppose gullible tourists lap it all up.'

I nodded uneasily.

'Anyway, tell me, are the French known for growing gargantuan flowers?'

I scratched my head. 'Truth to say they aren't. The Brits and Americans are into growing large vegetables and flowers and Australia holds a fair few in the larger species category.'

'What about vineyards?'

'Nothing doing. The largest vine was in California but perished in 1920 and the largest bunch of grapes was found in Chile.'

'Anything at all?'

'Well, the French created the world's largest bouquet in Annecy. It was 36 feet and 10 inches high with 9,299 flowers.'

He gave a grunt. 'I suppose that will have to do. Hopefully we'll get a good story on this Mr Fontaine tomorrow morning.'

Sarah strode towards us. 'We've got to have some pics taken outside in the courtyard. They're for Harris & Hubert's customer magazine.'

We trooped out. Sarah touched my arm. 'Penny for your thoughts, dreamer?'

After the strange things Mike had been telling me, I didn't much feel like sharing my thoughts with anyone. I had a feeling that ghostly encounters at the hotel would prove the very least of my problems.

★ ★ ★

Gerry had organised a seven-course French banquet at the hotel that night with an array of some of the region's finest wines and so the conversation flowed. John, a large, bluff gardening correspondent with a ruddy nose who wrote for one of the broadsheets and whom I had previously thought rather taciturn, became hugely animated after a few glasses of Pouilly-Fumé.

'There's nothing to beat the pinot noir grape, is there? Give me a good Sancerre any day – you can't go wrong.'

Roxanne took a sip from her glass and giggled. 'It's really nice, like some German wines I've tried. Sort of fruity.'

His eyes nearly popped out of his head. 'My dear girl, they are not remotely like German wines! *Quel horreur*!'

'Ooh,' said Roxanne. 'Now I've got him going!'

'Did you know, Roxanne, that in the Middle Ages, wines from the Loire region were feted above even Bordeaux?'

'Gosh, who'd have thought it?' she honked.

It was well after midnight before we all got to our beds. The narrow corridors which ran like a warren inside the chateau were candlelit, their dim rays creating a buttery glow around the walls, antique tapestries and suits of armour. After wishing everyone goodnight, Mike and I found the corridor to our suites which were situated away from the other rooms. I wished him goodnight and entered my room. By night it looked different, large and shadowy, the antiques rather grotesque and imposing. I was tired and so no sooner had I put out the bedside light than I fell asleep. In the dark, cold early hours of the morning I thought I heard a telephone ringing. Sleepily I fumbled for the receiver.

'Hello?'

Silence.

'Hello?'

I put the receiver back and laid my head back on the pillow thinking I'd been dreaming. It began ringing again. I sat bolt upright. An iciness coursed through me. Could it be a ghostly creature somehow infiltrating the telephone lines? I picked up the receiver again.

'Look, who IS this?'

A pause. 'It's me. Gerry.'

'Gerry? What on earth is the matter?'

'I have to talk to you. I need to explain to you that fate has brought you here. It is our destiny.'

I crooked the receiver under my chin and in the darkness attempted to find the bedside light switch.

'Gerry, I haven't the faintest clue what you're talking about. Perhaps you've had a little too much of the old Crémant and...'

'STOP!' he shrieked. 'My psychic told me I would meet a woman with the initial A, with your exact birth date and with a dog whose initial was N. She said we would spend the rest of our lives together.'

The man was clearly deranged or at least delusional.

'Gerry, there are many women whose names begin with A and who share my birthday. Probably the majority have dogs with the initial N unlike me.'

He laughed like a madman. 'But you're wrong. I rang my psychic tonight and she said N could refer to a good friend, not just a pet. Perhaps N could refer to Norris McWhirter. I mean he's your boss and a good friend. You see, it's all coming together.'

'I'm sorry Gerry but you're now talking complete gibberish so I'm going to go. Please don't call back.'

I slammed the phone down and sighed deeply. What was wrong with people? The phone was ringing again. I picked it up and replaced it without answering. It rang again. This time I was cross.

'I'm afraid I will have to come to your room to explain the psychic signs. You have to understand. You cannot escape your fate.'

The phone went dead. Now I was feeling unnerved. If the man had lost the plot I did not want him pounding on my door at this creepy hour of the night. I thought of Mike slumbering in a suite not far along the corridor.

I heard a creak in the corridor. He couldn't possibly be here already? I dialled Mike's internal line. A sleepy voice answered. He listened groggily.

'I knew he was loopy. Look, give me a sec and I'll come to your room.'

There was a knock at the door and the sound of Mike's distinctive gravelly voice. He plodded in to my room and sat on an upholstered chair.

'I tried ringing Gerry but got no reply.'

'Do you think he's on his way over here?'

He closed his eyes. 'God knows but I'll give him a piece of my mind if he does turn up.' We sat chatting for a few minutes until the telephone rang again.

'Pick it up,' hissed Mike, 'and say I'm here and wish to speak to him.'

I answered the phone. Gerry sounded totally contrite. 'I'm sorry, forgive me. I've been an idiot. I'll explain myself tomorrow.'

I took a deep intake of breath. 'No, don't explain anything. I'd rather pretend the whole episode never happened.'

He wished me a goodnight, the cheek of it, and apologised again. Mike shook his head.

'You know, I'm always telling my wife to watch out for nutty types like him. You never can be too sure.'

He got up and wandered over to the door.

'Ring me if anything else happens.'

I thanked him and went back to bed. After a fitful few hours of sleep, I awoke to hear a mournful howling somewhere within the bowels of the hotel. I checked my watch in the half-light and saw that it was five o'clock. Was it a hound? The cry began again and then a strange muffled muttering or chanting. I rubbed my eyes. Was it one of the phantoms Mike had been warned about?

I sank back into my sheets, put the pillow over my head and tried to resume sleep. By six thirty the chanting had stopped but I was unnerved and keen to leave my isolated cell. In the dining room I asked the waitress if she'd heard a strange howling. She told me she had only just come on duty but would ask the reception staff. She returned with a glum expression.

'They say, mademoiselle, that a nobleman from the court of Count Blois was once killed in a terrible sword fight in this chateau. It is said that he weeps and howls and walks about the corridors racked with pain and anger.'

'Great,' I replied.

We had one more day and night in Château-Renault before returning to Paris. Would I survive it? That was the sixty million dollar question.

★ ★ ★

A mere ten minutes' drive from our hotel in the heart of Loire country we found ourselves traipsing through the rich and expansive gardens of Monsieur Fontaine. A few moments later, he welcomed us into his musty greenhouse with its lofty glass roof and dusty panes, and introduced us to his prized possession: a cluster of towering, triffid-like chrysanthemums in pots. Several journalists in our party were taking photographs. Mike had already promised to provide me with shots for the book. I stood looking up at one of the enormous white blooms.

'They really are amazing. This one has four thousand and fifty blooms apparently and is 8 foot 3 inches tall.'

Mike snorted. 'Yes, but you have to look at the conditions. I mean the flowers are well protected and sheltered and are given high dosages of nutrients and the fertiliser, Bloomer.'

I laughed. 'I'm not very green-fingered so I wouldn't have a clue how to grow such monsters.'

I looked across the greenhouse and saw Gerry, his drawn and crumpled face observing me from behind a large pot plant. Mike stole a glance in his direction.

'Just ignore him and stick with me. Never wind up on your own with him.'

'No way,' I replied.

Roxanne sauntered over. 'Isn't it pretty in here? Got everything you need?'

I nodded. 'Monsieur Fontaine has been very helpful with authentication details.'

'Great! That's so exciting. And will you be able to mention Bloomer in the entry?'

I frowned. 'I'm afraid not. We're only interested in the record-breaking entity itself.'

'But surely these flowers wouldn't have grown so big without Bloomer?' she pouted.

'How do we know that? If it were claiming to be a record-breaking fertiliser we'd need scientific evidence and to look at competing brands.'

She clicked her teeth. 'Oh that's a bit of a bore. You can't just stick it in anyway?'

Mike raised his eyebrows.

'No, it just doesn't work like that.'

'Have you told Gerry that you won't put Bloomer in the book?' she asked.

'Of course. I made that perfectly clear before agreeing to come.'

She raised her arms in the air. 'That'll explain why he's been acting so moodily. I knew something was up with him.'

We watched as she ambled off towards Gerry.

Mike gave me a wink. 'This would make a great comedy script.'

'It might one day,' I replied.

He laughed. 'Just one more day. We can handle that, can't we?'

★ ★ ★

Another banquet. Another round of Sancerre, Pouilly-Fumé and Mousseux. Sitting at the far end of the enormous banqueting table in the chateau I was careful to keep a beady eye on Gerry. Sarah had been briefed by Mike on the strange goings-on at the hotel and somewhat disapprovingly glanced down the table from time to time, regarding Gerry with a mixture of ennui and pity. Just before we all set off for our rooms, Gerry caught up with me.

'Could I have a word?'

Mike stood like a rock by my side. I decided to confront the issue.

'OK, Mike. I'll be fine, thank you.'

I waited until he'd reluctantly walked away.

'I just wanted to apologise,' whimpered Gerry. 'I realise that my behaviour must seem quite odd but my soothsayer…'

I tried to be my most rational. 'I don't believe in soothsayers and I don't want to hear another squeak about any of this ever again. Understood?'

I strode off without looking back, sure that this time I would have a quiet night. All was well until about five o'clock in the morning when again I heard the same anguished moaning and chanting. Gripping my door key, I crept out into the corridor and set off on tiptoe along the cool stone tiles. The sound appeared to be coming from behind a large oak door. Carefully I turned the handle and peeped in. There, sitting cross-legged in what was evidently a small chapel, was Roxanne. She was swaying and moaning to herself and seemed in some distress.

'Roxanne!' I hissed. 'Whatever's wrong?'

She stopped abruptly in her tracks and turned round.

'Oh it's you! Nothing's the matter. I'm just doing my sacred mantra chanting.'

I blinked hard in the gloom. 'What?'

'Yeah, you know, cosmic chanting? I do healing vowel sounds every morning. It's so cool, you should try it.'

I stared at her in wonderment.

'I do creative visualisation techniques too.'

Weakly I headed back to my room, creatively visualising the plane back home.

★ ★ ★

Norris's shoulders were shaking with laughter. He examined the white petals of the pressed chrysanthemum in his hand and laid it on the table.

'You know, why is it you always have such fun on your trips?'

'Fun? Being pursued by a compulsive obsessive with a penchant for clairvoyants?'

He shrugged. 'The poor chap needs to visit a good psychiatrist. You know Boston in Massachusetts would be just the place. They have one shrink for every three hundred and twenty-eight heads.'

'I must call to let him know.'

Muriel opened the library door. 'I'm putting some tea on. Fancy a cup?'

'Absolutely,' said Norris.

His eyes followed her as she left the room. 'You know, AN, there was once a psychiatrist in New Jersey called Dr Albert L. Weiner, who had only ever trained in osteopathy and yet treated up to fifty patients per day using electro-shock and narco-analysis. He got his comeuppance in 1961 when he was found guilty of twelve counts of manslaughter on account of using unsterilised needles.'

'How horrific!'

He eyed me coolly. 'Oh, I can tell you far worse stories than that.'

'I'm sure you can. Anyway, how was the trip to Arles?'

'Less eventful than yours up the Loire but most enjoyable nonetheless. Madame Calment is a grand old dame and totally compos mentis, although her sight's not too good these days. She told me that she took up fencing at eighty-five and was still riding her bike at a hundred years of age.'

'What a phenomenon.'

He nodded. 'Yes, she is a one-off. It just shows you can do anything if you put your mind to it.'

'Well that's certainly the motto of our record-breakers but I'll never ride a bike at a hundred years of age. I can't even stay on one now!'

'Pathetic!' he exclaimed.

'Pathetic,' I laughed, 'but true.'

TWELVE

★ ★ ★

DEAD WOMEN, HANDSHAKING AND LONG CARS

I stood in the busy entrance hall of Foyles bookshop on the Charing Cross Road observing the hustle and bustle around me. Staff scurried around like white rabbits, a nervous and hounded look in their eyes. This wasn't too surprising given the reputation of Christina Foyle, the store's elderly and imperious owner. I had met Miss Foyle, her favoured title, a few times with Norris because by curious chance she happened to be his wife Carole's aunt. This made her a sort of aunt-in-law to Norris and she enjoyed the perk of having a well-known nephew by marriage who could be relied upon to do regular turns as a guest speaker at her famous Foyles literary lunches. He was endlessly amused by her authoritarian ways and admired her brisk, no-nonsense and, at times, ruthless manner. I felt a tap on my shoulder. Norris appeared from nowhere.

'Have you been here long?'

'About ten minutes.'

'So have I.'

'Well where have you been?'

He looked at me as if I was a simpleton. 'Reading, of course. You know I never like to waste time. I thought you'd be late as usual.'

He walked off overcome by a fit of mirth just as I began launching into an indignant tirade about his own appalling time-keeping habits. I caught up with him.

'I'd rather have liked to look at the fiction section.'

He was apoplectic. 'Fiction? What a waste of time. You should only read factual books – that way you might learn something. So what do you think of this shop?'

'It's an anachronism. I can't bear the fact I have to queue up all over the place to order and pay for things. I also take issue with the way things are set out. It seems so chaotic and unorganised.'

He paused. 'Good. Well you must tell Christina all this when we see her.'

He approached one of the desks. 'We're here to see Miss Foyle.'

There was instant recognition. 'Oh, Mr McWhirter. Of course.'

'You didn't say we'd be meeting her today?'

'Life's full of surprises, AN. By the way, you do know that Foyles is the biggest bookshop in the world?'

I rolled my eyes. 'It has a stock of four million books on thirty miles of shelving, employs about six hundred staff and handles nearly nine million letters per year. Satisfied?'

'Not bad.'

'But is it the largest?' I challenged.

He hesitated for a split second then smiled. 'Well, the most capacious store is Barnes & Noble on Fifth Avenue but it has only about a third of the shelving of Foyles.'

At that moment an elegant, fine-boned woman in her seventies approached us. The silvery-grey hair rolled back from her head in neat waves, and the small intelligent eyes latched on to Norris. She was wearing a soft-pink dress with an expensive-looking, colourful brooch. It shimmered under the harsh lights.

'So lovely to see you again, Norris.'

He dutifully planted a kiss on her powdery cheek and turned to introduce me.

With some impatience she whisked a hand through the air. 'We've of course met before.'

She looked at her watch. 'Norris, I really can't be long but I imagine neither can you. I just wanted to show you the new display area for the Guinness book. Come.'

We followed in her wake. She was a commanding figure who practically had the staff doffing their imaginary caps as she sallied forth. I stole a glance at Norris. He returned a surreptitious grin. She stopped abruptly beside a large bookshelf.

'What do you think? Good visibility from the entrance and if we have some decent point of sale material for the new edition we can make this quite a showcase for the book.'

Norris nodded. 'Excellent. I think Fred, our sales director, would appreciate that.'

She turned to me. 'What do you think?'

I felt a momentary stab of fear as the sharp, bird-like eyes rested on me.

'I think it's perfect. Even better if we could have a cut-out of the tallest man or some other eye-catching record-holder posing next to it.'

She frowned. 'You don't think that's a bit vulgar?'

I shrugged. 'It would attract customers and sell books which is, after all, the point of the exercise.'

To my relief she managed a pert smile. 'All right, well I'll leave you to sort out the details. I must be off.'

We watched as she marched along one of the wide corridors, her body erect, her head held high.

'Did you know that Christina was related to Charles Henry Foyle who invented the folding carton?'

'I can't say I did,' I replied distractedly. 'Gosh, I'd be terrified to work for her.'

'Nonsense,' said Norris. 'I think you'd get along famously. Like you, she's a practical joker.'

'Me?'

He rattled on. 'Oh, another interesting thing about her is that she once wrote to Adolf Hitler to challenge him about Nazi book-burning and he actually replied.'

'What did he say?'

'Tried to justify his actions, of course. Now why was it we were meeting?'

'To discuss my trip to Finland. You said you'd give me some background on record-breakers there.'

He sniffed the air. 'It's not a country known for record-breaking but I have some ideas. Let's have a cup of tea along the road. There is of course one very important word you must remember in Finland.'

I stopped outside the store and regarded him in anticipation. 'What's that?'

'*Suklaa.*'

'Which means?'

'Chocolate, of course. If all else fails, ask for *suklaa*. It might prove a sensible alternative to vodka.'

★ ★ ★

It was an exciting day for the residents of Turku on the south-west coast of Finland. Well, I imagined it was because Rainer Vikström, a wheelchair-bound local man, had decided to attempt the world handshaking record. Juhani, editor of the book's Finnish edition, had invited me over to Finland for a few days to witness the event, speak at the press conference and later travel with him up to Imatra in the east where we would take a drive in the world's longest car. Juhani was waiting for me at Helsinki airport and together we set off in his car for the two-hour journey along spiky spruce-lined roads to Turku. After forty minutes I asked Juhani whether all his compatriots had been abducted by aliens.

He threw me a confused glance. 'Aliens? What do you mean?'

Then he looked ahead at the painfully empty road and gave a deep laugh.

'Ah, British humour. It's true, we don't have much traffic here as you can see. Mind you, an elk might jump out at any time.'

So that's how the Finns got their kicks, I thought to myself.

'Can you tell me about the record attempt tomorrow in Turku?'

He stroked his beard. 'It's in celebration of the annual spring market in Turku, Manun Markkinat. A very big day.'

'And how many people do you reckon will show up?'

He paused. 'I believe President Roosevelt once shook 8,513 hands at an official function in Washington, so we'll have to beat that. Rainer's been training hard and the whole town is geared up for the attempt.'

I looked out of the window at the seemingly endless evergreen forests, gently undulating hills and clear blue sky. I wondered whether anything ever happened in this ordered paradise. At that moment, Juhani braked suddenly. An indignant elk did a quick sprint across our path and disappeared down a bank into a dark wood.

'You see?!' he cried excitedly, putting the car back in gear. 'An elk!'

'I can see you all live on the edge of your seats, Juhani.'

He tutted and waggled a finger at me. 'There's a lot to be said for a quiet life.'

Perhaps he was right, but after two hours on the road and having only spotted one elk and two other cars, I wasn't so sure.

★ ★ ★

The people of Turku were forming an orderly queue at the entrance to the busy marketplace. Sitting on the stage, I glimpsed the small group huddled by the rope and worried about the Finn's chances of breaking a world record, but, as I knew only too well by now, anything could happen. An oompah band was playing somewhere in the background and neat stalls of vegetables, fruit and flowers ran all the way around the wide market square down below us. Rainer Vikström was a strongly built man in his late twenties with chocolate-coloured eyes and an ultra-white smile. Stretching out an arm, he showed me his huge bicep as evidence of his strength. I just hoped more people would turn up.

Half an hour elapsed and then quite suddenly I was aware of a gigantic wave of humanity approaching the square. Where had they all come from? They walked steadily towards us.

Given that neither of us could communicate in each other's language, I gave Rainer a nudge and he returned a thumbs up sign. The atmosphere was becoming festive with a more cheery band striking up nearby. Soon Juhani was at my side.

'Things are livening up. There are people coming from all directions. I think he'll make it.'

The sun was hot and I wondered how long Rainer might cope sitting for hours up on the stage. He seemed nonchalant as he gripped each hand in turn, smiling benevolently up at the blue sky. At one point he caught my expression and said something to Juhani who turned to me.

'Rainer said to tell you that we Finns are strong and not to worry about him,' he said.

But what about us weedy Brits? As if on cue an official appeared and whipped a red cap out of a plastic bag and offered it to me. It sported antlers and a cartoon of a dead elk with a target on its head. Finnish humour, I imagined. I just hoped I wouldn't be snapped by a photographer wearing it.

The hours went by and still more people arrived. Those entering were immediately logged by two volunteers at the entrance who scrutinised their identity papers and checked that there were no duplicate entries. All the same, to be doubly sure I had a small manual counter that I clicked every time someone approached.

Juhani tapped my arm. 'How are we doing on numbers?'

'He's up to five thousand eight hundred people so we're on course. Do you want to stop when he surpasses the old record?'

He turned to Rainer, who indicated that he was happy to carry on.

'He's happy to keep going until everyone's shaken his hand. I feel we could be here for some time.'

Three hours later Rainer was still shaking hands. Aside from stiffness and cramp, he was doing OK and after a brief sandwich break, his energy levels were restored. After eight hours he pumped the final hand. His own was swollen and red but otherwise still attached to his arm. He shook his head and flopped in his wheelchair.

We waited with baited breath for the hand count. Rainer had shaken exactly 19,592 hands. After a great fanfare and press conference, Juhani and I set off for a celebratory dinner in the town with Rainer, the mayor and local officials.

'Now we'll see what you're made of,' laughed Juhani.

'What do you mean?'

'Tonight you'll be sampling the best of Finnish vodka.'

★ ★ ★

At some garishly bright hour of the night – the sky resolutely remaining blue because of Finnish summer light – I awoke with a splitting headache. What had they poured down me the night before? I remembered the schnapps, or was it vodka, and doing an interesting national dance with everyone around the table after a bit of elk and chips or something similarly tasty. We had then found our way back to the hotel, a modern wooden construction in what appeared to be a forest of spruce caught under the penetrating rays of a dentist's lamp. Juhani and I were given forest cabins and in some exhaustion I hurled myself into my wooden cot and tried to sleep. After an hour of tossing and turning I wondered what was wrong and then it struck me. The room was flooded with light. The curtains were drawn but it made not the slightest difference. It was like lying on a lilo in the Mediterranean Sea without sunglasses. At some godforsaken hour I fell asleep only to be abruptly awoken by the honking of the hotel's alarm clock. Had I set if before I went to bed? How efficient was that? Of course I hadn't. It was the telephone ringing.

'Good morning. Juhani here. I am in the foyer. Do you want breakfast? We leave in half an hour.'

I groaned. 'I'll see you by the car.'

After a chastening shower of cold water, all that seemed on offer, I emerged from the cabin and staggered through the forest to the main building. I hoped that any random elk would be sensible enough not to cross my path. I might just bite its nose.

Juhani was singing cheerily in his car seat.

I stared at him. 'What's wrong with you? Is this a display of the national character or are you unstable?'

He giggled and taking off his metal-framed glasses gave them a good clean on his shirt while studying the map.

'A good night, eh? Now you know how Finns have fun.'

'Yep.'

'I have some *piima* here. Do you want to try some?'

I surveyed the carton suspiciously. 'What is it?'

'Good for the stomach.'

I took a sip and nearly retched. 'That is awful.'

He revved the engine and reversed out of the car park. 'Now for a five-hour drive up east to Imatra. It's a good 350 kilometres.'

I lay back in my seat and tried to close my eyes. 'So what is *piima*?'

'Fermented milk.'

I groaned. 'Somehow, Juhani, I wish I'd never asked.'

★ ★ ★

Heikki, the chauffeur of the world's longest car, was driving cautiously out of the forecourt of Imatra's Hotel Valtionhotelli, an art deco-era royal lodge which could have been mistaken for a castle.

'Valtionhotelli. That's a name that just rolls off the tongue, isn't it?' I said to Juhani who was sitting next to me on one of the enormous sofas housed within the cream Cadillac.

'But back in 1903, this hotel used to be called Grand Hotel Cascade d'Imatra.'

'Why did they change it?'

He scratched his head. 'Maybe because the new name is easier for tourists to pronounce?'

I looked at him in amazement but discerned a note of dry humour in his voice.

'So, tell me about this car. It's a hundred feet long and has twenty-four wheels?'

'It was created by Jay Ohrberg, a specialist car dealer in California who designs all sorts of super-long limos for use by the film industry and exhibition and event companies. As you can see, it has sixteen windows running along each side and twelve sets of wheels to give it ballast. Heikki is taking it on an official tour of the country. You know it's not easy manoeuvring such a vehicle.'

'I'm sure it's not.'

As if to prove the point, some half an hour later we were about to turn a corner when the car ground to a halt. A crowd formed by the kerbside.

Heikki cursed. 'I will have to reverse. Corners like this aren't good when your car is 72 feet long.'

Quite. I looked anxiously behind and saw a traffic queue forming. 'Maybe we should carry on straight?'

'Yes but we need to loop back. We can't travel interminably along this straight road.'

He was right. If we did, we'd probably all die of boredom, resort to a few shots of Finnish vodka and take off on the first elk that swung by. Juhani and I got out of the vehicle. Given its length it took us some time to reach the cars behind us. I listened as he tried reasoning with the other drivers. They didn't seem remotely bothered about having to reverse but rather keener to get out and examine the beast ahead of them. Soon we had a crowd of fellow drivers inspecting every inch of the car. They peered inside the voluminous interiors with its kitchenette, television and large waterbed and goggled at the swimming pool and diving board on the back.

'Do you fancy a swim while Heikki works out how to turn the car round?' grinned Juhani.

'Shucks,' I said with a smile. 'I forgot my bathing suit.'

Heikki gave a toot. 'Now I know how to do this. All aboard.'

We swung back into the vehicle. Juhani looked at his watch.

'I think we'll be OK if we return now. We're meeting the mayor for dinner but first we have a fun excursion.'

I narrowed my eyes. 'Excursion?'

'Yes, you're going to love it.'

★ ★ ★

The Finnish press was out in force. Having arrived back in the nick of time, we now stood with the mayor of Imatra admiring the Cadillac at the front of the Hotel Valtionhotelli.

'We'll be leaving now on the excursion,' whispered Juhani.

He wandered over to the mayor and they had a few words. After some earnest discussion, we all set off across the woodland surrounding the hotel.

'We are now entering the oldest nature park in Finland,' Juhani advised me. 'It was created in 1842 by order of Tsar Nicholas I.'

'That was when this part of Finland was still under Russian rule?'

'Correct. It was in 1917 that we gained independence. You see Imatra was a great holiday resort for wealthy Russians at that time. They'd travel from St Petersburg to come and admire the spectacular Imatrankoski rapids, where we are taking you now.'

'So our little excursion is to see the rapids?'

He stopped and pointed to a far-off bridge. 'Unfortunately the rapids were dammed in 1929 but they are diverted from the hydroelectric installation during the summer months for the benefit of visitors. Come.'

We followed the mayor and other officials as they made their way across a small wood. The press lumbered behind, stopping occasionally to take photographs. As we neared the bridge which rose high above the river, there was a deafening roar as water cascaded and foamed into a gorge below. The mayor halted and beckoned to me. The press fanned out around him.

'Look,' he yelled above the din of the water. 'These are our famous rapids. Are they not magnificent?'

I leaned against the stone parapet. 'An extraordinary sight.'

He tapped my shoulder and laughed. 'Back in 1872 there was a ropeway built and you could cross the rapids in a basket. I'm only sorry we cannot arrange that for you today.'

The assembled press and the officials all found this very funny.

'Now I have a little something for you.'

Everyone gathered round. Juhani gave me an encouraging wink as the mayor stepped forward and sombrely handed me a dark blue box. Inside was a small bronze sculpture. I pulled it out and examined it carefully. It was of a naked woman seemingly asleep, her long curling hair spread out around her. She was mounted on a small wooden plinth which had a brass plaque engraved with the words 'Maid of Imatra' and the date. I smiled and thanked the mayor profusely but he was glum. The press snapped away as we stood together with the little bronze but I was puzzled. Why the long faces? Juhani sidled up to me. 'This bronze is in memory of all the women who threw themselves off this bridge.'

I wasn't sure if this was a stab at Finnish or maybe British black humour.

'Are you joking?'

'No, not at all. You see this place is famous for the number of women who leaped to their deaths as an escape from unhappy marriages or because of unrequited love.'

'How dreadful.'

He sighed. 'It got so bad that if a woman coming from St Petersburg bought a single ticket, the police would follow her.'

I wasn't sure whether to laugh or cry.

'And how long did this go on?'

He tapped his chin. 'It was still happening in the fifties. They'd flock here from Helsinki and Russia.'

I had a ludicrous image of crowds of weeping women, rushing like lemmings for the bridge or perhaps leaping from the basket attached to the ropeway only to hurl themselves into the raging waves below.

Juhani brightened. 'Of course now it is a rather good tourist attraction. We even have a drowning woman called Imatra in the park's fountain. Not a real one, of course.'

★ ★ ★

It was still light when we returned to the hotel despite it being eight o'clock. I dressed for dinner and met Juhani in the grand reception hall with its copper and stone fireplace. The woodwork was painted in gentle pastel tones and photographs hung from the panels depicting the last Tsar and his family. A gong sounded and we headed for a private room leading from the main dining hall. It had an impressive turn-of-the-century Russian feel to it, with heavy dark furniture and early 1900s-style decoration and art. The mayor rose to welcome me in front of the all-male VIP guests. In front of us lay gold and blue porcelain plates and an impressive array of glasses. The courses rolled by until the moment when large silver salvers were brought into the room high on the shoulders of the waiters.

'What are we sampling now?' I asked Juhani.

He gave a snort of laughter and began singing. At first I couldn't catch the tune but others swiftly joined in. It was – unmistakably – 'Rudolph the Red-nosed Reindeer'. More of that Finnish humour. I gave a slow clap and everyone laughed. A moment later glasses of ice-cold schnapps arrived to accompany the elk. I guessed it was going to be another long night.

★ ★ ★

I gave Juhani a hug at Helsinki airport. In my hand luggage I carried my gifts of Finnish Vodka and dead Imatra. Hopefully this time I wouldn't be stopped at British Customs. Trying to explain why I had chosen to bring back the sculpture of a suicidal woman might raise an eyebrow or two. Juhani reached into his briefcase.

'Here are some bars of Fazer Blue Finnish chocolate for Norris. It's very good quality.'

I found some local currency in my pocket and handed the marks over to him.

'I won't need these anymore.'

He refused to take them. 'Keep them for when you come back to see us.'

I waved as he drove away, wondering what Norris would say when I produced the large blue bars of Finnish *suklaa*. As for the vodka, I'd keep that to share with Jane back at my flat. A sensible alternative to chocolate, whatever Norris might say.

THIRTEEN

★ ★ ★

A SPORTING CHANCE

Fred, the sales director, was sitting at his desk.

'Can you try to be serious for a second, love?'

I pulled the red plastic ball off my nose and placed it on the boardroom table.

'Red Nose Day is a very serious matter, Fred.'

Chris tapped his pen against his head and grunted. 'So you're going to force our poor foreign editors to don those ridiculous noses for Comic Relief?'

I rounded on him. 'Why ever not? It'll make a great photo in *Publishing News*. Think of the PR value.'

Fred swivelled in his chair and sighed. 'Well, I'm all for it. I mean, it's a cheap stunt but it shows we're a strong international team supporting a good cause. I reckon it'll make a nice little diary story.'

Chris doodled on his notepad. 'I suppose we can just about splash out on twenty fifty pence noses.'

Fred yawned and rubbed his eyes. 'So we have a knees-up on the last night?'

'Knowing the foreign editors a little, I think there'll be a knees-up every night,' I replied.

The door opened and David peered at us. 'Sorry to interrupt but the Telex machine is playing up again and I can't find my toolbox.'

Alex held up a hand. 'Sorry, David, I borrowed it. I had a problem with the wall light over my desk.'

Chris dropped his head onto his hands and gave a desperate yelp. 'Perhaps we should just become a DIY outfit.'

'It might prove more profitable,' laughed Alex.

'I shall leave you all to your ruminations,' said David and closed the door softly behind him.

Chris massaged his forehead and blinked. 'Now then, where were we?'

★ ★ ★

Norris was sitting at my desk flicking through the programme for the editorial conference.

'This should keep them all busy. You don't think you might ask Juhani to bring some more of that excellent Finnish chocolate with him?'

'Was it that good?'

'Very, but there wasn't nearly enough. I could have done with a bar at the studio today. Those children ask some devilishly tricky questions sometimes.'

I laughed. 'I don't know how you dish out answers on the spot like that. Have you always had to do that on *Record Breakers*?'

'Yes, but it's a winning formula and certainly keeps me on my toes.'

'Rather you than me.'

A tall form, sporting a spiky thatch of red hair, hovered by the partition. It could only have been Stewart, the deputy sports editor. He gave Norris and me a smile.

'When are you two off to Gartree Prison?'

'In a week or so,' I replied.

'Not before time,' he said dryly.

'Oh, very funny.'

'Have you actually spoken to Vinny?' I asked.

He shook his head. 'I've been liaising directly with the prison staff.'

Norris looked up. 'Presumably he's trying to beat the record held by John Decker?'

'That's right. He'll have to do more than five thousand and ten finger press-ups in five hours to beat him,' Stewart replied.

I whistled. 'He must be unbelievably strong to do that.'

Norris briefly closed his eyes. 'We certainly shan't get on the wrong side of him when we visit.'

I caught Stewart's arm as he turned to go. 'You're OK about wearing a red nose, aren't you?'

'Do I have any choice?'

'A red nose?' queried Norris.

'Don't ask,' said Stewart, 'or she'll get you wearing one too.'

After Norris had left, Stewart took me aside. 'There are some IRA prisoners holed up at Gartree. Thought you should know, given what happened to Ross McWhirter.'

'Has Norris an inkling?'

'He actually broached the subject with me.'

I sat and contemplated our trip to HM Prison Gartree in Leicestershire. Under supervision, Vinny, one of the inmates, would be attempting a press-up record in the prison's gym. This new information concerned me. I only hoped that for Norris the visit wouldn't bring back too many sorrowful memories.

★ ★ ★

It was the last evening of the editorial conference held at the rather understated and clubby Grafton Hotel on Tottenham Court Road. Norris was sitting between Margarita and

Orlygur, the Icelandic editor, dryly recounting the mishaps that occurred while on a record-breaking roadshow in Austria some years before in the company of eighty record-breakers.

He cleared his throat. 'So we arrived in Faak…'

'Faak?' someone shouted.

Screeches of laughter erupted from the other end of the table. Lisa elbowed me.

'How much *vino* have they all had?'

Ignoring the hysteria, Norris continued. 'Chris Greener, the tallest man, had to help us carry the chap out of the train. He was completely sozzled. Thank heavens Count Desmond the sword swallower was there. A sensible chap in an emergency.'

David Hoy suddenly rose and tapped his glass with his coffee spoon. A hush fell on the table.

'I just want to thank you all for attending the editorial conference. I hear that the red nose photocall was a success and that the photo will be appearing in *Publishing News* next week.'

Several guests cheered while Donald raised an eyebrow and fixed me with one of his inscrutable smiles. David carried on with his speech until glasses were raised.

'*Skål!*' shouted Anne.

'*Shucram!*' rejoined Sami from Saudi Arabia.

'*Santé!*' said Philippe from France.

There was the further clinking of glasses and then, with a loud grinding of chairs, everyone rose and made their way to the bar. Norris pulled on his coat.

'David's giving me a lift. You'll stay up until they've all gone to bed?'

'Don't worry. I'll cut off the drinks at around midnight.'

He laughed. 'You can reward yourself with a lie-in tomorrow.'

'I take it you're joking?'

He turned at the door and winked. 'What do you think?'

★ ★ ★

Donald was sitting at his desk editing the mechanical world section. A fountain pen hovered in his hand. I wandered over to his desk and plonked myself down in a chair. He looked up absent-mindedly and pushed his wire-framed glasses back against his nose.

'To what do I owe this pleasure?'

'Guess who has just called me?'

He threw the pen down in front of him. 'Go on, surprise me.'

'Norman Painting.'

His eyes flashed with uncharacteristic excitement. 'Norman Painting, as in Phil Archer from the BBC *Archers* programme?'

'The same.'

He was in a state of shock. 'Well why was he ringing?'

'He called to thank you for sending him the latest book. He told me he'll be coming up for his fortieth year on the show.'

'Amazing. What else did he say?'

'Just that he loves being in the book. He said that he'd been playing the same role since doing a week's trial run back in May 1950 and hoped one day to clock up fifty years.'

'I hope you told him I was the show's number one fan?'

'Of course I did. He was thrilled.'

He smiled. 'I've got to convert you to *The Archers*.'

'It's for old people.'

'Cheers. Does that mean I'm past it at thirty-five?'

'Probably. Anyway, I've got to head off to St Pancras station to meet Norris.'

'To sample the delights of Gartree Prison?'

I nodded. 'Don't forget that you're going to Surbiton later.'

He looked blank and then slowly consulted his pocket diary. 'Surbiton?'

I rolled my eyes. 'You can't have forgotten! You're meeting the nine-year-old who's the youngest boy to have ever passed an A level.'

He smiled. 'Fooled you.'

As I reached the door, he looked up from his desk. 'There are a fair few murderers put away in Gartree. Watch your back.'

★ ★ ★

We were sitting in a small cafe near Market Harborough station listening to Hazel, an earnest middle-aged lady in pearls and a peach dress talking about rehabilitation at HM Prison Gartree.

'People often commit terrible crimes through no fault of their own.'

Norris tried hard not to interrupt, staring with a sublime expression out of the grimy window of the cafeteria and into a cloudless sky.

I felt irritated. 'Yes, but surely most murderers intend to kill their victims?'

She turned to me with a watery smile. 'Of course some people intend to hurt others but you cannot apply that rule to everyone.'

'Well Gartree's a category A prison so I'm sure there are some fairly unsavoury types locked up.'

'Of course, but they still need our love and understanding.'

'What, even cold-blooded terrorists?'

Norris made a non-committal grunt and gave me a warning kick under the table.

'Perhaps we should be making a move? It's almost two thirty,' I said.

Hazel regarded her watch. 'I suppose we could be heading over to the prison.'

'So how long have you been a prison visitor?' asked Norris.

'For more than five years. Of course it's all voluntary but I feel it's my duty to help those in need.'

I tapped the table impatiently. 'What support do the victims' families get?'

She stiffened. 'There are plenty of help groups for victims.'

'Yes, but it doesn't bring back their dead, does it?'

Norris sighed. 'And what sorts of activities are carried out at the prison?'

She clattered her spoon in its saucer. 'There's a cooking and studying area and the prisoners can work in the gardens or in various workshops and earn themselves some cash.'

'I see,' said Norris.

'And of course Gartree likes to encourage record-breaking!' she giggled.

He nodded enthusiastically. 'Of course – Gartree broke a record a year or so ago. The first prison to be successfully sprung by helicopter.'

She frowned.

'What happened?' I asked.

'Well, a Bell helicopter landed in the exercise yard and carried off two inmates, John Kendall, a well-known gangland boss and Sydney Draper, a convicted murderer.'

Hazel shifted uncomfortably in her chair. 'It was an unfortunate incident. You'll find that as a consequence, security has become very tight.'

'Did they catch them?' I asked.

Norris rubbed his eyes. 'Draper was only caught recently. He'd been on the run for more than a year.'

Hazel stood up. 'Right, I think we can make a move now.'

Norris prodded my arm. 'Drink up, AN. We haven't got all day.'

We followed Hazel out of the cafe and into her car and soon after arrived at a large foreboding edifice that sat like an enormous grey elephant amid fields and fallow grassland.

'This looks cheery,' I mumbled.

'It's a prison, what did you expect?' said Norris.

At the gatehouse we showed identification and the letter of authorisation from the governor. Keys rattled and gates groaned as we were led through a series of rooms until finally reaching what Hazel described as the recreation zone. The governor was there to greet us in a formal grey suit. Vinny, whose record attempt was being carefully monitored and logged according to our instructions by two prison guards and a sports trainer, had still not finished his finger press-ups so the governor suggested we visit the premises and chat with some of the prisoners. We popped our heads round the door of the cookery room and library and peered at Vinny doing his press-ups in the gym. The poor guy looked exhausted but he was obviously not one to give up easily. On arrival at the workshops I bristled slightly when Hazel muttered that IRA prisoners were working there. Were Ross's killers amongst them? I hoped not.

'So have you ever had any notorious prisoners staying here?' I asked.

The governor laughed. 'Are you an autograph hunter then? We've had Reggie Kray, a bit before your time, but also Ian

Brady, one of the Moors murderers. He's in Broadmoor now though.'

I pulled a face at Norris.

He leaned over to me. 'You should vacation here, AN, just the sort of company you'd enjoy.'

By the time we arrived back at the recreation area, various prisoners were milling about in their overalls. A pleasant-looking young man smiled over at me.

'How long have you been in here?' I asked.

'Two years and seven months.'

I nodded glumly. 'And when will you get out?'

He shrugged cheerfully. 'That all depends. I'm a lifer, so I'm not getting out any time soon.'

'Do you mind me asking why you're here?'

'I stabbed a bloke in a street fight. Shouldn't have really but in the heat of things, I sort of lost control.'

'Terrible.'

He sniffed. 'It was for him. He copped it.'

Norris tapped my shoulder. 'Can I possibly tear you away? Vinny has just broken the fingertip press-up record. He's managed 5,570 in 5 hours exactly.'

A huge cheer rose up among the prisoners. We rushed over to the gym to find the victor, his muscles taut and rock-like, standing modestly with a towel around his neck. His face was wet with perspiration and it seemed a miracle that he was still standing. Norris shook his hand and after congratulating him warmly, made a dignified speech and presented him with a signed copy of *The Guinness Book of Records*. The certificate would come later.

★ ★ ★

We waved to Hazel as she drove away from Market Harborough station.

'What a day!' I exclaimed. 'And what about Hazel?'

Norris walked slowly on to the platform. 'Sometimes, AN, it's wiser to bite one's tongue.'

We sat on a bench. 'What, even when people say really stupid things?'

'Especially when people say stupid things. What is to be gained from arguing a point? You're not going to change them.'

I thought about my irritation with Hazel. It was true; nothing I said would have altered her viewpoint and what was to be achieved by causing ill-feeling? I pulled my jacket up around my shoulders. It was March but the sky was already growing sullen.

'I hope it wasn't too harrowing for you being in there.'

He shook his head. 'No, it was fine.'

A train shuffled into the station. I looked through the windows of the nearest carriage.

'Oh God, it's heaving with people.'

Norris threw open a carriage door and smiled. 'Never give up, AN. Where there's a train, there's a potential seat. I feel we're in with a sporting chance!'

FOURTEEN

★ ★ ★

KOREANS, KIMCHI AND CAR-PULLING

Sharp light flooded the bedroom and for a moment I had difficulty remembering where I was. I eyed the alarm clock warily. It was six thirty and my room service breakfast would hopefully be arriving in half an hour. I stumbled out of bed and looked out of the window. I was staying at the Effingham Park Hotel, a sort of Dallas-style country house set in oodles of acres on the outskirts of Crawley. Given the 'all out' underground and rail strikes of 1989, I had decided to play it safe and stay at a hotel close to Gatwick before my flight to Seoul.

I dressed and showered and began flicking through my itinerary. The Korean Airlines flight would be leaving late morning and taking me first to Anchorage where it would refuel, and then on to Seoul. This was going to be a big trip – ten whole days visiting South Korea as it embarked on a week-long celebration of record-breaking, an initiative taken by the newly created Guinness Korea organisation. It was hoped that the first ever Korean edition of the book would be produced the following year. There was a knock at my door and a waiter, kitted out in a pristine white ensemble and bearing a gilt tray aloft one shoulder, entered the room. It wasn't balanced well because a moment later it came crashing to the floor, splattering orange juice against the wall and sending shards of pottery and glass in all directions. The poor chap apologised profusely and called the housekeeper, who immediately organised a clean-up operation. It was about 20 minutes later when the harassed waiter reappeared. This time he got as far as the table but as he bent down he tripped and sent the second tray flying towards the TV set. I stared at him in disbelief and then towards the door in case Spike Milligan and *The Goon Show* team had somehow been reincarnated and were hiding in the corridor. Miserable with embarrassment and inconsolable, the poor waiter rang the housekeeping department again.

I sighed. 'Listen, don't worry about breakfast. I'll get something at the airport.'

He pleaded with me. 'Please. Let me try again. Otherwise it will be very bad for me.'

'Are you Italian?'

'Yes, but that is not why I dropped the tray. I am new so maybe I'm a little nervous today.'

I thought he might lose the will to live unless I agreed a third attempt. This time breakfast would be on the house, he told me. The telephone rang. It was Norris.

'All packed and ready to go?'

'Almost. I'm just waiting for my breakfast.'

I told him about the Italian waiter's two blunders.

He pondered this. 'Maybe the poor chap's suffering from hypoglycaemic shock or even lithium poisoning.'

'What?'

'Hand tremors and hypertension like that can be due to a number of disorders. Mind you, if he's Italian, it could be

Wilson's disease. A lot of southern Italians are diagnosed with the complaint. Is he from the south?'

'I've no idea where he's from in Italy,' I blustered. 'Anyway, why were you calling?'

He coughed. 'David said you'd be meeting the Seoul Olympic Committee while you're over there.'

In 1988, the Olympic Games had been held in Seoul, the capital of South Korea. 'Yes, I'm handing out a load of Guinness certificates to commemorate the event. Why, what's the problem?'

'Well, when mentioning their achievements, keep off the fight that took place during the Olympic Games between Roy Jones, the American boxer, and Park Si-Hun, the Korean fighter. There was a bit of controversy over Si-Hun's win.'

'I haven't even heard of either of them.'

'Yes, well that doesn't surprise me, AN,' he replied witheringly. 'The thing is that Koreans can be very sensitive about these matters. Apparently there was a dispute about the decision to award Park Si-Hun the gold medal when Roy Jones was clearly the victor. All three judges were eventually suspended with one admitting to having made a mistake. Despite that the record still remained unchanged.'

'Oh dear, I see what you mean.'

'I'd just congratulate them on their table tennis victories and remember that the Koreans won twelve gold medals, thirty-three medals altogether.'

I sighed. 'Don't worry. I've got all the details here.'

'Good. Well enjoy the trip and bring me back something interesting.'

'I shouldn't think the chocolate will be up to much, so I'll think of something else.'

There was a frantic knocking on my door. 'Oh God, the waiter's back with my breakfast.'

Norris chuckled. 'Make sure you give him a wide berth this time.'

I replaced the receiver and opened the door. The man was perspiring heavily.

'Why don't you just let me have the tray?' I said encouragingly.

He shook his head vehemently. 'No, I can do this.'

He glided over to the table and placed it down without incident. I tipped him as he left. I glanced over at the tray and then at my watch and cursed. It looked as though breakfast would have to wait.

★ ★ ★

Anchorage wasn't the most enticing of places if the views from the airport were anything to go by. Molly, the jolly wife of an Irish diplomat, had befriended me on the plane and together we strolled around Anchorage airport eating butter pecan ice cream and conversing with a Korean family that had stopped us to ask in faltering English our opinions of President Bush and Mrs Thatcher. We were recalled to the plane after it had been refuelled and made our way back to prestige class to enjoy the delights of orange juice and honeyed peanuts before a lavish airline traditional Korean meal. The plump man sitting to the side of me told me he sold industrial mixers of every size to Korean factories. I listened politely while stifling a yawn. He asked where I'd be staying in Seoul.

'Hotel Lotte.'

'Ah, it's huge. Like a station. Very opulent. You'll get lost.'

I dozed off only to be jolted awake as the wheels hit the tarmac. It was three fifty in the afternoon and as I collected my case, I quickly referred to a notebook in my handbag in which I'd reminded myself that a Mr Yang-Kee, as opposed to Yankee, managing director of the Guinness Korea organisation, would be collecting me. Stepping into the arrivals hall, I was aware of a huge gathering of Koreans wearing garlands and waving colourful placards. At first I thought it might be a sort of demonstration but everyone was smiling and boards with WELCOME stamped across them were raised high. Distractedly I looked around the throng of people in search of Mr Yang-Kee. How would I recognise him? Would he wear some kind of identification? It was then that my eyes darted to one of the huge welcome boards. My name was plastered all over it. Could there be two of us with the same name arriving simultaneously at Seoul airport? It was unlikely. A minute later and I was besieged. Cameras flashed, TV crews rushed over and before I knew it I was giving a live interview to KBS TV. Very ceremoniously Mr Yang-Kee and several animated colleagues placed floral garlands around my neck and solemn greetings were exchanged. A number of Korean record-breakers had come to the airport, wanting to know whether I would be witnessing their attempts at the forthcoming 'Oddity' contest. That was an event I surely couldn't miss? My luggage was whisked from my hands and soon I was in the back of an air-conditioned limo and being driven at speed in the direction of, I hoped, Seoul. In the back three immaculately dressed Korean men with short shiny black hair and who spoke no English whatsoever smiled politely and nodded at me throughout the journey. As we neared Seoul I was overcome by the sheer scale of the buildings, the towering skyscrapers and the strange, eclectic merging of old and new architecture. At one point the car bounced along a pot-holed road which led into what I took to be the historical quarter.

'Joseon Dynasty City!' smiled one of my companions. 'Taejo Yi Seong-gye.'

I nodded uncomprehendingly and stealthily searched my guidebook, discovering that this was the downtown area and that Joseon referred to the Korean Sovereign State, which existed for five centuries from the late fourteenth century. It had been founded by Taejo Yi Seong-gye. At times our car could hardly move for the traffic and flow of people crossing the streets. With a ten million population in the city alone, it was hardly surprising that Seoul throbbed with life.

An hour later I looked out of the car window to see twin towers thrusting up into the endless blue sky like shiny silver bullets. The doors of the limo were yanked open and I was again faced with television crews and microphones and overwhelming pulsating heat. Would I be judging the Korea Oddity Record-Breaking tournament in Pusan? Would I be meeting with the chairman of SOSFO, the Olympic organising committee? Had I ever tried kimchi? My personal fan club followed me into the hotel. I didn't even need to register at reception. Everyone came with me into the lift, including the receptionist. Crammed in with 15 small and polite Korean men, I wondered what to say. We were, it seemed, heading for the thirty-fifth floor. Mr Yang-Kee, who appeared to have a smattering of English, solemnly addressed me.

'And how is great Mr Norris?'

'Oh, he's still great and of course sad that he cannot be joining us all here in Korea.'

A translation went round. Everyone nodded and peered at me.

'Mr Norris has twin brother?' questioned Mr Yang-Kee.

An awkward pause while I weighed up a suitable reply.

'I'm afraid Mr McWhirter's brother is no longer alive.'

Another rapid translation from Mr Yang-Kee. Fifteen pairs of anxious eyes searched my face.

'Why? He die of illness?'

'Sadly he was shot and killed by the IRA.'

'IRA?' asked Mr Yang-Kee.

'It stands for Irish Republican Army.'

He nodded slowly. 'I heard of these people.'

Silence. Would this lift ever arrive? It stopped for a few seconds. Oh God, it wasn't jammed was it? A snuffle followed by several more. White handkerchiefs were produced. Heads were bowed. My black-suited entourage was sobbing en masse. What had I done? A jolt. The lift was moving again. Ping. The lift door opened. How would I rectify this diplomatic disaster? I addressed them all by the lift doors.

'I just want to make it clear that Norris's brother was a brave man and is regarded as a hero in the UK. He was a fighter and believed in his convictions. Norris would want us all to celebrate rather than mourn his life.'

Mr Yang-Kee translated and everyone nodded approvingly. The hankies were refolded and tucked away in suit pockets. We all entered my suite, which groaned with exotic flowers, their wild colours jarring with the golden, sun-splattered walls.

'Come! Terrace big!' shouted Mr Yang-Kee. 'See all of Seoul.'

He was right. The view from the terrace was incredible. Seoul, a massive throbbing city of sun-spangled skyscrapers and slate-coloured towers seemed to stretch for miles.

'Later you meet Miss Kim. Your translator.'

'Ah, good.'

'Miss Kim be with you always.'

'Marvellous.'

They were gone. After I'd had a much-needed shower and a change of clothes, there was a knock at the door. Five of my entourage faced me, smiling broadly. They gestured for me to follow. Downstairs I was taken to one of the hotel's plush traditional restaurants where my five companions left me in the hands of a blushing Korean woman who removed my shoes and led me over to a smiling Mr Yang-Kee. I copied my host who sat on a low cushioned bench with his legs slotted into a deep well beneath the restaurant's table. It was a tricky manoeuvre to complete without looking inelegant and I didn't stop to contemplate how I'd get out again. A young woman bowed to me.

'I am Miss Kim.'

My lifetime companion had arrived.

'And now we have Korean banquet and Korean traditional dancing.'

I smiled, wondering when sleep might pop up on the menu. The courses came one after another. I hardly recognised a morsel but everything tasted spicy and delicious. I brought great joy to my fellow diners when I declared my love of kimchi, the pickled vegetable dish which I had sampled on my flight and which I would soon discover was served as a *banchan*, a side dish, with just about every course. I had a feeling it was going to be cropping up a good deal on the trip. An hour of dainty Korean dance followed. Just when I thought I might be able to retire to my room, I was informed that we were off on a group outing to Seoul city. It was getting dark as we walked the streets, exploring markets, malls, examining the tiny stalls brightly lit by paper lanterns and selling bananas, trinkets and things I couldn't even guess at. The streets were thick with humanity and the air was rent with the heavy perfume of garlic and sweat. We returned to the hotel around midnight when Mr Ji, a colleague of Mr Yang-Kee, arrived and suggested that together with Miss Kim, we watch some Korean soap operas on TV. I explained that my linguistic skills might not quite be up to that but he insisted so I sat in a comatose state in a hotel lounge watching Korean ladies in exquisite hairdos and thick make-up weeping on screen while Miss Kim sat entranced, and at times practically wept with them. Then Mr Ji had a bright idea. He thought it might be just the hour to set off to visit 63 City, Korea's tallest tower and the tallest building in Asia. We jumped into a taxi and set off towards Yeouida Island to view the landmark tower. Rain suddenly began tumbling from the dark sky and the taxi driver began shaking his head. An animated discussion ensued between the men.

Miss Kim calmly turned to me.

'The driver does not think it good idea to visit tower tonight because it is closed.'

'Perhaps we'd better return to the hotel?' I suggested.

She shook her head. 'Mr Ji and Mr Yang-Kee think he is wrong.'

The rain was now falling in heavy white sheets and I could hardly catch sight of anything beyond the window. We travelled a little further and then the car stopped abruptly. Mr Ji opened the passenger door and I climbed out and was instantly soaked to the skin.

'Here is tower!' he shouted above the rain.

I looked up and saw a silvery skyscraper bearing down on me.

'Here is Han River!' yelled Mr Yang-Kee, pointing at the darkness beyond.

We splashed over to the front of the building. Mr Ji tapped his head hard with his right palm. It made a dull sound rather like a boiled egg being tapped with a spoon.

'Tower closed,' he said.

We ran back to the car, our clothes dripping tears on to the glazed pavements.

In the car the two men were silent. Miss Kim fixed her gaze on the windscreen and I sat dozing in the back dreaming of pillows, duvets and crisp white sheets. At the hotel the two men bowed solemnly and disappeared into the wet night. It was three o'clock. Finally, I could take to my bed.

★ ★ ★

Mr Ji, Mr Yang-Kee, Miss Kim and I were standing in the midst of an excited group of people at the Hilton Hotel. I was here to present ten certificates to a host of Korean world record-breakers, mostly in the sports category. Before I had left the office back in Enfield, Stewart the sports editor had carefully sifted through the applications and witness statements, only agreeing to award certificates to those who had met our rigorous standards. Mr Kim Ock-jin, president of the Olympic Sports Foundation, came over and gave me a warm welcome, explaining that we would be lining up on a stage for the press photos. He would be receiving a certificate on behalf of Seoul for having hosted the Olympic Games with the most participants, 9,302 in total, and for having the involvement of 160 nations. When everyone had gathered I was to hand over the ten individual certificates and he and I would make formal speeches for the Korean TV networks. The manager of the Hilton bustled over and shook my hand. He would be receiving a certificate for the world's largest lantern which measured 3.7 metres high and stood proudly in the hotel's ballroom. We gathered on the stage and as I handed out each certificate, there was wild applause, cameras flashed and the TV homed in on our faces. Kim Ock-jin made a heartfelt speech in Korean throughout which I smiled uncomprehendingly and then it was my turn. As I spoke, Miss Kim stood at my side, translating directly to the assembled throng. The clapping continued for some minutes as we all took our bows. As I was ushered off the stage Miss Kim gently touched my arm.

'Now we pick up bags from hotel and go immediately to KBS TV office for interview and then to *Korea Herald*, *Daily Sport* and *Korea Times*.'

'OK.'

'Then we go *Joon Ang Ilbo*, *Han-Gook Ilbo* and *Han-Kyoreh Shinbum*.'

'Are these places?'

Miss Kim burst into hysterical giggles which she quickly tried to stifle. 'No, newspapers.'

'We're doing interviews with all of them?'

'Yes, then we take plane to Pusan for world record oddity contest.'

Five hours later Seoul's domestic airport appeared as a tiny dot from my aeroplane window as we headed into the sky for Pusan on the southernmost tip of Korea. On arrival at the airport the floral garlands were in abundance once more and there were more in store in my sea-facing room at the Westin Chosun Beach Hotel. At this rate I could give serious thought to opening my very own flower shop. I looked out of the wide bay and at a blazing sun. So this was Pusan, Korea's second-biggest city and the best place for fish, according to Miss Kim. If I'd had any illusions about lying out on the beach I was wrong. After a quick turn around we found ourselves in the lobby facing a barrage of TV cameras.

'Please, tell our viewers what you like about Pusan,' commanded one interviewer.

I fixed him with a beam. 'Well, of course I have only just arrived but I've heard about the marvellous fish, and the Jagalchi market and the Buddhist temples.'

He nodded enthusiastically and appeared to be translating directly to camera. Another man dived at me with a microphone. 'You meet Mrs Thatcher?'

I smiled. 'Yes, I have indeed.'

'She like Korea too?'

'Oh, I think it holds a special place in her heart.'

A few people clapped. Mr Ji hustled me out through the glass doors.

'Now we judge records on beach. See banners?'

Miss Kim clapped excitedly. 'See banners, yes?'

I squinted at the sun. Banners ran as far as eye could see along the beach.

'What are the banners advertising?' I asked Miss Kim.

'They say "Welcome to Pusan, Miss Anna Nicholas, Guinness representative".'

I gulped. Oh God. Norris and the editorial team would never, ever let me live this one down. I could envisage Shelley and Stewart hugging their stomachs at their desks. Down on the beach a stage had been erected and for the rest of the afternoon I watched a series of weird record attempts. Some would make it into the book, others would be relegated to the bin or nutter file. There was a car-cramming attempt in which 25 Koreans squeezed into a Mini. I feared for their lives in that stifling heat but they grinned cheerfully, their smiles smeared against the window panes of the car as the doors slammed shut, sealing them in their stifling tomb. Then there were endless push-up attempts, a man gobbling down a pile of octopus tentacles, a woman juggling coloured balls, a child coin snatching and a man pulling a fishing boat in from the shore with his forearms. The sun beat down and the would-be record-holders kept on coming. At the end of a long day I explained to Mr Yang-Kee that only three of those endeavours might make it to the book.

'No problem,' he smiled. 'Three more days here in big arena. We see hundreds more record-breakers.'

I asked Miss Kim to explain.

'We have many more record attempts over three days in a special arena here. Then we have weekend off and then we visit Mr Song. His son is called Super Boy and he can pull car with his teeth.'

I frowned. 'How old is Mr Song's son?'

'His name is Song Min-Ho and he is seven.'

'What? But Miss Kim, I cannot let a boy of seven pull a car with his teeth or any other part of his anatomy. It's just too dangerous.'

'He been doing this for years. Don't worry!' said Miss Kim.

I thought hard. Perhaps I should call Donald or Norris. I didn't want headlines appearing in the British press that we were condoning records that exploited children. What to do?

★ ★ ★

That night we visited a fish restaurant on the beach at which the most extraordinary dishes were on display. Open-minded and keen not to offend my hosts, I decided to try a little of everything. It was all going well until the abalone made an appearance.

'Try one,' smiled Miss Kim.

'Sorry, but that looks awfully like a big slug.'

She grinned. 'Yes, marine gastropod. Is nice and crunchy.'

I declined diplomatically saying that I'd just have a little more kimchi instead. This made the table of 20 or more guests roar with laughter. Next came a plate of something luminous orange and distinctly shiny and wobbly.

'This is sea squirt,' said Miss Kim. 'Different taste.'

Hmm. She passed a plate to me. Once again I politely declined, hoping that something a tad more conventional such as rice might be on offer next. It wasn't to be.

Miss Kim was thrusting another dish under my nose. 'This is very special. It's *gaebul*. Pink sea worms.'

'Wow, it looks as if they're still moving.'

She giggled. 'Of course, they moving. Still alive.'

I looked at her in horror.

More eruptions of laughter around the table as she translated my comments. Mr Ji laughed so much he had to stand up and blow his nose.

'After dinner some people are going to dog fight. You go?'

'Maybe I'll give that a miss.'

'You don't eat dog at home.'

I shook my head. 'No, not a lot, Miss Kim.'

As I headed back to the hotel, I watched as many in our group strolled off in the direction of a large open-air building. Later, I stood on my terrace basking in the subtropical heat and breathing in the fragrance of the sea. Tiny lights flickered around the bay and the distant mountains stood dark and erect against a grey marbled sky. It was then that I heard the distant yet distinctive sound of dogs barking but in an instant it faded away, perhaps carried off on the breeze. I retired to bed. Tomorrow was going to be a long day.

★ ★ ★

It was Monday morning. I had endured three further days of the Festival of Record Breaking Oddity in Pusan. There were many losers but also some clear winners such as Park Bong-ta, a 65-year-old park keeper who skipped non-stop for an hour at lightning speed and Kim Young-gi, who, at 50, managed two records: chin-ups with two fingers of each hand and then with one. A young Korean named Choi Ju-yong kept his head while bouncing a ball on it for five hours and Min Ji-Hung made a spectacular assault on the non-stop somersault record. A phenomenon that I had never witnessed before was the ritual of collectively reading out the Guinness rules and regulations before record attempts were made. Koreans believed in honour and fair play and wanted me to understand that they intended to abide by the letter of the Guinness law. On Sunday evening I had been invited to the home of one of the record-breakers, a fisherman who, to my amazement and humour proudly showed me a small shrine he kept to Norris in his bedroom. Two small candles glowed on either side of a large photocopied image of Norris. He explained to me that 'Mr Norris' was his inspiration and although he might not be as important as Buddha, he came a pretty close second.

After a restful weekend in which I visited the North Korean border, and just about every Buddhist temple, every museum and market in the Yeongnam region, I arrived at a strip of wasteland in Pusan where Song Min-Ho – or Super Boy – would try his teeth at car-pulling along a quiet disused road. A shy and polite child built like a sparrow, little Song Min-Ho bowed low and proceeded to meditate on a mat for some minutes. His father, Mr Song, approached me with a cheerful smile.

'My son has been training since he was three. Please don't worry. He pulls cars all the time.'

In some state of preoccupation I watched as two Cadillacs were towed within a few feet of me. The cars were chained together and at the front of the first a heavy rope had been attached to the grill. Without fuss, Song Min-Ho waited for the world media to get comfortable, rose from his mat and then, taking the looped end of the rope between his teeth, began to move slowly backwards, with the two cars facing him, along the road. I bit my lip. Would the cars run him over? Would his teeth fall out? What was I doing here?

Miraculously before my eyes, the two cars began to move, at first slowly and then at an enhanced speed. Super Boy continued to walk backwards at a measured pace and at an angle, his eyes glued to the vehicles gliding seemingly effortlessly towards him. Television cameras trailed him as he continued, step by step, and inch by inch, along the road. After about ten metres he stopped, took the rope from his mouth and gave a low bow. His father who had been shouting out a strange mantra throughout the attempt came over and hugged him. I walked up to Song Min-Ho and congratulated him, careful not to raise his hopes of gaining a place in the book. This was the sort of attempt we didn't want ambitious parents pushing their children towards in the future and there was no way that Donald would permit such a record to enter the new edition. Mr Ji called to me. 'Now we watch Mr Jung Sung-guk.'

'Who?' I asked.

'He pull cars with his ears.'

How could I resist? Mr Jung Sung-guk was 75 years old. Wrapping a rope around the fender on the Cadillacs he made two loops, attaching one around each of his ears. He then pushed back with his arms held wide until both cars began to move slowly forward. Like Super Boy he managed several metres. The crowds clapped and whooped. Mr Yang-Kee was full of smiles.

'Now we return to Seoul.'

'What, right now?'

Miss Kim nodded. 'Yes, we have meeting at Seoul headquarters and we have been invited to visit roof of very tall tower tonight. You lucky. Then you go home tomorrow.'

Whisked into a car we arrived back at the hotel, grabbed our luggage and caught the plane for Seoul with only minutes to spare.

'You do live by the seat of your pants,' I said to Miss Kim as we took off.

She looked horrified. 'What you say to me?'

I quickly explained what the expression meant and she looked visibly relieved. She blushed. 'I thought you say rude thing.'

'We have lots of strange sayings I'm afraid but you speak very good English. Did you learn at school?'

She smiled bashfully. 'I used to work from six o'clock in the morning before school and then until eleven o'clock at night. I went to university and worked hard.'

'Do you have a boyfriend?'

More hysterical giggles. 'Oh no. I never talked with boys. Only I have met men at work and of course, my father.'

'Don't you get lonely sometimes?'

She shrugged. 'Not really. I live with my parents and work all week so no time for fun. I like working hard.'

I thought back to my fun-filled days at university and felt a frisson of guilt.

'Maybe we can be pen friends?' she suggested.

'That's a great idea,' I replied.

After all, Mr Yang-Kee had said that Miss Kim would be with me always.

★ ★ ★

It was a wet and windy night in Seoul. Arriving back in town from Pusan, I had spent the late afternoon at the Guinness Korea office and then scooted over to the Foreign Correspondents Club to meet a stringer from the *Daily Telegraph* who was keen to file some copy about Song Min-Ho. He fully understood my apprehension about condoning dangerous records but admitted to being enthralled by the seven-year-old's attempt. He told me that he would be filing a piece for the *Telegraph* but promised to be non-committal about the chances of the record entering the book.

Later that night Mr Yang-Kee, Mr Ji and I found ourselves in the foyer of one of Seoul's tallest buildings waiting for a lift to take us up on to the roof. The chairman of the building was a friend of Mr Ji's and had invited us all to experience views of Seoul by night. The building had 55 floors but we would be travelling beyond the top floor to the roof itself in a private lift, accessed only with a special key. An entourage of ten or more polite and besuited men stood with us in the foyer awaiting the arrival of the lift. I still hadn't worked out the identity of this ever-present group, but they appeared and disappeared seemingly at will. The lift arrived and with great ceremony a porter turned a key and beckoned us inside. The chairman and various directors working at the building came too, so we were a snug group of about twenty. After a few minutes the lift doors opened directly on to a wide and exposed rooftop. Seoul sparkled before us. I stepped out and in some excitement went over to the railings and peered down. My heart missed a beat. We were very, very high up. Seeing Seoul from the top of the world was quite remarkable, the views so immediate and the glittering skyscrapers so close I felt I could reach out and grasp them. We wandered around, the chairman proudly pointing out distant landmarks and buildings to me until with a shiver he declared it was getting late and we should descend to the bar. We approached the lift door and then suddenly all hell broke loose. People began shouting, the chairman cursed and absolutely no one thought to tell me what was going on. Mr Ji clasped his fists into balls and strutted around the roof moaning. Finally I caught up with him.

'What's wrong, Mr Ji?'

'No lift,' he whimpered.

'What do you mean?'

'Man with key forget we up here.'

After some minutes of shouting, cursing and general histrionics, the men around me calmed down. It was getting very cold and standing on an exposed roof in the dead of night in a linen dress wasn't ideal but somehow I tried to see the positives. Unfortunately I gave that up because there weren't any. How long might we be up here? In twenty years might they excavate us?

An hour later as we sat huddled in small groups around the railings there was a sudden bang and the doors of the lift opened to reveal the porter with the key. He was snivelling and his legs were visibly shaking. I actually felt sorry for the guy. After a cold exchange with the chairman, he pressed a button while we all clambered in silently and soon the lift had descended to the ground floor. I had never been so happy to see a marble foyer.

'You want to drink ginseng?' asked Mr Ji.

'I'm a little ginseng-ed out. A double brandy holds more appeal.'

He looked blank. I marched into the bar and called over the barman. The ginseng would have to wait.

★ ★ ★

Miss Kim had heard about our ordeal on the roof the night before and hid her face in her hands.

'Terrible. I am real sorry. You must be so angry.'

I explained that I had been hungry rather than angry. We were standing in a large department store with Mr Ji and Mr Yang-Kee, both of whom were chewing furiously on salted raw fish. This seemed to be a habit, along with knocking back copious amounts of fizzy ginseng from cans wherever we were.

'What are we doing here exactly?' I asked Miss Kim. 'I have to catch my plane soon.'

'You have special surprise present for taking home.'

We were surrounded by traditional Korean wedding outfits and it was only moments later that three shop assistants ushered me into a large cubicle, undressed me and began wrapping fabric and silks about my body. Miss Kim giggled outside, occasionally telling me to be patient. An hour later I left the shop with a fuchsia and pea green traditional wedding outfit known as a *hanbok*. It included a *jeogori*, a decorated silk jacket, sash, long skirt and an exotic headdress. The white cotton socks and boat-like, decorated slippers were also included.

At the airport I had an emotional farewell with Mr Yang-Kee, Mr Ji and Miss Kim. They helped me with my luggage and after checking in, handed me a crate of ginseng cans and one more surprise.

'This is for Mr Norris. Very special gift.'

It was an enormous box.

'Very fragile,' warned Miss Kim. 'Ginseng floating in juice in glass container.'

Oh no. How was I going to carry this on to the plane together with my *hanbok* in its huge box, my crate of ginseng cans and my hand luggage? An official from Korean Airlines zoomed up to me and offered to help me on to the plane. I readily accepted the offer.

Many hours later I touched down at Gatwick. The cabin crew had been delighted to see that I was carrying a box with a *hanbok* inside and so treated me royally on the flight, even calling ahead to find an official to help me off the plane with my booty. All was going well until I pushed my overloaded trolley through the Customs area. A stern grey-haired official in uniform approached me.

'Hello Madam, so what have we got here? Anything interesting?'

'Not really,' I groaned. 'Just a giant ginseng root floating in fluid, a *hanbok* and a small crate of…'

He gave a snort of disbelief and shook his head. 'I'm sorry madam. Could you come this way?'

FIFTEEN

★ ★ ★

GOLDEN OLDIES

Norris and I jumped out of a cab in St James's and made our way to the offices of the Welsh Tourist Board where John Evans, the UK's oldest living man, would today be honoured on the occasion of his hundred and tenth birthday. The former miner from Swansea had only a few years before been fitted with a pacemaker and to the bafflement of the medical staff had left the hospital with no ill effects just three days later. This was his first ever trip to London and it had been orchestrated by the Welsh Tourist Board in conjunction with the National Coal Board, for whom he had worked from the age of thirteen until the age of seventy-three. The large function room was besieged with reporters and television camera crews from all over the world and it took some time for us to squeeze our way through the animated scrum. In the corner, John Evans, surrounded by his family and close friends, was sitting perkily in a chair with a grin on his face, evidently hugely titillated that his presence had created such a media circus.

The chairman of the National Coal Board lumbered up on to a rostrum and called for attention. A hush descended on the room as he spoke into the microphone, welcoming John Evans to London, and giving a well-rehearsed and humorous eulogy about the veteran's former days working as a miner in Swansea. As the cameras homed in, he invited the elderly man to accept a carriage clock on behalf of the Coal Board. With his cloud of wispy white hair and strong, animated features, the old man took the item with a quivering hand and, after inspecting it carefully, offered the chairman his thanks. Then with a twinkle in his eye, added with a chuckle, 'To think I worked for them for sixty years and all they gave me was this old clock!' To huge applause and laughter he returned to his seat, leaving the Coal Board's slightly embarrassed chairman to say the final word. Norris giggled. 'Poor chap seems a bit ruffled. I bet he wasn't expecting such a razor sharp riposte from someone of his years.'

We made our way over to the centenarian, introduced ourselves to the family and those guarding him from the barrage of press and approached John. His face creased with humour when Norris shook his hand. 'Well, well,' he said with his Welsh lilt. 'I had to wait until a hundred and ten to make it into the famous *Guinness Book of Records*, but it was worth it.'

The press seized upon the moment and soon Norris was surrounded as he presented a Guinness certificate and specially engraved medal in the Welsh language. Norris asked John Evans if he could see the clock he'd been given.

The elderly man passed it to him and gave a snort of laughter. 'And what use is that to me now? I stopped clock watching years ago.'

We left the jam-packed room and headed off for the station and back to Enfield. Norris looked out of the window at the blue sky while I scribbled notes.

'Not a bad morning. John Evans was a wonderful old chap.'

I smiled. 'And he was so mischievous and full of wit.'

'That's the trick of ageing gracefully,' he replied with a smile. 'Never losing one's sense of humour.'

Then he added dryly. 'Of course working with you I have no choice. It's the only way to survive!'

★ ★ ★

I was sitting at my desk when Shelley came over to me. 'When are you off to see my oldie record-breakers?'

I was always amused at the way the deputy editors treated the record-holders within their sections as treasured personal property. Shelley looked after the arts, entertainments and business chapters and was meticulous about keeping her records current.

'Well, we're off to visit rather a lot of older record-breakers over the next few days, a sort of oldies road show, but I presume you're talking about Reverend Canon Cook and his missus in Norwich? We're meeting them tomorrow afternoon.'

She nodded. 'It's just that Mr Cook rang me today and said that you and Norris were in for a surprise.'

'A surprise?' I said suspiciously.

She frowned. 'Thought I'd better mention it.'

An hour later I picked up my briefcase and headed for the door. I was puzzled. Norris and I would be spending a day in Norwich visiting the book's printer and one of our key book wholesalers, then finally paying a brief visit to the record-breaking Reverend Cook and his wife Helen, who during World War Two had written one another the most love letters ever recorded. There had never been any talk of surprises. What on earth could they have in mind?

★ ★ ★

Soon we were in the car and off to St Mary's Church in Diss, to meet the Reverend Cook and his wife, Helen.

'Now then,' I said. 'We're aiming for the six o'clock train back to London so we mustn't hang about.'

Norris looked at his watch. 'Oh, we've plenty of time.'

The driver parked outside the church.

'Seem to be a lot of people about,' he remarked.

He was right. There were a lot of people milling around somewhat expectantly. They smiled when they saw us approaching the church doors. I suddenly thought back to the surprise that Shelley had warned me about. The Reverend Canon Cook, for it was he, rushed from the side of the building to greet us. His wife followed behind.

'How wonderful to see you both! The press has arrived and as a special surprise we have organised for the whole parish to join in the fun!' said the Reverend Cook.

'We've prepared a special tea party at the vicarage in your honour.'

Having just enjoyed a rather strapping lunch with one of our book distributors, Norris and I stole a furtive concerned glance at one another.

'Really, you shouldn't have gone to so much trouble,' said Norris.

'Not at all,' said Helen, with a kindly smile.

Minutes later the local press was taking happy snaps of Norris as he handed over a certificate to them both. A local news reporter came up close with a microphone just as Norris addressed the throng.

'This is to certify that the Reverend Cook and his wife, Helen, sent each other no fewer than six thousand love letters during World War Two. This extraordinary record is a positive statement of faith and hope amidst the doom and gloom. In fact, they have told me that to this day they still own and use the original fountain pens from those war-torn days.'

With aplomb he signed a copy of the latest edition of the book, writing in neat black ink: 'With best wishes and admiration, Norris McWhirter.'

We were carried along on a joyous wave of guests and into the vicar's home. Our eyes widened when we saw the sumptuous fare before us. Helen and the ladies of the parish had evidently been toiling away to produce such a veritable feast. There were cream cakes, flans, scones and biscuits, trifles and chocolate treats. I sneaked a look at my watch and sighed, knowing that we were going nowhere soon.

★ ★ ★

It wasn't until after six o'clock that we finally waddled back to the car, our stomachs aching. We had missed our train and were resigned to a very long wait on Norwich station. The driver waved us off and in some exhaustion we flopped on to a bench in the gloomy entrance hall. There seemed to be very few people waiting for trains. Then seemingly from nowhere a strange hunched figure loped over in our direction. He sported long black tresses and wore a bright red anorak, yellow shorts and Doc Martens and grinned manically. The apparel alone would have made him look not out of place on a Gary Larson Far Side card.

'All we need,' I muttered to Norris. 'A nutter. And we've got to wait another hour or more.'

Norris looked up as the character loomed over us.

'You're Norris McWhirter,' he chortled happily.

'Yes,' said Norris pleasantly. 'I am.'

'Are you waiting for the London train?' he asked, his big round face quivering with excitement.

'We are,' Norris replied.

'I'm not,' he giggled. 'I just like stations.'

'Good for you,' said Norris.

'You've got ages to wait for your train but you won't get bored,' he screeched theatrically. 'I'm your number one fan and now I can ask you all about my favourite records until you leave.'

He jumped up and down like an excited baboon and then plonked himself next to Norris. I put my head on my knees and groaned.

'Marvellous,' said Norris with infinite patience, digging me in the ribs. 'Now tell me – what would you like to know?'

★ ★ ★

Given that there were so many memorable older record-breakers in the book, Norris and I had liked the idea of holding an oldies road show, visiting senior citizens the length and breadth of the country and celebrating their achievements in later life. At the same time we had teamed up with my previous employer, Help the Aged, to create an educational pack for schools which highlighted achievements by older individuals and featured various record-holders.

Aside from the likes of the Reverend Cook and his wife, another record-breaking Mr Cook had caught our imagination. His full name was Arthur Merrick Cook, the world's oldest motorcyclist at the age of 93. In fact, Arthur was to be one of the stars of the Help the Aged campaign and our visit was partly to promote the fact.

It was a sunny day when we arrived at his home in a quiet leafy suburb of Exeter. As soon as we rolled up in a taxi from Exeter station, he rushed out to greet us on the porch of his neat semi. I imagined he'd been anticipating our arrival for some time. He was a diminutive figure, neatly dressed in a tweed suit and white shirt with dark blue tie. His snowy head was almost bereft of hair and his kindly, watery blue eyes twinkled behind gold metal-framed spectacles. He and I had spoken some weeks earlier by telephone and he had confided that he was a widower and a regular churchgoer who lived alone but managed very ably to cook and look after himself with frequent visits from his daughter and fellow members of his local congregation. His pride and joy, a Suzuki 125, rested on gravel in his front garden and he lost no time in showing her to us.

'You know I rode my first bike in 1919,' he told Norris. 'I can't remember what it was but I once had an old Vesper. But my little Suzuki is a joy to handle and I take her everywhere.'

'She's a beauty,' said Norris. 'I can tell you look after her.'

He nodded. 'Indeed I do.'

'Don't you worry about the traffic?' I asked.

He patted my arm and with a pronounced Devonshire burr explained that he never faltered when he was on the road. 'Thank the Lord, I've never had an accident in my life. Do you ride a motorbike, young lady?'

'Heavens, no!' I tittered. 'A university friend took me for a spin recently but that's all.'

He beamed. 'Well then, let me take you for a quick ride around the block and you can see what I'm made of.'

Norris seemed to enjoy the idea. 'Oh, AN, what an excellent suggestion. She's a bit of a speed hog, so I'm sure she'd enjoy it.'

'But the local press will be arriving any minute,' I protested.

Norris wafted a hand through the air. 'They can wait. Besides, you won't be going far.'

It was settled. Reluctantly, I pulled on the heavy men's helmet that Arthur proffered, noticing Norris's amusement when it slid down on to my forehead, almost completely obscuring my vision. Arthur revved up the bike and I straddled it rather clumsily behind him and the next minute we were off, out of his short drive and roaring up the road. It was late morning in September and to my relief few cars were about. I gripped the elderly man's jacket as we turned a corner and closed my eyes as a cold breeze flooded my face and chilled my nose. In next to no time we were travelling back to the house at what seemed like great speed but Arthur was steady and fearless and appeared totally in control of the throbbing machine. To my embarrassment I noticed as we drew nearer that Norris was now accompanied by a group of photographers who began snapping madly as we tore up to the gate.

Dizzily, I alighted the bike and pulling off the helmet, attempted to tidy my hair. Norris came forward.

'That looked like fun! I knew you were a biker at heart.'

Arthur put his arm round my shoulder. 'You see, there's life in the old dog yet.'

'That's true,' I said, giving Norris one of my warning glances.

After several shots were taken of Arthur and Norris astride the bike, Norris handed over a certificate and a new edition of the book. The local TV station had sent along a reporter, as had one of the radio stations, and so it was a good half an hour before the interviews were over and Arthur, Norris and I were able to adjourn to his living room for tea. Arthur showed us the many framed photos of his wife and family and images of him on his wedding day, and as a younger man smiling astride one of his many bikes.

When we got up to leave, he shook Norris's hand enthusiastically. 'I'm enjoying being the centre of attention in my old age and it's a privilege to take part in the Help the Aged campaign.'

'Good for you. It's an honour for us to have you involved,' replied Norris.

Arthur and I hugged. 'Come back and see me for a spin some time, won't you?'

I nodded. 'I'll hold you to that.'

Our taxi had arrived, the engine humming softly as we approached. I waved as I jumped into the back seat. Arthur stood on the pavement, a sweet smile on his face.

'God speed, my friends, God speed.'

It was a late September afternoon when we finally arrived in Marske. We had enjoyed a whirlwind tour of golden oldies across the country and were now at our last port of call. The previous day we had caught up with Harry Corbett, whose Sooty puppet show had run on the BBC from 1952 until 1967, making it one of the most durable UK television programmes. We had told Harry that we were on our way to Blackpool to meet Norman Johnson, the world's fastest cucumber slicer, and he suggested we pop by one of the famed fish and chip restaurants in the area founded by his uncle Harry Ramsden. In fact, Harry Corbett's uncle had his own entry in the book for owning the largest fish and chip shop in the world. So after a delicious Harry Ramsden's lunch in Blackpool, we had spent the afternoon with Norman Johnson who in his seventies could cut 244 slices from a 12-inch cucumber in only 13.4 seconds.

Earlier today we had met with Mrs Gerty Land in Colne, Lancashire, who at the age of 90 (and 229 days) was the oldest person to have re-taken and passed her driving test and, having driven for 70 years, still pootled around her hometown in her Morris 1000. Now we would be meeting Mrs Charlotte Hughes; at the age of 110, her claim to fame was being the oldest woman to have travelled on a Concorde plane.

Norris threw me a glance. 'Are you daydreaming or map reading?'

'Neither. I was just wondering what flying on Concorde would be like.'

'Noisy and fairly cramped,' replied Norris. 'Have you ever spoken to Fred Finn? He's made six hundred and four flights on Concorde.'

'Funnily enough he rang me last week checking that he'd be in the next edition.'

I sat up straight and held the map in front of me. 'Look lively. We're only a few roads away.'

'Thanks for letting me know. Where next?'

'We need to take the second left and there should be a track to the right which leads up to Mrs Hughes' cottage.'

Norris yawned. 'You contacted a few local press?'

'Just a few,' I replied.

We turned left and a few minutes later, discovered a narrow lane to the right. Following the bumpy stone track we soon came to rest in a grassy area which was already occupied by three cars. Norris parked and sat back in his seat. 'I imagine these vehicles will belong to local reporters, AN.'

'Probably,' I said, grappling with my bag in the half-light. I opened the passenger door and looked beyond to a gravelly slope which I presumed led to the house. I took a few steps forward and was immediately aware of a huge swell of people up ahead and a mountain of parked cars. I could see television cameras positioned and a barrage of photographers pacing about outside the cottage. All eyes seemed to be fixed on our arrival. I popped my head round the car door.

'A slight situation up ahead, No.'

'What do you mean?'

'Well, it appears that we have rather a lot of media attending.'

He raised his eyes. 'The only possible reason they're here is because you invited them, AN.'

'Maybe I occasionally forget how popular you really are,' I said. 'After all, they do build shrines to you in South Korea.'

'Oh let's not mention that nonsense again,' he snorted. 'Now where is the framed certificate?'

I fumbled in the back of the car, found the bubble-wrapped package, undid the ties and drew out the frame. To my horror I found the glass had cracked.

'Oh bugger, the glass has shattered.'

Norris looked on calmly. 'What do you suggest?'

'I'll just have to remove the shards of glass and you can present it as it is. We can always post another to her later.'

Just at that moment there was the sound of feet on gravel and several photographers began descending the slope towards us.

'Keep them busy while I dismantle the frame, No,' I hissed from the back seat of the car.

He jumped out and welcomed the gathered throng while I grappled with the broken glass in the back. Norris stepped back at one point during the delicate operation and murmured, 'Take your time, there are only about a hundred press waiting here.'

Finally I grabbed the damaged certificate and extricated myself from the car. Together we strolled up to the small cottage, almost submerged by the avalanche of reporters.

'How in heaven's name can we all fit in there?' he whispered to me.

'What about staging a record attempt to see how many press we can squeeze into one tiny cottage?'

'I despair of you sometimes,' he sighed.

Norris dipped his head through the small doorway and I followed, as did several TV crews. We were welcomed by Charlotte Hughes's local MP who made introductions to the elderly lady sitting, somewhat dazed, in her armchair. Seeing that various television reporters were trying to cram into the tiny sitting room behind us, Norris was struck with a brainwave.

'Look everyone, I think Mrs Hughes won't be able to cope with such a scrum of people asking questions. Why don't I just present the certificate and have a few words with her which you can all record?'

The press readily agreed and positioned their cameras and sound equipment accordingly. When all parties were ready, Norris passed the glass-free frame to Charlotte and congratulated her on her transatlantic crossing. She was evidently very deaf so he had to repeat his words several times. He paused for a moment and, placing the microphone close to her, asked, 'Mrs Hughes, you were a teacher for many years. Do you still see any of your former pupils?'

She digested his words carefully and then with a disappointed shrug, replied, 'Oh no dear, they're all dead!'

The room erupted with laughter and Norris gained an exclusive sound bite that was to ricochet around the world, used by every major news outlet from London to New York. I turned to Norris back at the car.

'That question you asked was a stroke of genius,' I said. 'Did you cook it up beforehand?'

The corners of Norris's mouth twitched as we drove away. 'You might think that, AN, but I couldn't possibly comment.'

SIXTEEN

★ ★ ★

ALL ABOARD – TRAINS, BUSES AND FIRE ENGINES

It was early October and Lisa and I were already busy organising the press launch for the new edition of *The Guinness Book of Records* which was only weeks away. This time it would be a bigger and more complicated extravaganza involving a host of celebrities and record-breakers. In addition we would also be auctioning the 60 millionth copy of the book by private bid and there was still a great deal to organise. Norris had bought in to my bizarre idea of him dressing up as a bus conductor, and travelling around central London on a red double-decker bus, picking up various record-breakers en route. The double-decker, known as the World Bus, would hopefully become a record-breaker itself as it was soon to travel to 22 countries covering 40,000 miles in an effort to raise money for two charities, Save the Children and Intermediate Technology. The bus journey was the brainchild of three friends – Hughie Thompson, Richard Steele and John Weston – who would be joining us at the launch. So far we had secured the celebrity support of Bananarama, the UK's most successful all-girl group, Roy Castle and Cheryl Baker of *Record Breakers*, several MPs, Nipper (the HMV dog), an unstoppable juggler and the world's longest soft toy, a fairly hideous caterpillar.

Lisa tapped her desk. 'Didn't David ask you to pop upstairs some time ago?'

'So he did. I'll go now.'

She rolled her eyes. 'You're hopeless.'

'So everyone keeps reminding me.'

I grabbed my launch file and bounded through the department and up the back stairs to his office. The door was wide open.

'Come in, come in. I was expecting you,' beamed David, his pristine dark suit displaying not the slightest crease. I took a seat and pulled open my file.

'Oh, you can put that away,' he said breezily. 'I'm sure the insanity of your launch will live up to our expectations. I wanted to see you about something else.'

I viewed him with puzzlement. 'Oh?'

He shuffled some papers on his desk and picked up a letter. 'Our Japan operation is embarking on a curious event. It seems that in order to celebrate its thirtieth anniversary, Fuji television has commissioned a luxury train company, the *Nostalgie Istanbul Orient Express*, to conduct the world's longest train journey from France to Japan. It will apparently start in Paris and pass through Germany, Poland, Russia and China before culminating in Hong Kong whereupon it will be shipped to Japan. The train will cover 18,000 kilometres in total and the gauges of the wheels will have to be changed in several countries to enable the train to reach its goal.'

'How curious.'

He thumped his hand enthusiastically on the table. 'It most certainly is and I would like you to represent us there by welcoming the train and its occupants to Hong Kong.'

'What else do I have to do?'

'Make one of your habitual cheerleader speeches and hand out Guinness certificates to each passenger.'

'When is it?'

'You'd have to leave in two weeks.'

'It sounds like an amazing trip but I'm right in the middle of launch plans for the new edition and I have to sort out the book auction...'

He waved away my preoccupations. 'I'm sure Lisa can keep an eye on things in your absence. It's only a few days after all. Well, almost a week.'

'That's a long time away. I'm just not sure.'

He jumped up from his desk. 'First-class British Airways flights and a five-star hotel.'

I chewed the inside of my lip. Decisions, decisions. Could I possibly have time to flit there and back without jeopardising the launch? More to the point, could I honestly resist first-class flights and the chance to visit another exotic destination?

'OK. I'll do it.'

'Excellent. Perhaps you can check currency and flight arrangements with Ted in accounts?'

'Fine. By the way, who are the passengers on the train?'

'French people, mostly celebrities, VIPs and media.'

I got up to leave.

'Do let Chris know we've spoken about this. Important to keep your boss in the loop.'

I nodded and strolled down the corridor. Ted poked his head out from behind his screen.

'The pauper's back. What are you sniffing after this time?'

'Hong Kong dollars?'

He guffawed. 'I've heard about your little excursion. Don't worry, I'll have everything for you by next week. First class indeed! Don't start getting ideas, my young friend.'

'It is pretty exciting. I only fly business class normally,' I teased.

He clicked his teeth. 'Listen to her! Business class indeed!'

Chris loomed large in front of me. 'Off on a little trip, are we, full of Eastern promise?'

'So it seems.'

I followed him into his office.

'I was just coming to tell you about it, Chris. I've only just found out.'

He yawned. 'David's already asked me about this. I told him I'd be ecstatic if you disappeared to Hong Kong for a while. I might at last get some peace.'

'Charming. Now while I've got you, have you had any word back from your contact at HMV?'

He sat back in his chair with an enigmatic smile. 'What's it worth?'

'Oh come on!'

'OK. My chum at HMV has agreed to let us hold the launch party at the Oxford Street store and he'll even pick up the tab on food and beverages.'

'You're a genius!'

He sighed. 'Finally, you've seen the light. Now it's up to you to sort out the nitty-gritty. HMV's PR guy is called Gennaro.'

Downstairs Lisa was filing a broken nail while talking to some caller. The telephone was tucked under her ear as she chatted away. She stopped her filing and scribbled me a note. Apparently Joe Girard from Michigan was on the phone, the world's best car salesman who back in 1973 had sold a record 1,425 cars which averaged out at 174 per month with six sales per day. I'd tipped him the wink about the charity auction of the 60 millionth book. I took the phone from Lisa.

'Hi Joe, what do you think about the idea of bidding for the book?'

A laid-back American voice filled the earpiece. 'I think it's interesting. Count me in. So what's the score?'

'You just make an offer and if it's the top bid, you get the book.'

'What sort of figure are we talking about here?'

'I can't really guess but I'd say no less than £60,000.'

He exhaled deeply. 'That's quite a sum. I'll think about it.'

Lisa stared at me as I replaced the receiver. 'Are you mad? Where did you get that figure from?'

'Well it's the 60 millionth edition so it seems a fitting amount and it's for a very good cause.'

She shrugged. 'I think you're pitching it too high.'

'Look, Joe's the best salesman so I'm sure he's shrewd enough to judge its worth. Anyway, I'd like him to win it. He's a nice guy.'

Norris appeared from nowhere. 'Any idea where Donald is?'

'He's in Warwick handing over a certificate to Eddie McGowan for the world's longest car tow,' said Lisa. She pounced on the telephone just as it began wailing.

'Ah, so he is,' Norris replied. 'Now AN, are you ready?'

'For what?'

'To leave for the *Jim'll Fix It* show. Had you forgotten?'

'Not at all. I just like to unnerve you from time to time.'

'Very warped,' he muttered. 'Now this young girl who wants to meet me, can we give her anything?'

'How about a signed book?'

Lisa handed me my briefcase. 'Stop gassing you two and get going. The cab should be here by now.'

★ ★ ★

A few hours later Norris was sitting on a sofa opposite Jimmy Savile, famed presenter of BBC television's *Jim'll Fix It* show. At his side was Gemma, a ten-year-old girl who had written to Jimmy Savile requesting a meeting with Norris whom she described as her hero. The aim of the show was to make dreams come true and so Norris had readily agreed to make an appearance.

Jimmy Savile, his smooth platinum hair flopping across his brow, leaned forward in his big chair. 'Now then, now then, tell me, Gemma, is there anything you'd like to ask your hero?'

The little girl flushed with excitement. 'Erm, what's the smallest egg in the world?'

'Let me see,' said Norris. 'I believe it's laid by the Vervain hummingbird.'

She nodded.

'How's about that then?' exclaimed Jimmy, using one of his favoured catchphrases.

'Who's the worst driver?' Gemma persisted.

Norris's face winced and he broke into a smile. 'That has to be poor old Miriam Hargrave from Wakefield who on her thirty-ninth driving test crashed at a set of red lights. She made it on the fortieth attempt but has apparently never got to grips with right hand turns.'

Gemma giggled.

'Presumably you know the answers to these questions, Gemma?' said a smiling Jimmy.

'Yes I do – and Norris has got them right both times.'

Jimmy clapped his hands together. 'Well I never. Magic! Right, now I think Norris has a little something for you.'

Norris handed the little girl a signed copy of *The Guinness Book of Records* and shook her hand. Jim also handed her one of his own badges.

'And now,' said Jimmy. 'We have a little surprise for Norris.'

I watched as Norris's eyebrows twitched. 'Really?'

'You see a little bird told me that you'd always wanted to be a fireman.'

Norris's eyes darted to the studio audience where he endeavoured to pick a face out in the crowd. I lowered myself in my chair.

'Yes, this little bird asked me to arrange for you to spend a day with a real life fire crew and have a chance to travel in a big red fire engine.'

Norris maintained a spectacular composure. 'I'll be talking to that little bird later.'

In truth Norris had grown used to my little pranks, often anticipating them, but this time he genuinely had been caught on the hop. He'd mentioned to me that his childhood wish had been to ride on a fire engine so I tipped the wink to Jimmy Savile and *voila*!

'And now Norris, here's a proper fireman's helmet and a "Jim Fixed it for Me" badge.'

As applause broke out, Norris plonked the yellow helmet on his head, his eyes still searching the audience.

At the end of the recording I hung sheepishly around the studio doors until Norris emerged carrying his battered old leather briefcase and fireman's helmet. He waggled a finger at me.

'Such scheming! You can be sure that retribution will follow.'

'Not even a thank you, when I made your childhood dream come true?' I asked aghast.

'Well I'll tell you something AN, you'll be coming with me on that fire engine whether you like it or not!'

★ ★ ★

The aeroplane banked sharply to the right and a few minutes later we headed north-east, flying unnervingly low over a crowded harbour, a grey smudge of skyscrapers and overcrowded down-at-heel city dwellings. Ahead of us a mob of green hills struggled for prominence in a sea of grey mist. The engine roared and the plane rattled and soon we edged ever closer to the bay. I sat up in my seat, startled by the closeness of the airport to the sea. We seemed to be clattering down the runway directly into the harbour but the plane braked hard and we drew to an elegant halt.

'Victoria Harbour,' said the elderly Chinese passenger next to me. 'Now we are in the heart of Kowloon Bay. This is Kai Tak airport.'

I smiled and nodded. If this wasn't Kai Tak airport in Hong Kong I was in big trouble.

'Terrible. Too many people in Hong Kong,' he continued.

Before long we were off, heading in an eager crowd towards the arrivals area. I collected my luggage and walked into a massive sea of people. The din was unbelievable as porters blew whistles and cabbies and opportunistic vendors yelled out to the new arrivals. I felt a slight nervousness when I viewed the huge mass of humanity before me. How on earth was I going to find my Guinness Japan contact in this scrum? Suddenly I felt someone tugging at my sleeve. A young Japanese man with a wide smile was thrusting a name board in my face.

'You Guinness lady, yes?'

'How did you know?'

He seemed to find that very amusing. 'Ha ha, you don't look like anyone else. White English girl with funny hair.'

'Thanks a lot. And are you Nori?'

He nodded. 'Like great Norris McWhirter. He Norris, I Nori. Very funny.'

It seemed that I was to be guided around Hong Kong by a perennial joker. Nori clapped his hands loudly and a small subservient porter came running over. We squeezed through the heaving mob into a waiting car whereupon the driver screeched out of the parking bay with his hand inextricably linked to the horn. We careered through jam-packed streets in which old coaches painted in rhubarb and custard hue billowed charcoal smoke, cars hooted and swerved, and pedestrians scurried along the pavements like startled bantams. High up and strung from one side of the street to the other were row upon row of gaudy, multicoloured flags sporting Chinese symbols. They hung down forlornly like long-abandoned washing on a line clamouring for our attention.

'Adverts,' said Nori pointing towards them. 'In Chinese writing.'

'Yes, I can see that.'

We zigzagged around slower vehicles, the driver honking furiously and yelling out in high-pitched hysterical tones. It was with some relief that I soon found myself facing a large pink hotel facade.

'Hotel Nikko on Mody Road,' said Nori. 'Very nice and comfortable for you.'

At the reception desk I was greeted with great excitement and hurriedly shown up to my room by a small welcoming committee.

'You are on private Nikko floor with special harbour view,' said the receptionist with enthusiasm. 'Unique room.'

The lift zoomed up like a rocket to the fourteenth floor where another small party was waiting to greet me in a wide sunny lounge. I was tempted with fresh juices, bowls of fruit and sweet cakes while all I really wanted to do was flop on to a bed. Nori, my comedian of a host, was already working on a new joke.

'Hotel Nikko and your name is Nicholas. Is almost the same! Ha Ha.'

Arrangements had apparently been made for dinner that night at a local restaurant followed by an evening tour of Hong Kong City.

'Later we will go on Star Ferry across bay to Hong Kong Island. Then we go on famous tram up to the Peak. From there you see all of Hong Kong.'

'Fantastic, Nori, but first I really would like to clarify arrangements for tomorrow.'

He giggled. 'You worried? At eight in the morning we meet passengers arriving in record-breaking train at Hung Hom station. Then you give press interviews. In the evening we dine at Tai Pak restaurant on Jumbo floating island.'

I frowned. 'So when will I be presenting the Guinness certificates?'

'At Tai Pak. You must make speech too.'

'Can you let me have a list of the VIPs I'll be meeting there?'

'Sure. You ask many questions.'

'I like to double-check everything.'

Nori broke into peals of laughter. 'From now on I call you Miss Double Check. Very funny.'

I pondered whether Nori's insatiable desire to find everything *very funny* might just begin to wear a little thin by my seventh day in Hong Kong.

Nori was still chortling away. 'Tonight you try traditional dim sum. I am Japanese but I love Cantonese food.'

'Excellent. Well I'll see you later.'

'Eight o'clock in reception,' he said.

As he headed for the hotel's immense glass doors I called to him.

'How many people will be attending the floating restaurant event?'

He turned briefly. 'Not many. Maybe four hundred.'

'WHAT?' I shrieked.

His face crumpled with laughter as he pushed the doors open. 'Very funny!' he said and disappeared into the traffic and chaos of downtown Kowloon.

★ ★ ★

It was a cool and grey morning and a whiff of ozone blew from across the bay as I stood out on the street waiting for Nori. Having woken early, I breakfasted on rolls, honey and fruit at the hotel and then took a stroll along the busy Kowloon waterfront watching huge ships docking and observing the frantic activities of local fishermen. Returning to the hotel I waited on the broad and busy Mody Road until a black limo came into view. It stopped abruptly at my side and Nori beckoned me into the back seat. Ten minutes later we arrived at the unprepossessing and modern Hung Hom station, formerly known as Kowloon Station. At eight o'clock the passengers who had all travelled from Paris on the world's longest train journey, would be briefly breaking their trip to spend a night in Hong Kong before continuing their train journey aboard a ship bound for Japan.

We found the right platform in the underground network of brightly lit tunnels and walkways and came face to face with a barrage of press and TV cameras. In a moment I was surrounded. What did I think of the record? Fantastic. Would it be in the next book? Yes. Would I be welcoming the guests? Er, yes, that's why I was here, and on and on it went.

At precisely 8.05 a.m. the blue and silver sleek train slowly drew into the station. The words *Nostalgie Istanbul Orient Express* ran in stylish gold lettering across the exteriors of the eleven pristine and shiny carriages. A number of heads were poking through open windows waving excitedly as the train came into view. The ladies who had travelled all the way from Paris were the first to alight. They were dressed in chic, knee-length suits and tailored dark jackets and blazers and many had opted to wear pearls and silk scarves, a recent craze for the better dressed and the Sloane Ranger brigade.

As each person descended I shook his or her hand and we smiled for the cameras. Few of the passengers spoke English but I managed to make polite conversation with my gauche French and rusty German. I deduced from one of the guests that many of them had parted with a good deal of money to join the train while others were famous French actors or politicians and had been given complimentary tickets. By nine o'clock the media had taken all the photos they needed, and the television crews had departed. We accompanied the guests up the stairs to the main concourse of the station and waved goodbye as they set off in a private luxury bus to their hotel. Nori and I stood waving as they departed.

'Well that went off OK,' I said with a sigh.

He nodded enthusiastically. 'Yes, all good Miss Double Check. Well done. Now you can take it easy. Best to conserve energy for tonight.'

'Oh, I'm sure it's not that big a deal.'

He laughed manically. 'You be surprised. You be surprised.'

★ ★ ★

At seven in the evening, Nori and I caught the complimentary shuttle boat from the waterfront of Aberdeen Harbour to the gaudily lit Tai Pak floating restaurant. We walked into the vast banqueting room.

'Many people coming, Miss Double Check,' trilled Nori, scanning the gilt chairs and dining tables that ran in golden waves around us, all set with pristine white linen and flower decorations.

'The world media will be here. Your speech must be perfect or your bosses in London will be very angry.'

I shot him a nervous glance, at which point his face creased with laughter. When he'd composed himself he suggested we try the microphone and meet the lady who would be doing simultaneous translation during my speech. Moments later I was greeted by the chairman and committee of the Guinness Japan organisation. After formal introductions we had a brief rehearsal and then the guests began flooding into the room. The translator, a beautiful porcelain-faced Chinese girl named Miss Wong, bowed softly and whispered to me that if eighty guests from the train were accepting certificates from me, we would need to be speedy. A deep echoing gong sounded and soon a hush fell on the gathering. I sat on the stage alongside a group of Chinese and Japanese officials who nodded courteously whenever I sneaked a look in their direction. After thirty minutes of formal speeches in Chinese, my moment arrived. From the side of the stage Nori beckoned to me and I approached the mike. The translator strode over and our joint ordeal began. Well, actually it nearly didn't begin at all because as the chairman came over to introduce me, the sound system failed and he was left mouthing like a distressed goldfish to the baffled and unhearing throng. Finally engineers leaped into action and the sound was restored. All eyes bored into me as I waded through my words, rather like an oarsman in a lake of treacle.

'... and so it gives me immense pleasure to present these eighty passengers of the world's longest train journey with Guinness certificates. These valiant souls have travelled 18,000 kilometres, and through many countries including France, Germany, Poland, Russia and China to be here today and still their journey isn't over. Tomorrow they will set off by ship to Japan. Now if you would like to come up and join me...'

One by one they trooped up on to the stage, shook my hand and collected their certificates. If these elegant French souls were stars of stage and screen I didn't know it. I recognised no one. At one point I was halted in my delivery by an elderly Frenchman who jabbered away at an alarming rate in his own language and kissed me violently on both cheeks. A lady in lilac, overcome with emotion on receiving her certificate, began sobbing and had to be helped away by attendants while a sassy blond approached me and began asking me in broken English where I'd bought my lemon silk suit. The reality was that, broke as always, I'd fallen on the mercy of my sister who'd quickly run up a skirt and bolero jacket from some old shot silk she had in a cupboard. The last of the certificate holders came on stage and Miss Wong, the translator, smiled at me in relief. The room thundered with applause as we descended the steps and took our places at one of the banqueting tables.

The chairman handed me a glass of ice-cold champagne.

'Here's to the longest train journey. Twenty countries so far, and just one to go – Japan.'

I turned to Nori. 'Tell me, what other things are expected of me over the next few days?'

He smiled. 'We have many press interviews and you will meet many groups of Chinese people who would like to break records.'

I wondered if I'd be invited to any Oddity contests similar to those in South Korea.

Nori rattled on. 'Then we buy present for Mr Norris too and special souvenir for you.'

I shot him a wary glance, shuddering at the thought of what might be inflicted on me to bring back to Mr Norris this time.

'Mr Norris like Peking duck?' Nori suddenly asked.

I flinched, envisaging a gaggle of dead ducks sharing my first-class seat on the plane.

'Or maybe Japanese warrior samurai sword? he suggested helpfully.

That would certainly go down a storm at Heathrow Customs.

A waiter appeared with more champagne. I held up my glass.

'You're laughing. What's so funny?' asked Nori.

'You, Nori. You're very funny indeed.'

Over the next few days I determined to make the most of my time in Hong Kong. I enjoyed squashing on to the ferries at Kowloon and listening to the loud incomprehensible chatter of the locals about me as the island's skyline came into view. On my own one day I took the *Ding Dong*, the green double-decker tram that stops off at various of the island's districts, and even managed to successfully reach my target destination on a local bus by using exaggerated sign language. Nori arranged for me to have a sail around the harbour on the newly restored *Duk Ling*, one of the last remaining authentic Chinese sailing junks, the romantic old boats shaped like the crescent of the moon with three deep sails. Originally these boats were owned by fishermen and were used for trading over hundreds of years. I watched elderly men performing Tai Chi in the parks and took photos of the giant Buddha and decided that I could spend several weeks in Hong Kong and still not see it all.

On my final day Nori turned up with a surprise gift for Norris, carefully wrapped up in a box with tight string and heavy industrial tape. He politely refused to tell me what was inside, repeating that it was a 'surprise' and so I gave up asking. If fate decreed that I should end up returning with a dozen ducks and a samurai sword in my luggage, then so be it. Whatever else, it would give Norris something to laugh about.

★ ★ ★

It was a cool but bright morning in mid-October. Norris, dressed as a London bus conductor, was chatting with Roy Castle and a scrum of press photographers on the pavement outside the Trocadero Centre in Piccadilly. A crowd of curious onlookers studied their every move. Parked on the roadside was the battered old red double-decker World Bus.

Roy called to me. 'When are we pushing off, love?'

I came over to the group, glancing at my watch.

'Careful, Roy,' warned Norris as he fiddled with his ticket machine, 'she's holding her clipboard. That's a dangerous sign.'

'I've just spoken with Mariella Frostrup, the PR consultant for Bananarama, and she says the girls are on their way to Hamleys now, so that's a relief. You never know with the pop fraternity.'

'Too right,' sniffed one of the paparazzi.

Norris hopped on to the bus and rang the bell loudly. 'All aboard!'

Richard, Hughie and John walked down the aisle.

'Are we off?' enquired Richard. 'I'd better get in the driving seat. First call the Houses of Parliament?'

'That's right,' said Roy. 'Norris and I will just take it easy while you boys do all the hard work.'

'Nah, Richard's doing all the driving this morning,' grinned Hughie. 'We're just here for the ride.'

At the front of the bus sat Sue Arnold, a journalist from the *Observer* magazine whom I'd invited on the trip. I was a huge fan of her satirical weekly column and rather mischievously wondered what she might make of the three Bananarama girls, let alone the world's longest soft toy, Nipper the dog and the other record-breakers joining the bus. With a tinkle of the bell we were off. People cheered from the pavement and Norris gave them a cheery wave in response.

The press had installed themselves upstairs and cigarette smoke soon began drifting down the stairwell.

'What a lot of addicts,' observed Norris. 'I'm glad they're not puffing down here.'

The bus swerved as it headed off into the traffic. It was early and the rush hour was at its zenith but Richard took it in his stride. Before long we were chugging up to Parliament Square where the MPs Diane Abbott, Michael Mates, Rosie Barnes and Matthew Taylor clambered on board. A reporter scuttled down the stairs.

'OK to answer some questions?' he asked.

'Be my guest,' said Diane.

I wandered down the aisle to find Norris handing tickets from his machine to all and sundry.

'What are you doing?'

'I'm a bus conductor, AN. What do you think I'm doing?'

Sue Arnold beckoned to me. 'So why are these MPs on the bus?'

'Michael Mates had the most votes in his constituency, Diane Abbott is the first black woman to be elected in parliament, Matthew Taylor is the youngest MP and Rosie Barnes won a landslide by-election.'

She tapped a pen against her head. 'I'll go and have a word with them.'

I watched as she lurched down the bus. Who were we picking up next?

Ding-a-ling. Ding-a-ling. Norris was having a ball. The bus drew to a halt outside the Strand theatre where the director and some of the cast of the play *No Sex Please, We're British* jumped on. It was the longest-running show in London. The lower floor of the bus was becoming quite congested with reporters and photographers traipsing up and down the stairs to interview record-breakers. Richard was hooting at cars and cyclists as he now made his way along Regent Street. There was an enormous crowd outside Hamleys, where the girls from Bananarama stood. We stopped with a jolt as screaming crowds cheered and yelled from the pavements.

'Oh gawd, what a larf!' yelled one of the bananas as I called to them.

'Come on Keren, get on for chrissakes!' yelled another.

The three girls, wearing high fashion, heavy make-up and towering heels alighted the bus. Keren, her hair sleek and dark, had squeezed into tight faded jeans and a black bolero with matching T-shirt while Sara had her short blond hair teased and lacquered into a quiff at the front and wore a hugging white and black minidress. The third and recently joined member of the band, Jacquie, sporting heavy black kohl around the eyes, swept her long sleek black hair onto her shoulders. She had donned a white jean jacket and matching miniskirt set off with a black studded belt. Behind them a long and scarily bright pink caterpillar called Lots-a-legggggggs was hurled on to the bus. It had one thousand legs, and was 250 feet long with a weight of 300 pounds. Norris stood back as reporters grappled with it.

'Good God, what is that thing, AN?'

'The world's longest toy,' I replied.

'Honest to goodness, this is the craziest stunt ever,' yelped Roy.

Norris rang the bell with difficulty as Lots-a-legggggggs got stuck between the platform and stairwell.

'Heave-ho!' a photographer yelled.

A TV team tried to lever the huge folds of soft pink fur fabric up the stairs while reporters on the top floor yanked at its head.

'Oh God! This is weird!' cried one of the bananas.

'WAIT!' someone screeched from the street. 'What about Nipper, the HMV dog?'

An employee from HMV rushed on to the bus with a little Jack Russell on a lead just as Richard pulled off from the kerb. There were screams of laughter from the bananas upstairs as we chugged along Regent Street en route to HMV where the launch reception was to be held.

Sue Arnold appeared.

'What a madhouse!' she exclaimed with a wry grin. 'Now why is the HMV dog on the bus exactly?'

'It's representing HMV which has the world's largest record store.'

She flexed an eyebrow. 'Thanks for clearing that up. I'm off to interview Bananarama. Wish me luck.'

I steered Norris to the conductor's cubbyhole. 'Do you think it's going OK?'

He nodded. 'Fine, though just as well we're getting off at the next stop. That wretched toy is a potential health hazard. It's already nearly flattened the Bananarama girls.'

As we came into view of the record store on Oxford Street, Hughie laboured down the bus towards us.

'Quite a mob on here, eh? Looks like we've arrived. Thank God for that!'

We stopped at the front entrance of HMV which had been cordoned off for the purpose. In a noisy tumble everyone scrambled into the store. A large media throng greeted us inside the shop and crowds of young girls screamed from the pavements outside. Stopping to sign autographs, the Bananarama girls eventually made it into the store and joined Cheryl Baker, Roy Castle and Norris on stage. A moment later Sam Scurfield, the unstoppable juggler, performed a record-breaking routine juggling CDs. As the crowds cheered, the Bananarama girls signed the 60 millionth copy of *The Guinness Book of Records* and collected their certificates along with other record-holders who had been present on the bus. Nipper came up to the stage and after having his paw dipped in ink, left his imprint in the book. Before we knew it the speeches were over and it was time for the reception. The champagne flowed and everyone was in the best of spirits. I slithered through the crowds to the front doors. Norris was hot on my heels.

'Gosh I need some air.'

He nodded and, taking off his bus conductor's hat, wiped his brow.

'It's bedlam in there but everyone's having a whale of a time.'

'All the same, I'm glad they only happen once a year.'

His eyes wandered down Oxford Street. 'I've been meaning to ask you, what happened about the auction bids for the 60 millionth book?'

'Sorry, I forgot to tell you. Yesterday, Joe in the States beat all the other bids with the sum of £60,000.'

He smiled. 'Just fancy that. I wonder how he arrived at that magical figure?'

'I've no idea,' I said. 'But it couldn't have been sold to a nicer person or a more dedicated Guinness fan.'

He pulled out a handkerchief and blew his nose.

'Hang on. Is that the embroidered handkerchief gift I brought you back from the Guinness team in Hong Kong?'

'Maybe.'

'You shouldn't be using it!' I exclaimed. 'It's very valuable. It's supposed to be framed.'

'Why on earth would I do that? Life's for living.'

'And what about that damned samurai sword I risked life and limb for on the way back from Hong Kong? I'm sick of being frisked at airports on your behalf.'

'It doesn't happen that often.'

'Trust me, I even know the name of Heathrow's senior Customs officers now.'

'Well, that could have its uses.'

I sighed. 'This job really is insane.'

'You're right and that's why you're the best woman for the job. As they say, if the cap fits...'

I was about to reply, but with a rascally smile he pulled on his own cap and re-entered the fray, immediately engulfed by a wave of adoring fans.

SEVENTEEN

★ ★ ★

THE WORLD'S WORST WHIFF AND OTHER TV DISASTERS

The sky was looking grumpy as I hurled myself on to the slowly moving bus. Gripping the centre rail for support, I swung on to the partially exposed platform and took a gulp of breath. Fast footsteps descended the metal staircase.

'Dozy cow! Don't do that again. If you'd have lost your balance, you'd be a cropper by now.'

'Yes but I didn't,' I replied triumphantly.

Eric shook his head resignedly. 'Well, don't say I didn't warn you. If you got up earlier in the morning, you wouldn't have to rush.'

'It's only seven o'clock.'

'Even so.'

I took a seat on the four person mangy banquette near the conductor's cubbyhole. The material was hard and shiny through use and bald patches covered the surface, reminding me of one of my old and beloved childhood bears. Fresh air streamed into the bus and froze my cheeks. I pulled my coat tightly around me.

'Anyways, what's new in the world of record-breaking?'

'Well, after the excitement of the launch we're slowing down a little. Mind you, there's a lot to do on the press front.'

'Bet there is. I mean everyone buys the book for Christmas. Them reporters will be doing reviews, won't they?'

'Loads. We'll be kept very busy.'

'Good. Stop you getting up to mischief.'

I suddenly remembered that I had brought Eric a souvenir from the launch. I fumbled in my bag and got out an envelope. 'This is for you.'

'For me? Not one of your tricks, is it?'

He pulled out the print showing Norris dressed as a bus conductor with Roy Castle smiling at his side aboard the World Bus. On the back Norris had written: 'To Eric. Thanks for keeping AN in order. From a fellow "clippie".'

Eric studied the message closely. 'Gordon Bennett. What a diamond geezer.'

So engrossed was he that he nearly forgot to ring the bell as we approached a request stop. A young man hopped on, dragging hard on a cigarette as he clambered up the stairs.

'I dunno what to say. Thanks, love. That means a lot to me.'

He walked over to his cubbyhole and secreted the photo somewhere in its depths. He came and sat next to me on the near empty bus.

'Where'd he get that old Gibson ticket machine and uniform?'

'London Buses lent it to us for the launch.'

'Nice of them.'

'Yes, I thought so.'

'They don't make gentlemen like Mr McWhirter any more. He's from another time, love. I remember him on the box reporting on the Olympics.'

'He was a BBC sports commentator for years on radio.'

'Wasn't he an athlete?'

He broke off to let someone pass down the bus.

'He was a top runner at Oxford University like his brother, Ross. He even represented Scotland and Great Britain in the early fifties.'

'Go on!'

'There aren't many things Norris can't do but I bet he's a lousy singer. I've never heard him sing.'

'He can't be good at everything, can he?'

The bus stopped and Eric stood back as several people jumped on to the platform. He swung along the aisle. 'Any more tickets, please!'

I listened to the tack-a-tack-tack and sharp ping as he turned the knob on his machine and a ticket spewed out, creamy and rough.

'Can I have one?' I asked as he tottered back up the aisle.

'Nah, have it on the house. If an inspector turns up I'll say you've just got on.'

'Are you sure?'

We laughed a small conspiratorial laugh. I didn't like taking something for nothing but on this occasion I felt I should, knowing that it was Eric's way of saying thank you.

When my stop came in to view, I picked up my bag and stepped down on to the platform.

'Send Mr McWhirter my thanks,' said Eric. 'Tell him I'll put it on the wall next to the Queen, God bless her.'

I stood on the pavement and smiled, picturing Norris dressed as a 'clippie' and Queen Elizabeth side by side above Eric's mantelpiece. A drop of rain landed on my cheek reminding me that I didn't have an umbrella. With a wary look at the darkening sky, I ran as fast as I could towards the office.

Alex was already ensconced in the kitchen making coffee. He pulled another mug from the cupboard when he saw me. It was just after seven thirty and a sullen and cold October day leered at us from the grubby window. Crossing the room I snatched a glance at the gunmetal sky and watched as a thread of starlings shot past like a streak of iron filings and were gone. Alex gave a big sigh.

'So another book put to bed. It's been quite a year, looking back.'

I nodded. 'I was just saying to Eric, my bus conductor, this morning that I couldn't believe I'd been here more than two years.'

'I know what you mean. It's the same for me.'

I pulled out a chair and sat down. 'I remember back to the day Norris first interviewed me. Actually, you could hardly call it an interview.'

Alex laughed. 'I'd have loved to have been a fly on the wall. Did he ask you to quote from Thucydides?'

'You're pretty close, as it happens.'

He propped himself against the table, his hands curling around his mug. 'It's sad that he's talking about retirement. It would be strange not having him pottering about the office.'

The subject of Norris's retirement had been broached on several occasions by David and the other directors but it was something I didn't want to contemplate. Besides, who knew what any of us would be doing in the future? All the same I hoped it wouldn't be any time soon. We had become quite a team and I relished my time with him. In reality it didn't feel like work at all. It was more like having bizarre and madcap adventures with an eccentric and fearfully intellectual uncle. I wondered what it would be like not having his presence in our midst.

'Anyway,' Alex said. 'Whatever happens, I'm sure he'd continue to take an interest in the book. After all, it is his baby.'

I drained my cup and yawned. 'I can't see him ever truly retiring for that very reason. He'll be keeping a beady eye on proceedings for many years to come, trust me.'

'I hope you're right. Anyway, why are you in so early today?'

'I've got a lot to sort out before I set off to Maidstone to take part in a kid's show. It'll take up most of my weekend.'

A sardonic smile played on his lips. 'Oh this sounds like good sport. What's it called?'

'*No. 73.*'

'You're kidding? That's a huge prime-time show. In fact, there can't be a kid in the country who doesn't tune in on a Saturday morning.'

'I know. It's become one of those cult shows with audience participation. I'm slightly dreading it for that reason but Norman's coming, thank heavens.'

Alex knitted his brow. 'Who?'

'You know, Norman Johnson – the fastest cucumber slicer from Blackpool?'

'Does he wear a black eye patch?'

'Sometimes, but normally glasses with a blacked-out lens.'

He chuckled. 'I remember now. You invited him to last year's launch at the Savoy. Quite a character.'

'He's one of my favourite record-breakers, a real sweetheart with a wicked sense of fun. He'll be attempting a new record on the show.'

Alex walked slowly towards the door. 'Well, I wish you luck. Is it just an interview?'

I shook my head. 'Sadly not. I have to pretend to be a guest in the *No. 73* house which is apparently full of wacky characters. The idea is that I interact with all of them during the show.'

He covered his face with his hands and took a sharp intake of breath. 'Oh no, that sounds really embarrassing. I hope you know what you're doing.'

I wandered out of the kitchen after him. 'When all's said and done, it's great publicity for the book.'

'Rather you than me,' he mumbled.

★ ★ ★

An hour later Pam, the marketing manager at the *Guinness World of Records* exhibition, telephoned me.

'Just to reassure you, we've couriered Princess Pauline and Robert Wadlow directly to the studio in Maidstone along with the chocolates and crown jewels.'

'Fantastic. I hope you can do without them for a few days.'

'We'll manage but do look after them. These exhibits cost a fortune. Are you actually filming tomorrow?' she asked.

'We have a day of rehearsals because it's a live show.'

'Heavens. Let's hope you don't forget your lines, then,' she laughed.

'Don't say that, Pam, I'm nervous enough.'

'By the way, I've bubble-wrapped the bottle of ethyl mercaptan and put it in a secure box. Whatever you do, keep the top securely fastened. It looks harmless enough but one whiff and you'll want to throw up.'

When I'd finished the call I popped into Donald's office. 'Have you perchance ever sniffed the smelliest substance in the world?'

He drew deeply on his cigarette. 'Thankfully not. Are you talking about ethyl mercaptan?'

I nodded. 'The producer of *No. 73* is very keen to feature it on the show along with the other artefacts from the Guinness exhibition.'

A wry smile crossed his lips. 'It's just a clear liquid but I wouldn't inhale it if I were you. It's supposed to smell really foul.'

Lisa appeared at the door. 'Can you come and check through all the gubbins you've got to take with you?'

Donald raised an eyebrow. 'Best of luck, anyway.'

I walked back to her desk.

Lisa folded her arms in a no-nonsense way. 'Now, I think you should wear a Guinness T-shirt, don't you?'

I looked at the voluminous red garment with its glaring *Guinness Book of Records* logo and groaned.

'It's a bit naff.'

Her charm bracelet rattled impatiently as she held up the item for perusal. 'Don't be such a fusspot. It'll be fine.'

Eileen's chariot appeared round the corner, the plates chattering like teeth as it drew to an abrupt halt by my desk. Thin and wiry but with the strength of a horse, Eileen raised the heavy silver teapot and poured me a cup of tea. Next she shovelled some custard creams and garibaldi biscuits on a plate and handed it to me. Lisa rather hastily bundled the Guinness T-shirt into my overnight case, perhaps suspecting that I might change my mind, and thumped three copies of the latest edition of the book down on the top. She had a struggle zipping up the bag. While I threw files and notes into my briefcase, Shelley appeared at my side wearing a rather coy expression. She was joined by her fellow deputy editors and Muriel.

'Aye, aye, something's up,' I said.

She handed me an envelope. Inside was a good luck card from the editorial team.

I read all their individual messages. 'That's so kind of you all.'

'Don't go all misty-eyed,' said Stewart, 'We can't wait to see you cock up.'

'Don't be a meanie,' hooted Shelley. 'Nothing will go wrong.'

'Yeah, right!' exclaimed Stewart and sauntered back to the sanctuary of his desk.

★ ★ ★

Miraculously, it was a sunny day for early November but the weather was the least of my concerns as I stepped gingerly into the cavernous building which housed the *No. 73* studios. I had already spent the best part of Friday rehearsing for the live show and now it would be the real thing. The action took place in the studio-created *No. 73* house in which a stream of oddball guests appeared and disappeared through various doors as in a Brian Rix farce while the show's regular presenters, all purporting to be inhabitants of the house, chatted to the invited guests. At the rehearsal we had been given our scripts and so I spent much of the day getting to grips with my lines and trying to fathom my role in the various scenes. It had inevitably not been plain sailing, with props collapsing, people forgetting their lines and guests not turning up at all. But as the producer maintained, everything would be OK on the day and so having spent much of the night fretfully sitting up in bed learning my lines, I felt vaguely confident that we'd all breeze through the show. Having ironed out any problems during the rehearsal, what could possibly go wrong?

I heard a jaunty tread behind me followed by a wolf whistle and spun round to see Norman Johnson, the world's fastest cucumber slicer. He was wearing his chef's tall white hat and a pair of spectacles with the left lens blacked out. I'd never asked Norman about how he had lost his eye and though we often met at record-breaking events, it had never cropped up in conversation.

'My darling girl!' he whooped. 'How are you? Radiant as ever on this beauteous day!'

We exchanged a bear hug.

'I'm feeling a bit nervous, Norman.'

He cawed loudly like a manic kookaburra and hit me lightly on the head with a cucumber. 'Forget your nerves! Today's the day to set a new cucumber slicing record and you'll be there to witness it.'

'Very thrilling, Norman. Now what about your scenes? How did they go yesterday?'

He scratched the white tuft of hair emerging from the base of his chef's hat. 'Ah, very well, although the vet and his fox didn't turn up. They'll be here today, apparently.'

'Is it a pet fox?'

'Oh no, wild, I believe. I think the vet's making some sort of foxy loxy appeal.'

A deep rumble of laughter rolled from his belly.

'There were lots of Japanese people in long gowns running round with swords yesterday and a man dressed as a squirrel. Did you see them?'

'Were you on the amber nectar again, Norm?' I quizzed.

In truth, the day before, there had been so many mad people dashing on and off the set, I had given up trying to work out who was who or what was going on.

Someone was calling our names. 'Cooeee! Over here you two. We just need a group meeting with the producer and then we'll get cracking.'

'That's Sarah, the researcher. Come on, Norm.'

We hurried over to the young woman with the clipboard and soon we were receiving final instructions from the producer.

'Remember,' he was saying. 'This is a live show. If there's a disaster we just keep going. If you forget your lines, make them up. OK?'

We all nodded dutifully.

'The bottom line is that the show must go on.'

Norman started humming 'Glory, Glory, Hallelujah' until I gave him a sharp nudge in the ribs. A moment later we were whizzed through to costumes and make-up and before I knew it I was hiding behind a studio wall in a make-believe garden with plastic bushes and flowers. On top of the wall was the *Guinness World of Records* life-size plaster replica of Pauline Musters – Princess Pauline, as she was nicknamed – the smallest woman in the world. She was wearing her prim Victorian outfit and a pretty miserable expression. Perhaps she thought she might suffer the same fate as Humpty Dumpty as she stood up there, waiting nervously for someone to send her flying. But of course she wasn't thinking at all because she was just a chunk of plaster. Silly old me. Now the script was simple enough. Neil, one of the young and chirpy presenters, was supposed to be birdwatching through binoculars from a roof and on seeing Pauline the midget perched on the wall was supposed to yell out, 'Who are you?'

Then I was meant to reply, 'It's me, Princess Pauline!'

The presenter would then scramble down a ladder only to find me hiding behind the wall pretending to be Princess Pauline. How hilarious was that? While I awaited my cue, examining a particularly hideous garden gnome, I was aware of an excitable cameraman hissing at me.

He seemed to be mouthing, 'NOW!'

Thinking that I'd missed my cue, I hurriedly called out, 'It's me, Princess Pauline...' which collided nicely with Neil's cry of, 'Who are you?'

Lowering the binoculars in his grasp, Neil looked momentarily confused before registering that something had gone slightly awry. Quick as a flash he improvised.

'Oooh, did that little woman on the wall really say her name was Princess Pauline?'

A studio hand prodded me and I leaped out from behind a bush, almost giving Neil a heart attack.

'Well, if it isn't my old buddy, Anna from Guinness!' Neil trilled. 'Fancy pretending to be that dwarf woman! Who is she, anyway?'

Thankfully I didn't screw up the script from there on in and meekly allowed myself to be pushed and prodded between fast-moving scenes. At one point, finding myself in the brightly lit studio kitchen with cameras trained on me, I was nearly flattened by one of the presenters as she whizzed on to the set on roller skates. The Japanese theatre group whom Norman had spoken of suddenly leaped on to the set – evidently unable to speak a word of English – flashing swords, clutching at their stomachs and uttering loud, blood-curdling screams.

'They're acting out *Macbeth*,' one of the presenters chirruped to the cameras, presumably to reassure viewers who might otherwise think they all had a bad case of gastritis. The show rolled on and it was only when I had left one of the sets for a quick break that I heard a scream. Norman came racing up to me, a large kitchen knife in his hand.

'Are you good with foxes, love?'

'What on earth do you mean?'

'The fox has escaped in the studio!'

'The fox?'

'Yes, he was with the vet and apparently managed to escape from the cage in the dressing room. The producer's frantic! Can you come and help search for him?'

'But I'm in the next scene. I'm talking about Robert Wadlow, the tallest man.'

'Heavens, I hope the fox doesn't dart on to the set,' said Norman with a nervous giggle.

'God forbid!' I muttered.

'I'm supposed to follow the vet and fox scene with my record attempt,' he said. 'What'll they do?'

One of the researchers rushed by. 'We think it's loose in the kitchen!'

'Anna!' a researcher was hissing. 'You're on with Neil now. Hurry.'

I gave Norman a shrug and tore in through a stage door directly on to the set.

'Oh here's my friend Anna again!' Neil said theatrically to camera. Then turning to me with a broad smile; 'Oh goodie, look at all these fabulous things you've brought along today. Come on, tell us all about them.'

On a large table in front of him were the replicas of record-breaking items couriered from *The Guinness World of Records* exhibition. Composing myself, I began chattering to Neil about Robert Wadlow, the tallest man, and then began to relate the history of the most expensive golf shoe, and the smallest book.

'And this here is the largest box of chocolates in the world?'

'That's right,' I said, suddenly distracted by a streak of russet fur off set.

Several people were following in pursuit and it was all I could do to hold Neil's gaze. As he began quizzing me about the 74-facet Cullinan, the largest cut diamond in the world, I stole a glance at one of the cameramen and saw Norman gesticulating wildly behind him, doing a fox impression, twitching his nose and drawing his hands together in front of his chest. It was all I could do to maintain a straight face.

'And now,' I heard Neil saying. 'We come to the exciting bit. Tell everyone what's in that little bottle, Anna?'

In some horror I regarded the phial before me. In the rehearsal we hadn't bothered to talk through all the items on the table, leaving them boxed up, and so I'd forgotten to warn the producer that the innocuous-looking clear liquid was in fact the real and noxious thing.

'Well, Neil,' I heard myself saying cheerily. That's ethyl mercaptan, the smelliest substance in the world.'

'Get away with you. I don't believe a word of it.'

'I'm afraid it is. Just one sniff and you'd be reeling.'

He chortled away. 'Go on, I'm not scared. Open the bottle.'

I tried to flash a warning with my eyes. 'Seriously, Neil, I really don't think I should do that. It reeks of drains and rotting cabbage and sewers and pigs' bottoms…'

'Pigs' bottoms?! How do you know what a pig's bottom smells like? Come on. Give it to me!'

He stretched out and grabbed the tiny bottle. 'Here I go!'

I gave him a wide berth but even at a measured distance the unmistakably gut-rotting, foul, nauseating stench wafted over me. I pinched my nose, gagged and averted my gaze. I watched as Neil reeled back. A delayed shock.

'Oh heck! That is terrible. Really horrible, disgusting, revolting… I feel truly awful.'

I leaped forward and secured the top on the bottle but the damage was done. Neil, pale then turning a sickly green hue, swallowed hard and valiantly tried to continue.

'Well, that has been… [gag] really amazing… [gag]. I think it's time for us to make tracks, eh Anna?'

There came the sound of spluttering and deep groans off camera and several cameramen dived into the darkness beyond overcome by nausea as the lethally repellent ethyl mercaptan vapour seeped into every part of the studio. Neil stumbled out of a door with a weak wave as his co-presenter on roller skates whizzed onto the set. As I left the set I could hear retching and much swearing in the near distance. Norman grabbed my arm.

'What were you doing? Trying to poison that poor chap, you naughty minx? Look, no time to lose, I'm on now. Have you got the stopwatch? Hurry!'

Norman disappeared through a door into the *No. 73* house. I lingered a second, recovering from the wave of nausea washing over me but my repose was short-lived. Someone was yelling at me. 'Quickly, get on set!'

I arrived to find Norman grinning manically at the camera in his pinstriped apron, a massive cucumber in front of him on a cutting board and the lethal-looking kitchen knife in his right hand. I sidled up to him and waited for my cue.

'Oooh Norman! That's a big cucumber you've got there!'

Boom, boom!

'Yes, that's because I'm about to set a new record today, Anna. Where's Neil?'

'I think he's been delayed, Norman.' Grin to camera.

Neil crashed through the door. 'Right, come on Norman,' he beamed, 'Let's get going.'

Holding the knife aloft, Norman waited until he was given the word and then began slicing away like a demon. Meanwhile I stood with the stopwatch, aware that ethyl mercaptan was still seeping into the skin of every poor mug in the vicinity. As Norman slashed at the cucumber I kept a wary eye out for the runaway fox. Where the hell had it got to? Neil stood wanly by Norman, until he let out a small gasp, his eyes drawn to the table. Following his gaze, I noticed blood oozing down the chopping board. It seemed Norman was cutting off more than just cucumber slices, possibly his own fingers. I wondered whether he'd noticed. The cameraman had already homed in on the scene so heaven knows what the audience were making of the bloodbath on screen. Norman cut his last slice.

'Two hundred and sixty-four slices in 13.4 seconds! A new record has been set!' yelled Neil.

Norman was rushed off to get his hand bandaged while I made for the dressing room. To my relief I discovered the fox had been cornered and was now appearing live with the vet in the living room of the *No. 73* set. I found Norman nursing a big bandaged hand in his dressing room'What happened?'

'That knife was bloody sharp,' he tutted. 'Nearly took my finger off.'

I bit my lip. 'So I saw!'

'Still, as the producer said, the show must go on. And what about the fox!'

'I know. It was like a madhouse! Anyway, it's all over. You've got the record and we've survived. Hopefully we can go for a drink now.'

'I could kill a beer, love.'

We stood up and wandered out of the room whereupon a cameraman whistled to us.

'Everyone's looking for you. They have a disco scene now with the pop group and all the guests. It's the show's grand finale. Quick!'

'Do we have to go?' I pleaded.

'Too damned right, you do!' the man replied.

Norman and I found our way back to the main studio and were pushed into a dark area in which the presenters and other guests were gyrating to blaring music while glittery orbs hanging from the ceiling flashed and changed colour. I cringed.

'This is seriously embarrassing,' I murmured.

'Dear oh dear!' wailed Norman above the din. 'I can't see a damned thing! At least you've got two good eyes.'

'Dance!' someone hissed into my right ear. Norman and I began swaying and he suggested we do the foxtrot. It seemed a welcome and appropriate alternative, although I didn't know the steps.

'Who are those young lads singing up there?' asked Norman, taking my hand and whirling me around.

'They're called Westworld.'

He seemed impressed. 'How d'you know that?'

'It's written on their drum kit,' I shouted back.

He snorted loudly, his chef's hat shaking wildly under the lime and pink strobe lights. Soon, oblivious to the rest of the room, we did our own shambolic disco foxtrot as the credits rolled. I was wearing the outsized red Guinness T-shirt and voluminous Andy Pandy blue trousers while Norman sported his kitchen whites. We must have seemed like two deranged inmates escaped from a hospital secure wing. It was then and only then that I was struck by the cold realisation that this was live TV and that the entire Guinness team would have been watching every moment of the unabridged pandemonium on the show. As for Norris, I imagined him staring stoically at the screen and with a weary shake of the head, muttering: 'Pathetic! Utterly pathetic.'

★ ★ ★

Norris was sitting by my desk, flicking through a copy of *Whitaker's Almanac*.

'You know, this was always my favourite book as a child. I was never into fiction.'

'That's a shame. I hope to write a novel one day.'

He sniffed. 'I suppose I'll break the rules for you. Of course, Barbara Cartland thinks I read her oeuvres.'

'Surely not?'

'I believe so.'

I selected a book from the shelf above my desk. 'Barbara sent me this but I haven't found a moment to study it.'

'I dare say,' Norris replied wryly.

I glimpsed the back cover. 'I love the names of her protagonists. This one is Prince Clement de Metternich.'

Norris rapped the desk. 'That's a bit cheeky. She's obviously pilfered it. There was a German-Austrian Prince von Metternich in the eighteen hundreds.'

'Maybe she admired him.'

Norris smiled. 'By the way, do you know who has the longest name?'

'No.'

'It's Major LSDOF Tollemache-Tollemache de Orellana Plantagenet Tollemache-Tollemache, but his friends call him Tolly.' He guffawed. 'It's rather good, isn't it?'

'Yes, very droll.'

'Well, talking of droll moments I'm still dining out on your outstanding performance with Norman on *No. 73*.'

'Oh, be quiet.'

'It was, as Muriel said, a triumph. That fox obviously deserved an Oscar too. Actually, Roy and I were discussing it at the *Record Breakers* studio this morning. He was very impressed. Thought you might be made for comedy.'

'Ho, ho, ho.'

'What's more concerning is that you weren't remotely affected by that ethyl mercaptan. You know the Soviet communist culture is all about withstanding pain and learning to block out physical and olfactory trauma such as noxious odours.'

I shook my head. 'So you're implying I'm a communist?'

'It would explain a lot. You did say that you travelled a great deal to the Soviet countries as a child,' he goaded. 'You've even got Mao Tse-tung's little red book on your shelf!'

I looked up at my bookshelf and laughed. 'That's true, actually.'

A grin lingered on his lips and then with a sudden seriousness, he rose from his chair. 'You know we must talk about the future.'

'In what way?'

'Well, about my retiring as editorial director.'

I paused. 'So it's true? When are you leaving?'

He seemed to find that funny. 'I have no intention of going for some time yet but I do want to wind down on adjudicating records and travelling. Donald's already doing a fair bit and with you helping to shoulder the load it means I can be freed up a little.'

'To do what?' I asked.

He fiddled with a thread on his old tweed jacket. 'I have a notion to write a book about inventions and, as you know, I'm hard at work on my islands title. And then there's my political work with The Freedom Association. It seems a sensible time to consider my obligations here.'

'Will you still do the promotional tours with me?'

'Some.'

'What about *Record Breakers*?'

'I'll continue with the show for a while longer.'

'So what'll I do?'

'Keep on doing what you're doing until you decide to do something else.'

I snorted. 'That's a great help.'

'This is excellent experience for you. Everything changes with time. You have to learn to accept that.'

I stood up and stared out of the window and down at the street far below. 'Won't you miss anything?'

He laughed. 'Of course, but new people arrive with their own ideas and have to be given a chance. You and I will always remain in touch. I dare say we'll work together on things beyond Guinness so my cutting down on time here is an irrelevance.'

He shovelled some files into his briefcase. I noticed that the tawny leather was flaking. I pondered the many miles it must have travelled, the countries it had seen and bizarre events witnessed. Lifting his sleeve, he examined his watch face.

'Are you aware that the grey fox is one of only two canine species able to climb trees?'

I observed him carefully. 'No, I wasn't.'

He gave a cursory nod. 'I thought you might like to know that.'

Pulling his thick camel coat off a chair he stepped out into the corridor just as I heard the distant jingling and juddering of Eileen's tea trolley. He paused a moment as if in deep contemplation and then with the most impish of smiles he winked and bid me goodbye.

ACKNOWLEDGEMENTS

When writing this book I found myself once again in touch with many old friends and colleagues from my *Guinness Book of Records* days. It has been a nostalgic and wonderfully indulgent experience. Some of those who have gone the extra mile include David Hoy, probably the kindest and most understanding MD I could have wished for during my time at Guinness, Muriel Ling, a good friend and colleague, and my long-standing friend, Beatrice Frei.

Several record breakers whom I worked with at *The Guinness Book of Records* have come to my aid and offered tremendous support. Topping the list is Dean Gould, champion beer mat flipper and coin snatcher who runs the website Record Holders Republic, and Chris Greener, who until 2007 was the UK's tallest British-born man and is still the second tallest in the country. My thanks must also go to Ralf Laue of *The Book of Alternative Records* and Martyn Tovey of Guinness Record Book Collecting. I would like to extend my gratitude to Alison Wheatley and the Jumeirah Carlton Tower Hotel in Knightsbridge for offering their generous support. It is a venue associated with a great record breaker who features in my book.

I would like to offer my inestimable thanks to the McWhirter family for their kindness and continuing friendship. In particular I would like to thank Tessa McWhirter for her tremendous support and also Alasdair and Jane McWhirter for their great encouragement.

Finally, it would be unforgivable not to mention my diligent and talented editor, Lucy York at Summersdale, and last but never least, Alan and Ollie for their incredible patience, encouragement and humour through thick and thin.

OTHER TITLES BY ANNA NICHOLAS:

A Lizard in My Luggage
978 1 84024 565 3

Cat on a Hot Tiled Roof
978 1 84024 683 4

Goats From a Small Island
978 1 84024 760 2

Donkeys on My Doorstep
978 1 84953 038 5

BIGGEST
FASTEST
DEADLIEST

THE BOOK OF FASCINATING FACTS

DAN BRIDGES

BIGGEST, FASTEST, DEADLIEST
The Book of Fascinating Facts

Dan Bridges

ISBN: 978 1 84953 084 2   Hardback   £9.99

THE WORLD'S BIGGEST ISLAND:
Greenland, Arctic, 2,175,000 km^2 (840,000 m^2)

THE WORLD'S FASTEST BIRD
peregrine falcon, dives after prey at 124 mph (200 km/h)

THE WORLD'S DEADLIEST LAND ANIMAL:
golden poison frog of Central and South America

Ever wished you could remember everything you learned at school? Ever felt the answer to a tie-breaker was on the tip of your tongue? With this treasure trove of lists you can fascinate your friends with facts on astronomy, history, invention, the natural world and a wealth of other subjects.

Go on, dip in – there's still time to win *Mastermind*, or at least a round of Trivial Pursuit!

Have you enjoyed this book?

If so, why not write a review on your favourite website?

Thanks very much for buying this Summersdale book.

www.summersdale.com